THE BOOK OF THE WOUNDED HEALERS

(A STUDY IN PERCEPTION)

JOSEPH CARRABIS

ISBN 979-8-9878048-9-6

Library of Congress Control Number

Characters, events, places, and things described, depicted, or referred to in this work are fictitious. Any similarity to actual persons, events, places, or things is purely coincidental.

Editing by Jennifer Day, Susan Carrabis

Cover by John Bernard Scullin

http://skolenimation.com/

Book formatting by Jennifer Day

Printed and bound in the United States of America First printing July 2024

Published by Northern Lights Publishing www.northernlightspublishing.com

The lyrics in *Chapter 22 - Hungry Universes* from "Behind Blue Eyes" by Peter Townshend, The Who

The lyrics in *Chapter 40 - Dancing with Death* are from Robbie Robertson/Aaron Neville's "What About Now?", Medicine Hat Music adm. by EMI April Music Inc. ASCAP/PRI Song, Inc./Sunset Beach Music BMI.

The lyrics in *Chapter 62 - The Far Distant Shore* are from John Cougar Mellencamp "Hotdogs&Hamburgers."

PRAISE FOR THE BOOK OF THE WOUNDED HEALERS

What a remarkable story (read the entire book in one sitting, as it simply draws the reader in). Ben's flashbacks are well-integrated into the narrative and add meaningful value. They reveal important aspects about his character and contribute to the story's emotional impact.

The story on the surface seems light, but there is a lot of heavy subjects (beliefs) being discussed that are very much on people's minds these days, and I suppose many minds over the decades. I feel like Oliver. I ask for More, Please, Sir.

A metamathemagical tour de force of how our self-understanding can be both liberating and crippling.

I dreamt scenes from the book. That tells you something deep's going on.

A beautiful use of meta-language to describe language.

A thought-provoking novel! Every quote, statement, or anecdote had me pausing to contemplate.

The use of mathematical symbols and objects to understand non-mathematical implications of meaning not derived from mathematics blew me away.

The zingers at the end of each chapter carried me out of the theoretical and into the feelings of those involved is brilliant.

Joseph Carrabis is a gifted writer who draws the reader into deep contemplation and self reflection with each turn of a page, all the while skillfully weaving a story that grabs your attention and holds on till the end.

Excellent for thought and conversation.

I loved the description of the sun doing its work, and the elevators being like valves in a heart. Bravo!

I never really stopped to consider how many feelings we have and that we always will have them. That one really had me thinking.

"Obligation breeds resentment, choice breeds acceptance." - LOVE THAT!

Joseph has created a book that allows us to view life and ourselves through the eyes of beings who have no reference points or background of our society. He encourages us to look our own values, beliefs and prejudices, often with eye opening results. Nicely Done.

A self-help, self-discovery book disguised as science fiction, and it manages to pull both off beautifully!

A sci-fi story that'll make you think!

Before you know it, you're incorporating what Ben's learning and saying and it changes your life.

So subtle, you're drawn into Ben's healing.

A WalkAbout in NYC

Carrabis pens another good one!

CONTENTS

First, to Susan
(because everything should be)

Second, to AJ
(because he said I could)

Thanks to
Jennifer "The Editress" Day

Thanks to First Readers
Bob Merry, Liz Tuckwell, Rika Chandra, and Ross Pickering,

and to
Andy, Martin, Tina, Steve, Brian, Sarah, Paula, Neil, ... Without you,
this book (and probably the bulk of my work) wouldn't exist

Deep thanks and appreciation to my sensitivity readers
Phil Williams, HR Professional, Ph.D.
and
Othneil Archer, RBN
for helping me understand experience I could never have

Note to readers: If you find yourself in these pages, welcome. Remember
the World Equation. It helps a lot.

ALSO BY JOSEPH CARRABIS

AUTHOR'S NOTE

The language used in this book may offend some readers. My goal is to use all the tools at an author's disposal and all the tools in my author's toolbag to create as exacting a sensory experience for the reader and to be as accurate to my creation as possible. Sometimes that means language which may offend some is used to create such exacting sensory images.

I've learned to accept my limitations and hope you'll do the same.

PREFACE

We often envision healers as individuals who are whole, who have conquered their own pain to offer solace to others. But what happens when the healer themselves is wounded? Can they still offer healing? Or does their own pain become a barrier?

This masterpiece delves into the intricate interplay between trauma, healing, and perception. Through a series of poignant narratives, the author invites readers to contemplate the profound ways in which our experiences shape how we see the world and ourselves.

Structured as a collection of interconnected stories, each offering a unique perspective on the healing journey, Joseph introduces us to a diverse cast of characters, from war veterans struggling with PTSD to survivors of abuse grappling with the aftermath of their experiences. These individuals become vessels through which he explores the complexities of trauma and its enduring impact.

Central to the Joseph's exploration is the concept of perception. He argues that our perception of reality is not merely a passive process but an active one, influenced by our past experiences, beliefs, and emotions. Trauma, in particular, can dramatically alter our perception, leading to distorted views of the world and ourselves. The characters in the book embody this idea, as they navigate the challenges of healing while grappling with their distorted perceptions.

One of the strengths of this book is its ability to evoke empathy and understanding. Joseph's writing is both sensitive and powerful, allowing readers to connect deeply with the characters' experiences. By sharing their stories, he challenges us to confront our own biases and preconceptions about trauma and healing.

This book also offers valuable insights into the healing process, as Joseph keenly emphasizes the importance of self-compassion, connection with others, and a willingness to confront difficult emotions. He also explores the role of therapy, mindfulness, and creative expression in facilitating healing. While acknowledging the challenges involved, he ultimately conveys a message of hope and resilience.

The concept of a wounded healer is not entirely new. Throughout history, many individuals have experienced deep personal trauma and yet have found ways to use their suffering to help others. Think of figures like Buddha, Jesus, and Rumi, who all experienced great suffering but went on to become sources of inspiration and healing for countless people.

You are about to embark on a thought-provoking and compassionate exploration of trauma, healing, and perception. The author's writing is both insightful and engaging, making this book a valuable resource for anyone interested in understanding the human experience. Whether you are a survivor of trauma, a mental health professional, or simply someone seeking to deepen your understanding of the human condition, this book offers valuable insights and inspiration.

- *Dennis J. Pitocco, Chief Reimaginator, 360° Nation*

THE BOOK OF THE WOUNDED HEALERS

Le coeur a ses raisons que la raison ne connait pas.
- Pascal

The limits of my language are the limits of my world.
- Ludwig Wittgenstein

There are places in the heart that do not yet exist. Pain must be so they may be.
- Leon Bloy

"Praise our choices, sisters, for each doorway
open to us was taken by squads of fighting
who paid years of trouble and struggle,
who paid their wombs, their sleep, their lives,
that we might walk through these gates upright.
Doorways are sacred to women for we
are the doorways of life and we must choose
what comes in and what goes out. Freedom
is our real abundance."
- Marge Piercy, *The Sabbath of Mutual Respect*

Only if words are felt, bodily presences, like echoes or waterfalls, can we understand the power of spoken language to influence, alter, and transform the perceptual world.
- David Abram, *The Spell of the Sensuous*

"I have learned that the head does not feel anything until the heart has listened. And what the heart knows today, the head will understand tomorrow."
  - James Stephens

"Speech is civilization itself. The word, even the most contradictious word, preserves contact. It is silence which isolates."
  - Thomas Mann

"We cannot use inner language to make ourselves understood except to those whom we meet at the outer limits of things."
  - Jean Arp

Any idea, person or object can be a Medicine Wheel, a Mirror, for man. The tiniest flower can be such a Mirror, as can a wolf, a story, a touch, a religion, or a mountaintop.
  - Hyemeyohsts Storm

These memories are painted in primary colors because they are childhood memories. I am not attempting to be fair to my middle-class schoolmates. I am only telling you how they looked to me at the time. Obviously, I now have much more sympathy for children from the middle-class. - Rita Mae Brown, "Starting From Scratch"

DOWNTOWN

CHAPTER 1
FIRST MEETING

How many heartbeats does it take to change the world?

Three creatures stare down at me like I'm the one who doesn't belong. People flee South Street Seaport under the FDR, across the Greenway and South Street, scream their way up Fulton, John, Beekman, and the Slips. Mounted NYPD officers yell commands no one pays attention to. Sirens get closer but the sound of squawking seagulls, screeching pigeons, shrieking blue jays, clomping horses, screaming people, and crying children drowns out everything else.

The asphalt's covered with my bloody handprints from crab-walking over smashed sunglasses, trampled phones, and broken souvenirs to get away from these things.

I look past them to the white sand desert they just crossed, a desert which used to be the East River and Brooklyn, and protect my eyes from a gale force sirocco blowing sand in everybody's eyes.

Foot patrol officers shout emergency instructions and are ignored. Car alarms go off all over the place as people run blindly and smash into them, into vendor carts, into each other. People trip over curbs and barriers. Some fall and are trampled. Some people scream and curse as legs and arms and hips break because those still moving aren't careful and race over them like they're ascending wobbly stairs. Only foot patrolman Distasio helps the fallen, lifting one in each arm, carrying them and dragging others intown.

Ten minutes ago I stood in line with my son, Jiminy, to get him a brown sugar and cinnamon zeppoli and me a hot Italian sausage sub with extra onions and peppers. It was our first day alone together since I went north to the Home for Mental Wanderers and he always wanted to go to South Street Seaport so here we were watching tugs and ferries go up and down the East River.

Jiminy pointed. "There's rainbows on the water, Dad!"

I didn't have the heart to tell him it was diesel slicks from the river traffic. Kids that young deserve some magic in their lives. One foot patrol officer, Distasio, tall, tanned, broad chest, muscular arms and legs, and blonde with a pencil-thin mustache, followed Jiminy's gaze, looked back at us, and smiled. I nodded in return and wondered if he were a real cop or some movie or tv star and we were being filmed unawares. Other patrol officers walked in twos through the crowd, bronzed arms and legs protruding from uniformed shirts and shorts, their arms often resting on the equipment in their utility belts, and smiled and nodded under their patrol officer caps and behind their aviator sunglasses. Two mounted policemen on South Street stood resolute like the NYPL Lions, Patience and Fortitude, their only movement their horses shifting weight from one leg to another and the occasional nod when a parent asks if their kid can pet their horse.

Seagulls, pigeons, blue jays, grackles, and other birds seem to be in the line with us and caw and squawk like tourists as their heads bob back and forth looking for scraps on the ground. A guy got in line behind me and I realized he was the one who worked the dolphin tank they brought in for tomorrow's aquarium exhibit.

"Big tank," I said.

"Yeah. State of the art."

"What's the netting for over the top of the tank."

The aquarium guy nodded towards it without taking his eyes

off the fat Italian-looking gentleman ladling peppers and onions into an open subroll. "If we didn't have the netting there he'd kill himself trying to leap into the open sea. He sees the netting and knows he can't do it."

"I thought they worked more by sound than sight."

"Yeah? Works so far."

I walked over to the dolphin tank, the sub in one hand and the zeppoli in the other. Jiminy's right beside me, a big coke in each hand slippery with condensation. The dolphin just swims and swims and swims in circles, its eyes out to the sea.

Until I got next to the tank. Then the dolphin stopped and moved next to me. It looked me in the eye, and I imagined it asking me, "Hello? Hello? Is anybody there?"

Jiminy looks up at me. Between chews of zeppoli he says, "You sure it's okay us being here, Dad?"

I look down, frown, and quickly scan the crowd, quickly become a bigotry sensor, searching the multi-racial, multi-ethnic porridge of humanity for signs of prejudice, malice, hatred for a black man with a biracial child, and detect none, everyone caught up in their own moment to interfere with ours. "Of course it is, Jiminy. Why are you asking?"

He looks down and swallows hard. "I...I don't want to...your work. I know it's important."

Yes, it was. Past tense. Was. So important I damn near destroyed my marriage, my family, my life, and it's why I escaped to Happy House. I knew I was in trouble, couldn't bear what I was doing to people, and just left. Emailed Grace Krazinski, the math department's secretary, a link to LakeShore Psychiatric in northern New Hampshire with "Get me there." She made all the arrangements, got me a cab to La Guardia, the next seat on Southwest, told LakeShore when and where to pick me up, and gave me a hug as she put me in the cab. "You'll be okay, Ben. You're too brilliant not to be okay."

I looked up as she closed the door. "I haven't told Gayle, I - "

She gave me a thumbs up. "I got this, Dr. Matthews. Go get well."

Suddenly Jiminy wrapped his arms around my hips and I felt the cokes sweating against my butt through my pants. He looked up at me and screamed, "I love you, dad."

"I love you, too, son."

We heard some applause and saw a crowd gathered around a good juggler. People threw real, folding money into his hat. Between bites of zeppoli, Jiminy asked if he can have a dollar to drop in the juggler's hat. I handed him a wetwipe because his hands were all sticky and took one for myself because my sub's dribbled oil all over mine.

"He's really good. Here's a five. Let's be generous."

Jiminy smiled, all proud and adult-like, and placed the fiver on top of the cash already there.

The juggler winked at him and called to the crowd, "Everybody ready for the big finale?" His juggling balls dropped into a box beside him. He reached into the same box and pulled out a machete, a bowling ball, and a tomato. "Please, folks, be quiet. This is going to be real difficult because, as you can see, these are different colors." The adults laughed and the kids oohed.

"Ready?"

We all watched the tomato, bowling ball, and machete fly around him in a big circle. Jiminy is wide-eyed. "He really is good, dad."

I pull Jiminy back a few steps just in case. "He sure is."

A stray wind came off the water, a hot breeze more like mid-August instead of early May. The seagulls, pigeons, grackles et al took to the air and flew inland in great sweeping dives.

Jiminy pointed south towards Governors Island and Brooklyn. "What's that?" A desert of pure white Caribbean sand stretched from the edge of the seawall south and east.

The wind increased until it felt like staring into a high-power hair dryer turned on full. Ice cream wrappers, crumpled napkins, Seaport Points-of-Interest and visitor guide sheets, ticket stubs, all the trash thrown on the ground got whipped intown and the wind strengthened like it wanted to push the Seaport towards TriBeCa and the World Trade Center.

Jiminy wrapped his arms around my legs and tucked himself into me. I dropped my sandwich and picked him up just as some lady's umbrella flapped open and lifted her off the ground. Another lady screamed and pointed at the juggler. I tucked Jiminy's head in my shoulder and headed towards the subway. "Don't look, Jiminy."

But he wasn't looking at the juggler, he's straining his head over my shoulder looking where Brooklyn and the East River used to be. Other people looked that way, too. "Dad?"

I put Jiminy down. The wind still blew strong and hot. The mounties steadied their horses and worked crowd control. One of the mounties called to the other and pointed towards the desert.

Three creatures, their images shimmering in the heat like a mirage, walked across the sand towards The Battery and TriBeCa South. The desert echoed back at us the horses' snorting, the birds' squawking, the crowd's screaming, the sounds of traffic, the car horns, ... The mob mentality fairy threw her dust at the crowd and panic clusters sucked up people like an amoeba preparing to divide.

Both mounties talked into their lapel mikes and steered crowds towards the patrollers, towards Fulton, Beekman, John, and the two Slips. The patrollers did their best and got swept up in the surging crowd like shrimp in an undertow.

I bent down to get Jiminy but he's gone. "Jiminy!" Everybody's screaming and yelling. I envisioned his little body trampled by the people around me. "Jiminy! Where are you?"

I grabbed one of the mounties' legs and yelled up at him, "My kid's lost. Help me find him."

He looked out over the desert and yelled back, "I've got more to worry about right now, mac."

"No!" I grabbed the reins of the horse. "Listen, - "

The mountie kicked me in the gut and I fell to the ground. His horse bolted and I rolled out of its way.

Squad cars screeched to a halt all along South Street and car doors slammed.

The sirocco receded and South Street Seaport's late May ocean breeze returned. The echoes faded to "chatter chatter," "chatter chatter," the sounds of people at a party; you know they're saying something but you can't make out the words. It didn't matter. Everybody ran including most of the foot patrol. Only blonde mustached, muscular matinee idol Distasio earned his pay and guided people back from the Seaport to safety. Police rushed out of their cars with their guns raised and ready. My eyes burned with sand and grit. I couldn't breathe, I couldn't see Jiminy. The only things around me were returning seagulls, pigeons, and other birds. I didn't know what they returned for because all the trash was blown up South Street and the escape routes. The birds looked at me like I'm their Christ and about to pull loaves and fishes out of my ass.

A shadow came over me. I looked up.

The three creatures stared down at me. Their chatter chatter, chatter chatter became near-words. They demonstrate syntax, structure, but the sounds aren't yet words, have no meaning, until the one in front says, "We are Healers from the Land of Barass." It points to the one on its right. "He is Cetaf, who cries for his own pain." It turns to the one on its left. "This is Jenreel, who tends to his own needs. I am Beriah. I will tell you how I feel. We are Healers from the Land of Barass."

The echoes across the desert, the sounds of the city, of the people, their babbling, their near-word jargon. These creatures sought response-cues, determining which sounds rose above noise to meaning.

They acquired our language walking across a desert? Of course! *DUH!* Like a child echoing the sounds its hearing and learning which ones its caregivers respond to.

My research kicks in. Did they spontaneously learn our language because they somehow knew we'd take too long to learn theirs?

I stare at them, my jaw slack as gurgling sounds leak up my

throat. What am I supposed to say? Greetings? Welcome to Planet Earth? Please help me up?

Beriah offers his hand. It has four fingers, one opposing the other three. I take it and it feels like I'm holding hands with a six-foot-tall chicken.

Beriah is only an inch or two taller than me. If shape and size are indications, he is the same weight as I am. He's red everywhere, the only exceptions are his eyes which are black pupiled and gold irised, there is no white, only black upon gold upon black like a weird bullseye. His head has a brownish, rough, horny kind of skin where we have hair. His features are human enough except for his eyes and lips which are big like a frog's. I think he is seeing everything even though he is looking at me. For a minute all my other fears are dwarfed by the image of a large tongue snapping out of his wide, thin-lipped mouth and pulling me back in. He wears a sleeveless robe which ends at midcalf. The rest of him, as far as I can tell, is just like us.

Cetaf, the one on Beriah's right, is yellow with the same features and color variations as Beriah, except he is nine feet tall and six feet wide. A walking wall. His legs and toes are like an elephant's, but his face is more like a man's than Beriah's, except it is flattened, like a boxer's. Jenreel is the most human looking one of the three, except he is blue with similar color variations, about seven and a half feet tall and thin as a wraith.

The desert vanished behind them and they didn't move.

"I've lost my little boy."

Beriah's grip is strong and sure and he didn't brace or budge as I stood up. Our hands remained clasped like arm wrestlers waiting for a table and referee.

"Then you must find him."

CHAPTER 2

HOW DO WE CHOOSE? HOW ARE WE CHOSEN?

I turn up Beekman.

The creatures follow.

The tall blue one, Jenreel, stands beside me. "Experience can guide our understanding. It should not lead our understanding."

"Huh?" and I realize I'm remembering something from my Baltic College days, an intrusive thought, something I worked on understanding from my time at Happy House.

There was a Ted Crowder - he pronounced it Crow-der. I'll explain in a bit - a Dean of Christian Life at Baltic College, a small evangelical college I attended in Michigan. I came to him with some questions, he told me to kneel and pray.

He smiled and nodded, his head bobbing like a plastic cat's in the rear window of a car, as I tried to articulate what I wanted to ask.

The only problem was I had trouble articulating the questions I wanted to ask and he had trouble giving answers other than those he'd learned from a book. I went into his office, I remember, because it was at the end of the hall and either I turned into his office or I went up the stairs to the cafeteria. The food wasn't that good and there were some things I wanted to know.

Simple, no?

Ted Crowder was a fundamental evangelical Anglican. From New Zealand. He was the first man I'd ever seen who had a single eyebrow running over his left eye straight to his right, a single bush so thick that if he was from Australia I would have expected to see a joey in it. It was also my first experience with a New Zealand accent (hence Crow-der, not Crowd-er). I didn't know until then that a New Zealand accent sounds exactly like patronizing.

This is why we go to college: to learn things.

When not kneeling and praying he saw to the spiritual needs of the campus. This meant making sure the bookstore didn't stock any Rolling Stones, Beatles, Frampton, CSN&Y, Joni Mitchell, Harrison, Yes, ELP, The Who, Procul Harem, Harry Chapin, Billy Joel, Elton John, Wings, and is this cross-stylistic enough so you get the idea? Gospels and Christian Rock were okay.

Have you ever listened to Christian Rock? As Ted defined it?

I'll make it easy for you: there is none. Pat Boone, Nat King Cole, Andy Williams, and a small number of sister college choirs do not any kind of rock make.

The only magazines allowed, aside from spiritual publications, were the likes of *Good Housekeeping* and *Modern Bride*. All the spiritual publications were evangelical fundamentalist in nature and scope.

This should not be a surprise. Remember this. People went to Baltic for this.

Dean Ted believed his role was to monitor the Christian life of each student, regardless of whether that student wanted said monitoring or not. I know this and will explain how in a moment.

I went to Dean Ted because I was confused about who I was and who was god and what was happening in my life.

I wasn't a "Christian" back then. Evidently Baltic admitted a select number of non-Christian students each year so the students could practice their evangelism.

Imagine being invited to go somewhere and discovering the

only reason you're invited is to be someone else's experiment? Tuskegee still exists and airmen abound.

Ah, the joys of being Black in America.

I explained things to Dean Ted the best I could. He smiled and nodded and checked his watch and picked up a well-worn Bible and opened it for me and told me what to read.

"The only thing which will save you, Ben" he said in that interesting New Zealand twang, "is accepting Christ Into Your Heart As Your Personal God And Savior." He emphasized each personal word with a personal index finger jab into my personal chest. He personally pointed into a gospel. "See, right there. You shall know the truth and truth shall set you free."

He rolled his "r'"s so nice.

"Satan and God are fighting for your soul and you must help God to win, Ben." He checked his watch again. "There is no choice other than Heaven or Hell. Central Valley and that Jewish girl you see there, Ben, that's Hell. Your friends here are Heaven, Ben. Now you must decide."

I remember thinking either-or. Never both-and. Black or white is only available in the quantum infinitesimal slices of a moment, if even then.

Or the racial prejudices of majority America.

Which you choose is based on what you study. Take your pick.

But I was raised in the post-Civil Rights / pre-Obama America. You didn't say such things to White America - or White New Zealand - if you were alone.

What I wondered was, if God is so strong, why does he need help? Second, I'd never mentioned going to Central Valley or dating anyone there. How did he know?

God I must be important for them to keep an eye on me like that. I wanted to do a Clevon Little/Blazing Saddles riff: Where da white women at?

"Kneel down here with me, Ben, and we'll pray together for your soul." He checked his watch.

Which I did because I had learned the lessons of the playground well: young black men do what patronizing white men say.

Besides, God seemed to be on a clock. Either that, or Dean Ted had a quota to fulfill.

But the real question?

The real question arising from all this is "How did Jenreel know?"

One block west of the Seaport and an Army colonel, her nametag reads "Harley," holds out a strange looking mobile and points to a list of questions on the screen. I swat her hand away. "You ask them if you're so damn curious."

"Dr. Matthews, you're a mathematical linguist." She tosses me the phone like it's full of angry hornets and backs away. "So far they've only talked to you. Lingual something with them." The phone bounces on the asphalt at my feet.

I watch Colonel Harley turn and hurry away. "Hey, you found out who I am pretty fast. What is this, my fifteen minutes of fame? Can I post to YouTube? I noticed my phone can't get a signal. Amazing finding a dead zone in the middle of New York City, don't you think? Or did you folks disable all personal telecommunications with some kind of electronic perimeter? Control the message and you control its meaning, right?" I shove my first in the air *ala* Tommie Smith and John Carlos at the '68 Mexico City Olympics. "I love my 40 acres. Had to shoot my mule to feed my family, though. Maybe that's why you gave us a creature that couldn't reproduce?" People stare from behind police and military rifle-walls. I stare back. "Who am I kidding? That would have been both sophisticated and subtle. Our government? Nah."

I turn to Beriah. "Am I the only one you'll talk to?"

"No."

"See?" I turned back to the colonel again but she's gone. The strange-looking mobile lays on the ground in front of me, its screen and the questions face up. I pick up the mobile, check it for damage

- nothing, not even a scratch - wonder why my screen cracks every few months.

"Fuck. Okay." I read the first question. "Who are you?"

"I am Beriah."

"I am Cetaf."

"I am Jenreel."

"Yeah, yeah, right. Where did you come from?"

The Healers look back down at the block we just covered. Beriah points. "We come from there."

"What are you here to do?"

"Me."

"Me."

"Me."

Echo. Echo. Echo.

Step back. I am a mathematical linguist. My research is in spontaneous languages. Think Chomsky's Universal Grammar across species, a true primary language, what linguists call the "One-Tongue," which allows communication regardless of who's communicating, and you have it.

A pattern was forming. There was a syntax, not to the words but to the event.

"What's not you that is you?" This wasn't on the list. I improvised. It is what my research would equate to "Where are your homes?"

"Wozanni," said Cetaf.

"Wijica," said Beriah.

"Tuktel," said Jenreel.

"I thought you were all from the same place. How come you all look the same?"

"We look the same because we don't look like you, Ben."

I put down the strange looking mobile. "Why did you choose me of all the people at the Seaport?"

"We chose each other."

"We did? I don't remember having any choice to make. When did I make a choice?"

Beriah gazes up at the World Trade Tower. "To know the choices one has made all one needs do is observe where they are at that moment in their life."

I look around at the litter, the crowds being pushed back, the military, the news helicopters being driven away by gunships and fighter wings, and the three creatures standing quietly at my side. "Huh?"

Cetaf the Walking Wall's gaze goes from following Beriah's gaze to looking me in the eye. "Our goals determine our life. The thought becomes the action. The belief becomes the deed. We can only succeed. Most often when we're not paying attention to what we've made our goals. Regardless, every attempt is a success."

I wonder if this is where it really begins. In a very few sentences, in a moment when I truly listen. I stop shouting my message and start listening to theirs.

Is this the basis for true communication?

I realize why we each make our choices. I look at the three of them, slowly aware of how long this journey, my fifteen minutes, will be, and whisper. "Hello?"

I listened to Dean Ted smile and nod and bob his head to his sofa pillow god as he told God to listen up now, we got ourselves another Boy for Jesus here.

I said, "Okay, Jesus. I've sinned. I want you in my life. Amen."

Dean Ted leapt from the floor and shook my hand, lifting me from the floor and steering me towards his door. "There you go, Ben. All's right now. You've accepted Christ as YOUR PERsonal LORD and SAVior and YOUR LIFE will CLEAR itSELF of ALL MYSterIES Now."

He said it like that. I swear it.

By now I was out of his office and he closed his door on me, nodding and smiling and bobbing all the while.

I started up the stairs to the cafeteria, suddenly sure the food wasn't that bad. As I turned up the second flight of stairs, I saw a shapely pair of legs in a skirt that could never have been purchased in the bookstore clacking in CFM stilettos before CFMs stilettos existed.

I'm sure Dean Ted smiled and nodded and bobbed.

Ted Crowder. His solution to anything was to kneel and pray.

Why did he offer solutions which didn't even work for him?

What does it mean to live outside of oneself? If I spend all my time monitoring your spirituality, what time do I have left to grow my own?

I mean, how can I feed you if I'm hungry?

CHAPTER 3
HELLO?

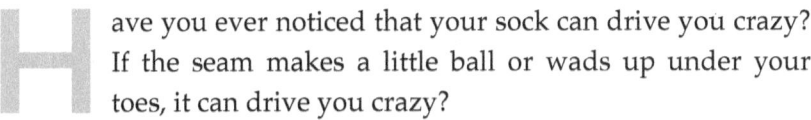ave you ever noticed that your sock can drive you crazy? If the seam makes a little ball or wads up under your toes, it can drive you crazy?

Cetaf nudges my arm.

"What?"

"It hurts."

I watch a corporal being ragged out by a lieutenant. The reason for this ragging is the corporal ordered some men to move back as we moved forward. The corporal did this just as every other corporal I've known to do it, the way he learned to do it by watching the DIs at Basic, by yelling at the top of his lungs and degrading his men in front of others.

The problem, it seemed, is Frog Lips, Elephant Toes, The Wisp, and I are the others, and the lieutenant is concerned the corporal's behavior may cause these three to shit sparks and otherwise cause more damage to our ozone layer.

He does this by spinning the corporal around and spittily saying he is dismissed, go away, be here no more.

As I watched the corporal being punished for doing his job how he thought he was supposed to do his job, I remembered Mrs. Woodbury, grammar school fourth grade. My strongest memory of Mrs. Woodbury stems from third grade, not even in her class yet. I had to get the boys in my class in line at the end of recess. We'd all go back into the school, nice and orderly, side by side, all in a line. It was my first day with this monumental responsibility. Everybody was making noise. I did to them exactly what my father did to me when I was making noise and he wanted it quiet. I yelled at the top of my lungs, "QUIET!" Mrs. Woodbury grabbed me by the shoulders and spun me around, slapped me hard across the face and shoved me into the school. All by myself. All the kids, boys and girls, laughed. I didn't know what I did wrong. Never even let myself cry.

"What hurts?" I ask Cetaf, my mind returning from its journey down memory lane. "Where?"

There are tears in his eyes. This walking wall sheds tears like a mourner on overtime and does nothing to stop or hide it. From me.

From anybody, really, but it is my arm he nudged.

He held his face in his hands and shook it from side to side as if caught in some kind of rage. "These are the strongest tears of all."

I looked at Cetaf, Jenreel, and Beriah. I looked up and down the street, at military types coming closer and police types moving away. "I don't know what to do."

Jenreel and Beriah move to either side of Cetaf and touch him. Jenreel stands in front and wraps his arms as much around Cetaf as he can. "The first communication must be instructions on how to build a receiver."

"What? How is the other group supposed to receive the communication if they don't have a way to receive it? How are they supposed to even know a message's been sent?"

Beriah stands to Cetaf's side and rests a hand on the giant's shoulder. "Exactly."

I stare into the sky and shake my head. Maybe I had to come from where they did to understand?

They stood there, like that, long enough for me to begin to understand.

Streetlights came on before we moved.

I did cry, eventually, on my way home. I climbed so high in a tree I knew nobody would follow, shoved my fist in my mouth to muffle my tears, and sobbed so hard my other hand cramped clasping a branch so I wouldn't fall.

I got word my son is safe. Gayle said not to worry. She's taking Jiminy to Hawaii. Lots of people are leaving the city. I don't know why; it's been two days, and we've only moved four blocks in a straight line up Beekman.

The fact that they never leave me makes going slow. We sleep in the street, a lot safer than you might expect it to be in New York City. I find that Cetaf, when lying down, makes a comfortable mattress. He never actually sleeps, I think. Every time I wake up at night, he is looking straight up, as if he can see the stars.

I roll off Cetaf as the sun splashes daylight into the city. "Okay, guys. It's morning. Where do we go today?"

Beriah points up Beekman to Pearl. The only problem is we'll hit Southbridge Towers once we cross Pearl.

"What do we do when we hit the brick wall?"

"We turn left."

Word is, Frog Lips, Elephant Toes, and The Wisp are the front end of an invasionary (envisionary?) force, scoping us out then relaying troop size, strength, level of technology.

CHAPTER 4
THE RUSSIANS HAVE LANDED

Fourth grade, now a student in Mrs. Woodbury's class, and we're watching a US-centric documentary about the 1960's Space Race. One of the kids in class asked why the Russians always landed on land and we always landed in the ocean. I remember Mrs. Woodbury dismissing the question. "Oh, we could land on land if we wanted to..." I don't remember the rest of her answer. What I do remember is knowing, knowing even then, that Mrs. Woodbury was lying, that we couldn't land on land and that water was safer for us. What I remember most was knowing in that sacred unspeakable way only a child can know, even as Jiminy would know, that Mrs. Woodbury was afraid of the truth, afraid to admit that the Russians could do something we couldn't.

The man is in the fifth-floor window of Southbridge Towers, looking onto Pedestrian, with a gun aimed at Beriah. He isn't dressed as a laborer, which surprises me. He is smartly attired, and I have the impression he is well educated and successful.

Beriah stares up at him. "We represent an end to all he believes is true."

"Huh?"

"The man up there, the man aiming the weapon at me."

"Aren't you going to do anything about him?"

"There is nothing I can do."

"You can duck, you can hide. You changed Brooklyn and the East River into a desert to get here. Don't tell me there's nothing you can do."

"The man holds the weapon, not I. We changed nothing, only took the path which opened for us."

I'm not listening. "But he's going to kill you."

"No, he's going to kill himself."

I have trouble with this. The gun is aimed at us. "How can you say that? He's aiming at us, dammit."

"He aims at us because he sees a world beyond that which he knows, beyond that which he has worked to make real. He sees in us a truth incongruous to his truth. Our destruction means his world is safe, nothing is new, his security is affirmed. Either he destroys us, or he starts over. But we are already here. By being there he acknowledges we are here. Destroying us would not destroy his memory of us."

"Huh?"

Beriah waves at the man. It's such a human movement I wonder where he learned it.

But then again, he could want to make sure the man in the window hits him and no one else. "No. No matter what he does, he cannot destroy us."

There is a gunshot. A deep, dark blast which echoes along the city's canyons and blots out the sun as thousands of pigeons take flight. I dive to the crash of glass and metal, thinking his first shot went wide, soon there will be another, and I curl into as tight a ball as I can.

Jenreel, Beriah, and Cetaf look down at me. All three offer me their hands. They are fine therefore I am shot. I run my hands over myself while still on the ground, realizing that to do so meant the bullet hasn't penetrated anything above my waist.

There are no wounds, no holes, no penetrations, no broken bones. Only a bruised knee from when I went down. The Healers help me up.

"Are you okay?"

Beriah's face, if completely human, would show concern. "No. We are the Healers from the Land of Barass. I am Beriah." He motions toward Cetaf.

SNAFU.

I interrupt him. "Yeah, yeah. You're not hurt? I thought I heard a gunshot. I'm sure I did." I look up to the man in the window and see him hanging there, half in and half out of the window, his tie a creek from which blood streams down the building's side.

Homo Sapiens is the current point in a line which started two hundred millennia ago, from one female in fact - an "Eve." At that time, there were three distinct lines, all modern human-like life coming from that same point in time, Eve1, Eve2, and Eve3. The other two lines died out meaning, if there was ever a One-Tongue, it was a product of Eve_1's line.

Class is starting. It started long ago but I didn't know how to attend.

How did they know what would happen? Are their eyes so much better than mine? I look into first Beriah's then Jenreel's then Cetaf's and wonder if their eyes are the color of Eve2's or Eve3's.

Maybe yes, maybe no. What I begin to learn is their use of language and how different it is from my own. Does one's language dictate one's truth?

What is the truth? Even in the face of undeniable evidence, it is still only that which we are willing to accept as true. The Russians landed on solid ground and the man in the window, much like Mrs. Woodbury, couldn't accept the truth of it.

It is tough to become a beginner.

CHAPTER 5

PLACES YOU'VE NEVER BEEN

ncontinent". Every time I hear that word I think, "It must have been a hell of a war."

Across South Street from the Port Authority's Downtown Manhattan Heliport is the Viet Nam Veterans' Plaza. The city is still deserted, at least at this end, and a mixture of police, National Guard, Army, Marines, and Special Forces surround us. Some have their weapons on us, others are buying doughnuts and coffee from some street vendors. The police are told to remove the vendors, this is a secured area. The police say, "Back it up, get out of here," then count their change, their mouths full of donut. Out in the East River are warships, their guns set to level Manhattan. Above us, swarming like locusts and nearly blotting out the sun, are Cobras and BlackHawks, combat helicopters in steady formation. Further above are bombers which I can hear but not see. The sky, where it shows between and above buildings, is bluer than I remember seeing except for up north in New Hampshire where pollution is petitioning for repatriation. Clouds and mists rise off the river, both due to the warbirds' blades. Despite all the activity, there is no wind and the smell of the river hangs on us like old, rotted clothes. There are no birds where we stand, but several pigeons wait for the soldiers and police to drop their donuts and flee.

Movable versions of The Wall, The Memorial Flag, The Book, and a few other, similar memorials are on display in Veterans' Plaza. Beriah and Jenreel walk towards them. Our ocean of defenders moves with us. The birds race forward and scramble to gather crumbs and avoid boots before they take to the air again.

Beriah places his hands on The Wall, presses his fingers into the names, and closes his eyes.

"Is everything okay?"

Jenreel leans against The Book, his face and eyes looking at the guardians of our peace occulting us as much as possible from onlookers. "These serves as a memory for those who passed in conflict."

"Yes." I notice some officers and older enlistees are acutely attentive to us.

"We don't have such things."

The secret of world peace is at hand? "You don't have conflict?"

Cetaf bends over The Memorial Flag. "There is always conflict. We don't have such memories."

"Are there no fighters, no soldiers, no warriors where you come from?"

Jenreel shakes his head. "Of course there are. They're all dead."

"Don't you wish to remember them?"

"Time spent dwelling on the past can blind one to today."

"There are those of my people who say, 'If we don't study the mistakes of the past we are doomed to repeat them'."

"Each morning be a blank slate that the new day may write itself upon you. Be wise as serpents and as harmless as doves."

Frog Lips, The Wisp, and Elephant Toes are Zen Christians? Did they read Earth literature before they came, deciding whether or not they'd enjoy this holiday spot?

The police and soldiers shrug and move away. The Healers

don't threaten their job security after all, they're just Joseph Campbell students. Birds land on Cetaf and he picks up crumbs and scraps to feed them.

"I don't understand." This has become my stanchion in the short time I've known them. "Doesn't that leave yourself open to repeating your mistakes?"

"It leaves you open to experiences unique to this moment. Sometimes experiences follow patterns. Respond differently to the pattern and it breaks. Mistakes are not repeated."

"But - "

Beriah waves his four fingered hand palm up at the memorials. "As long as you need to mark how long you've been free of a drug, you're still doing a drug. You must become "Do something else" to be free of a drug. If you continue to accept your disease, you can never accept your health because the two do not leave room for each other. Continue to glorify conflict by remembering it and you'll never be free of it."

"But you said there would always be conflict."

"How often one enters conflict is not an indication of their spirit. How one engages conflict is an indication of where their spirit is. How one responds to conflict is a pattern learned somewhere in time."

A disfigured handful of homeless vets huddle in their P-coats and khakis. They stand still as our slow parade moves past, their ears and eyes and fingers and nostrils and tongues twitch and flick and blink and fidget and flare as they relive wars seconds and minutes and hours and days and years away.

Something one of the Healers said, something about experience and understanding, merges with something I heard at Happy House, something about BMIRs, Behavioral Manifestations of Internal Responses, about little twitches and flicks and blinks and fidgets and flares we do when an unwanted memory takes hold of us unannounced, simply pops into consciousness for some reason, takes hold for a moment, until going back down into momentarily forgotten memories.

The two dance together, arm in arm, both wanting to lead, fighting for control, until I shake my head and dismiss them both.

The Healers watch me but say nothing. I dismiss my mental minuet with a nod towards those we pass and wonder if my battle-fields are any different from theirs. "Poor bastards. They would have been better off protesting their wars."

Jenreel looks past me to them. "I think they are."

CHAPTER 6
TOURISTS VERSUS LOCALS

A path I'm unaware of brings us to Legion Memorial Square where a sign on a lamppost reads like the top paragraph of a newspaper story: Who What When Where Why. There is no How.

Our entourage of news, police, national guard, and other personnel still move in a fifty-foot perimeter around us, camera lights and floods on trucks keep us in a shadowless blue-white concrete and asphalt landscape. In the middle of the night I wear sunglasses and feel myself getting a tan from the false-front sunlight's intensity. I wonder if warships still glide up and down the East River, training their guns between buildings in order to find us. The guarding is now in distinct shifts and I've made uneasy friends who leave groceries in our path or toss me soap when they're brave enough to approach.

One tall, thin man comes by a little more often than most. His heavy beard sweeps his chest and his hair needs to be both washed and combed. I want to ask him what he wants, what can I do for him, and don't. His skin is darkened by the sun and his eyes appear brown when they're not obscured by the winds.

What am I to do with you and these creatures? is what I think he wants to ask inside his ratty jeans. What part in my life do you four play? is what I hear in the wet rustle of his wool socks and squeak of Knapp work shoes. What part of the ritual is you? his sweat stained red and yellow on black flannel shirt calls out. Which is me? And if I do it right, just right, oh so right, will things get better for me? And if I don't, will things get at all?

I know he wants to ask these things because they are clear in the miasma which surrounds him.

The question he asks by his presence, his person, his being as it comes and goes before me, is the one echoed in my own eyes, Why has this happened to me? All I want to do is make sure my son is okay.

"Still seeking your little boy?" asks Beriah.

"Well, no. I know he's safe. I wish he was with me." I quickly correct myself. "I mean I wish I was with him."

Beriah nods and we walk on.

Most of our path is swept clear because of the slow passage of our host. There is a Manhattan map on the ground, a Hagstrom Quick&Easy Map. It is crushed and covered by a confusion of boot-prints, so its folds are forgotten but it's laminated and much of its yellow and green and red and black and blue printing has survived. I pick it up. "Great! Frog Lips, look, a map of where we are. Now we won't have to wander around aimlessly. You guys can figure out where you're going and just get there. Great, huh?"

Beriah frowns. As much as a frog can frown, he frowns. "We aren't 'wandering'. Perhaps you mispronounced what you wanted to say. Our path is clearly laid out before us."

Cetaf looks at the map in my hands. "Besides, all maps are made by tourists."

"Will Jesus-fucking-Christ somebody reboot the clue server?" I turn to our entourage and shout, "Will somebody please hand these guys a clue-phone?" I spin back to Cetaf, Jenreel, and Beriah. "Just what do you think you are, locals? You sure don't look like Jack

Lemmon and Sandy Dennis. I've been walking with you guys for two weeks and I haven't seen any path."

Jenreel strikes an Indian scouting for cavalry pose as if he's in an old John Wayne western. One hand shades his eyes. "Truth waits for eyes unclouded by longing."

"Fuck you." I think about it and don't find the image comforting. "No, skip it."

I hear a voice slightly above the milieu of our host. It is from a network announcer. "Somebody tell that prick to watch what he says. We're going to have a bitch of a time cutting this to pass Standards."

Most know the Healers don't answer questions which are asked. If they do answer, the answers have little to do with the questions.

I don't know what I'm doing here. I don't know why I was chosen. I decide to do something totally selfish: I sit down and cry.

There is much commotion along the inner circle of our host. "Dr. Matthews, are you okay? Is something wrong?"

Can assholes ask questions or did I just hear an articulate fart?

"Dr. Matthews? Is everything alright?"

I look to see who's asking these questions. Faces are hidden behind camera lights and laser sights. Some of our younger escorts keep their weapons trained on us until sergeants and officers order them to stand down. One man-child not old enough to shave has trouble reholstering his gun.

The question is repeated. "Dr. Matthews?"

In answer I wail louder. The Healers stop. They don't join me on the street. They stand around me. Cetaf holds his hand out to me. He doesn't touch me. He just holds his hand out where I can see it. I take it, his hand engulfing my forearm and I know he can snap it if he wants to. Instead I feel my arm against a strong wall and realize he is merely there. He will help me up some, but I'm the one who must stand.

"Thank you."

He smiles and we start to walk again. One step and the man-child's gun fires. Our host fall and run. The man-child's face is white and he's looking at his weapon as if his best friend had just betrayed him. His shirt is turning ruddy with his blood. A second man-child's face appears behind the first, this one's eyes wide, his face white with fright as he clutches his falling comrade.

I frown. How was he floundering with his holster such that he shot himself in the chest? Before the thought becomes words I remember a lesson of my fellow travelers: the best answers have little to do with the questions asked.

Calls and commands run through our crowd. "Corpsman!" "Medic!" "Ambulance!" "Lou, wrap him!" "Pack him!" Suddenly all eyes are on the Healers and there are no more sounds other than kestrels perched high overhead and waking because they think they see the sun.

"Dr. Matthews?"

I look into the lights and shadow my eyes. "What?"

"Could you ask your friends?"

"Ask them what?"

"They...They're healers, aren't they? Buck's shot himself right in the chest."

I don't know what to do and turn to Frog Lips, Elephant Toes, and The Wisp. "Can you heal him?"

Jenreel looks at the dying soldier then in the direction we're traveling. "How? His damage seems extensive."

"You're healers aren't you? Or can you only heal your own kind?"

An ambulance arrives. There is nothing for them to do. They cover the body and leave.

"Like all things, we only heal ourselves."

"But you told me you're Healers from the Land of Barass."

"Yes, we are."

"What kind of healers are you, damn it?"

"The only kind we know. We heal ourselves. Once we gain the power to understand our own wounds, then, perhaps, we can help others heal themselves from similar wounds."

Newspeople's pens and pencils zig and zag on notepads, camera shutters click, recorders pause in their recording. There will be headlines: Physicians Who Heal Themselves!

I flag a rifleman. "Somebody shoot them and put me out of my misery."

CHAPTER 7

THAT WHICH MAKES US HAPPY, THAT WHICH MAKES US SAD

1-800-MD-TUSCH

Jenreel points at the sign as we enter the #9 train at South Ferry. Cetaf and Beriah are at street level. Ever since the war memorials they are fascinated by people's stories. We stop at each historic marker, each memorial plaque. Thank god we didn't go to Ellis and Liberty Islands!

I feel the train lurch and worry that Cetaf and Beriah might be left behind.

The doors pulse shut and I'm reminded of a sphincter constricting.

"The sign is for a doctor, a type of healer, who specializes in problems of the rectum and anus."

"Isn't that how you people relieve yourselves of waste?"

I nod.

"You people have trouble relieving yourselves of waste?"

A bag lady bumps into me and knocks me back. Her hand clutches the pole in front of me and she stands between Jenreel and me. "Children don't. Kiddies go whenever and wherever they need. That's why they's always smiling."

She smiles wide and proud and releases her bowels. The smell is obvious, although she is so wrapped in rags nothing escapes.

A chime sounds and the doors clamp again but open quickly, stopped from sealing by some of Notre Dame du Bags' luggage. She waddles out and Cetaf and Beriah come in. People make room for Cetaf as he squeezes through the door.

Jenreel points her out to Cetaf and Beriah as she crosses the platform and bumps into people. "She has no problems of the rectum and anus."

I nod. "I think that's why she's so happy."

Cetaf and Beriah also see the TUSCH sign.

Jenreel explains, "Some of them have trouble getting rid of their waste. The ones who don't smile, evidently."

I look around the subway car. Nobody's smiling. Some are twitching. One or two mumble to themselves.

My eyes come back to Jenreel and he cocks his head at me. "You're not smiling, Ben."

"Constipated."

"Oh."

CHAPTER 8
THE RULES OF BADMINTON

When we were thirteen, I told Denny O'Malley the idea of badminton was to try and keep the birdie in the air for as long as possible. I didn't know if these were the rules but I wanted them to be the rules. Denny said nothing and played by these rules all day long. We laughed and had a good time, kidding each other when the shuttlecock missed a racket and fell to the earth where it stayed until our laughter picked it up again. Because of my joy, I forgot I made up the rules.

The next day Denny returned with a different look on his face. He told me I was wrong and my rules were stupid. How could anybody win with such stupid rules?

This from a thirteen-year-old?

"I looked it up. It's just like tennis. You score it pretty much the same way."

I winced slightly looking at him, fearing, preparing for what might happen. "We had fun, didn't we?"

"We're going to have more fun today."

I didn't fear Denny would hit me or beat me. That was not Denny's way. What I feared was another tearing away of the joy of childhood, another day of boyish laughter never to be repeated or known again.

Not exactly true. That whole day we played by my stupid rules I waited for that crushing blow, the slap on the face of my mother shouting, "You did it again, didn't you, you little bastard. You wet the bed and you said you wouldn't. God damn what's wrong with you, boy? I'm going to put a clothes pin on that thing of yours and you won't pee in the bed again!" from the porch as I played with my friends and followed by the laughter which bit deeper than any shark's teeth, which punched harder than any fist could.

I knew Denny would go look up the rules. He was having too much fun not to.

The World Trade Center is busy again because the world must trade and three aliens walking with a black man isn't news anymore. Cameras and news crews remain, but no longer offer step by step coverage and analysis. A copy of USA TODAY flutters by on West Street, pinned down here and there by a light rain, the first since the Healers arrived. As the pages turn past me, I read Gayle and my mother have sold the rights to my life story to Warner, and Mike Straczynski has been approached to write the screenplay.

Gayle says it's to make sure Jiminy has all the money he'll need. My mother says it's to pay her back for all the sheets she had to change. I like Straczynski's work. He's okay.

Although wetting, the rain isn't invigorating. It carries the smells and airs of the city in it and leaves black rivers on your face and clothes when it runs down.

Although there is no direct sun, there is enough heat so more rain steams back up off the streets than stays. Since they came, I've only been able to wash when someone tosses me a bar of soap by an open hydrant. I look for a hydrant now but there are none. In renovated areas the city has gone with submerged emergency facilities; pop a tile and the hydrant's there.

There's not much traffic because the streets are being kept clear lest the Healers begin emitting death rays from their eyes. Three week's walking and I know the only thing deadly about them is their monotony.

There is a slight rumble which I've never experienced before. I don't know if there can be earthquakes on the Island and the idea doesn't please me. I look out over Battery Park City and North Cove to see the waves where they belong on the North River. The birds are still pecking and seagulls circle the River Terrace construction site like vultures seeing the workers' scraps as dying cattle scattered across the range.

It takes me a moment and then I know. Without the traffic and the greater number of people, without the chaos normally contained by the city, I feel the engines in the Path Tubes rumbling to their World Trade Center stops.

A green-on-black armored truck pulls up going north and stops outside the Towers. Four men in gas masks and short sleeved green-on-black guard uniforms get out. Each has a line of grenades on shoulder straps and carries an automatic rifle.

I dive to the asphalt. "It's a hold up! Get down."

I'm the only one who dives.

Three more similarly dressed men climb from the back of the truck. One checks his watch and hollers, "Go."

There is a certain precision to such things. The first four run into the Center and the last three stand watch. One of them pulls his shirt away from his skin and waves at us like we're old friends. "You bring this heat with you?"

Before the four in the Center return, police cars show up.

Camera crews still follow us. Did the thieves forget? Some people begin to run.

There are pedestrians but no traffic and the police form a semi-circle around the truck. Those who did not run now join me on the ground. Only the Healers remain standing to witness what unfolds

The police bring up their own shields and SWAT teams draw near. They arrive so soon I wonder if they, also, have been following us all this time. I haven't seen this much activity since I dropped my sandwich ten or twelve blocks ago.

The three by the truck train their weapons on us. The friendly one shouts, "We go or there's interplanetary war."

Jenreel starts walking. Cetaf and Beriah follow. I crawl on my belly as fast as I can to keep up. They move directly between the three and the police. I don't crawl as fast. Once directly between the two groups and directly in the line of fire of both, they stop. Cetaf lies down on his belly flat. Beriah and Jenreel sit on either side of him.

Jenreel smiles. "Finite to Zero-Sum achieved."

I realize I'm the only one who can be shot without harming anyone else and scamper on all fours until I'm in the middle of Cetaf's back. He is quite large. My position isn't safe and he provides some cover for this scene's antagonists should either side venture close and begin firing. Both sides are still far enough away so doing so would only force a firefight.

Not far away, some pigeons walk in circles and begin cooing. Cetaf smiles at them and waves.

I flatten on Cetaf's back. "We'd be safer somewhere else."

Jenreel shakes his head. "This is the safest place right now. Neither side can afford to play the game."

"What game?"

He points at the thieves and the police. "These two groups want to play a finite game." He points at the thieves. "This group demands we play without asking if such is our wish."

"Yeah, so?"

"So when we're included in a game we don't wish to play, our own rules can apply."

"We changed the rules?"

"Yes. They wished to include us in a finite game in which we would be the ultimate losers. I did not wish to play. I changed the rules so we would either win or no one could play."

The first four, slumped over low to the ground, each carrying a sack a third as big as they are and swinging their weapons around them as they move, run down the middle of the Center and join their comrades by the truck. I hear one ask, "What the fuck's going on?" Another comments, "Jesus Christ, Paul, can't you get anything right?" One of them stands up and trains his weapon on the police on our opposite side.

A policewoman stands up and takes aim on him.

He squats back down.

So does she and a policeman behind her pops up then down.

Another of the felons does the same.

I can't stop myself. "I know this game! It's Whack-a-Mole!"

A moment or two later we're in the center of a curse-throwing calliope, thieves and police uniformed pipes popping up and down to a jagged, light rain damp, early June hot, south-west city beat: "I'm gonna get you motherfucker!" "Drop it, asshole!" "Move and you're dead!" "Kiss my ass, cocksucker!" "You're surrounded, shit-head!" "Blow me, cunt!"

I want to grab a gun, hold it to my throat, jump up, and cry out, "One move and the nigger gets it." I mean, it worked for Cleavon Little in *Blazing Saddles*, didn't it? Instead I turn to Jenreel. "How long are we not going to play the game?"

"The goal of a finite game is to end with a single victor and a single vanquished. We've already stopped playing."

"But those guys stole money. Money that doesn't belong to them. The way this is going they'll get away with it."

"We haven't been forced into that game."

My arms go wide, my hands up to hold this scene in place. "It's not a game?" I pull my hands and arms in as I have no wish to be a target in whatever game people are playing.

"Yes, it's a finite game, just in the way in which that money was earned was a finite game. All that is necessary for either is to find those willing to play. You can adapt the rules of finite games to become zero-sum, but then no one wins. After a while of playing zero-sum, players who wish a victor and vanquished either stop playing or develop other games where such can exist."

When did the Healers study Nash?

Beriah waves an all-inclusive hand at both sides in the game. "We only play infinite games."

Jenreel scoots beside him. "The goal of an infinite game is to continue being played." His hand reaches out to Beriah's and I wonder if they're going to high-five each other. "All life is designed as an infinite game."

"They have guns! They're going to shoot us! We're going to die!"

Beriah shakes his head. "You count death as a loss. It isn't. It's only a change in the game."

Jenreel concurs. "All life is designed as an infinite game."

Cetaf adds his two cents. "The players may change, the game continues regardless. All players share the same last move, hence everybody wins. It's more fun that way. Life is designed so that everybody wins."

Beriah glances at both sides simultaneously. You can do that when you have frog eyes. "Humans must do a lot of work to keep things so finite."

Cetaf begins to move and both Jenreel and Beriah stand up. I stand with them and we continue north on West. Both teams shout at us. They alternate aiming their weapons at us then back at each other. One of the police screams, "Hey! What the fuck you trying to do? Get us killed? You can't just get up and go like that. Get back here!"

One of the crooks stands, points his weapon at us, and hollers agreement. "Yeah, that's right, get back here."

I continue walking, the Healers and I, and holler back, "Sorry, we choose not to play."

Somebody fires and the pavement chips up about a foot in front of me. Suddenly there is a firefight behind us as the two teams open up on each other.

Jenreel nods. "Zero-sum."

I'm not sure. "No. This game seems to go on forever. Doesn't that make it infinite?"

"You people make violence and inequality an infinite game? No, you simply haven't exhausted all the players."

Beriah invites me to walk beside him. "Yes. There are some who choose not to play."

I think back on all I've known. Yes, there have been some who didn't choose to play the game.

"All you need to do is find others who'd rather keep on playing than win any game."

Denny was a good tennis player and we played badminton by the good rules most of the next day. As we played, the kidding shifted, with more statements of placement and difference than equality. Denny told me we were having fun.

I guess Denny found fun in different places than I.

Perhaps he was angry at my saying "These are the rules." Perhaps it was that betrayal that caused Denny to play the way he did. Perhaps if I had simply said, "I don't know what the rules are. Let's play this way," the game would have gone on forever.

I didn't know if what he told me was true, nor have I ever looked it up. The real rules never mattered. I know now my rules are as good as any, all that's necessary is finding people who want to play.

At the time, Denny could not play by my rules, whatever his reason. I guess Denny needed to know where he was in the order of things. Trouble is, that means you can only cooperate with your equals.

CHAPTER 9

AT THE INTERSECTION OF LOOSELY WOUND TOILET PAPER AND WADDED SOCKS

Take the A train. But only to Fulton Street, at East New York and Broadway. A white haired, lightly tanned white man, his hair swept back and looking like it cost more to comb than this train is worth, sits wrapped in a black greatcoat. It serves a vivid contrast, like vanilla rum ice cream frosting on Devil's food cake. It is hot and muggy down here. You can tell the one because everyone is sweating and the other because steam from the track cleaners hangs like an early morning mist around a fish trawler, flies and stench serving as gulls and fish tripe.

The man is barefoot. His toes are manicured. Despite the filth around them, his feet look healthy. The arches are strong. The great coat stops mid-calf and his muscle tone is obvious. He plays racquetball three times a week. He plays before daylight, before the courts are in demand, charging himself for the day before his competition arises. He plays to win. He opens his coat wide every time someone walks past. Underneath he is immaculately dressed. His pants are tailored and hemmed to stop just above the end of his coat. It is a great coat, and every time he spreads its black, devil's food wings people turn away in disgust, then out of the corner of their eye look back, and he catches them, and he laughs.

Cetaf is absorbed by the people and their reaction to the racquetball-playing man. Some are oblivious. Some show open interest until the game is played. Some show disgust before the serve then disappointment when racquetball-playing man fails to return their volley.

The train halts and the man rises. He stops in front of us, smiles, opens his coat. Cetaf, Beriah, and Jenreel smile and applaud, something they learned by watching others on the streets. The man bows and leaves.

Another man, a dirty man in a dirty gray raincoat, unwashed long black hair stringing over unwashed ruddy face, grease-stained jeans and black high-top Keds, rises from the back of the train and walks over to us. He smells like he's bathed in the track cleaners' steam. "I've been watching you for the past three stops," he says in a crisp academic accent. "You people are sick. You applaud that man's depravity."

He opens his raincoat and holds it open as if putting his hands in pants pockets. Only he has no pants pockets. He has no pants. No shirt except for a collar and highly cut tie. His jeans are only pantleg trunks running from just above the knee down, suspended by garters which cinch his thighs, pinching hairs as they band beside his groin. The tie's color matches the stains on the pants. He begins to pace, a professor explaining the notes upon his board or some speaker removing the barrier of a lectern between himself and his audience. "I don't know about the world you creatures come from, but that kind of behavior isn't tolerated here."

He turns from us and walks to the front of the car. There he stops and places a leg on a bench, resting his elbow on his knee and looking like some ancient mariner standing upon the bow searching some far distant shore, works his penis like a proud tiller as he rows for home.

Aye, laddies, there's a man fer ya.

The masturbating sea captain fascinated Jenreel. "Our reality is as fragile as our lives. It can be destroyed, distorted, or enlarged by so many things."

Cetaf follows his gaze. "Yes." He closes his eyes and reads from a book he won't touch for several days yet. "A spaceship landing, the death of someone by whom we gauge our own mortality, a shaman writhing and sweating over a twisted child to align the child's colors into the four directions, a surgery performed without needles or knives," he turns to me, "or three beings being, walking on unseen sand."

Jenreel nods. "How we handle our changing realities determines who we are. If there is no room in us for these things, their existence destroys us."

Certain things can catch you off guard at the strangest times. Consider a few sheets of toilet paper rolled less tightly than all the rest. You tug on the end, the toilet paper spins on its spindle, then all of a sudden the sheets spun less tightly jump up as if to get your attention. Usually it's something like, "Hey, you missed one little turd down at the bottom of your crack." Other times it's "Well, I got some good news and some bad news. The good news is you're about to receive the best blow job of your life. It will be performed by someone with no other sex partners and no history of venereal disease. It will change you in ways you can't presently comprehend. The bad news is it will be performed by an as yet unprobed monster from Stephen King's id."

Other times, it's a wad of sock bunched up in the toe of your shoe.

CHAPTER 10
CHOICE VERSUS OBLIGATION

By the time we get to Manhattan Community College, CNN stops following us. The police, escorts, news crews, and curious are more news-worthy than we are. Even the *Enquirer*'s and *Midnight Sun*'s psychics have forgotten us, more concerned with some women in Toronto having Beriah's child.

He hasn't even been here a month.

CNN pays a crew to follow us and keep a directional mike on us at all times. People tire of Beriah's snoring, even though it sounds more like a cat wheezing at night.

All we ever do is walk. We never challenge anybody and, now that the word is out, nobody challenges us. People have even stopped coming to be healed, although I hear there is a cult in Indianapolis which worships us from afar.

We stop in front of a boarding house on Albany. The manager comes to the door as he sees us walking across the street.

Beriah reads the sign in front. "We can sleep here."

I scan the sign and, ever articulate, agree. "Huh? Yeah, yes."

We start up the steps and the manager opens the door towards us. "You looking for a room?" He scans up and down the street then up at the windows on the buildings across the street. He keeps the door between us, him inside and the four of us outside, only his head and chest peering past the edge as if he were some Hollywood Indian gazing from around some tree at a wagon train of settlers crossing the plains. The image is insane. He stands behind a glass door.

"Yes, we are."

He continues to look up and down the street.

I reach for the door. "May we come in?"

He looks at us hard, as if maybe to figure us out. He licks his lips. The skin just below his nose starts to glisten. "I - "

The Healers walk away. The man points at their backs. "Guess you won't be staying." He steps back inside and closes the door before I can turn around.

"What's wrong? Didn't you want to go in there?"

"Yes."

"Then why didn't you? He couldn't keep you out. It would have been against the law."

Beriah doesn't stop, doesn't ponder, only explains. "A law created by one to create an obligation in another."

Cetaf doesn't glance back, keeps moving forward "He didn't want us there."

Thinking I was learning, I said, "He was just afraid of you. He doesn't know you."

Beriah stops, considers. "Perhaps...Perhaps he resents us."

"How can he resent you? He doesn't know you."

"Knowledge has never been a prerequisite to resentment. Besides, obligation breeds resentment, choice breeds acceptance."

CHAPTER 11

THE FEAR IN SANTA CLAUS' EYES

One summer I worked at a meat packing and processing plant called JilSom. It was run by Irwin Goldfarb, a man who was given the job because his family didn't know what else to do with him, who always drove a Corvette paid for in cash until someone gave up trying to explain and simply told him leasing through the company was better, who had two black, foresty eyebrows trying to mate along a ridge like a mogul where his forehead met his face, spent as much time under the hair dryer as did his wife but never with her, and yelled during staff meetings that God Damn It, It Was A Good Thing He Was Around Because His Company Was Being Run Into The Ground By The Flunkies He Had Working For Him And They Were Lucky To Have Their Jobs Anyway.

I wondered if he'd ever been to New Zealand.

He said this each week to his senior staff. Obviously he was correct because his senior staff, being vilified thus each and every week, never left. He also made it a point to let the workers, especially those spending their first day on the job, know how he felt towards his staff.

One of his staff, Jones, a man in charge of receiving and

lorrying - placing things in the warehouse-size freezer so they could be found quickly and orderly - confided in me one day he was going to be president of the company in five years. He told me this in front of his crew. He was a Santa Claus-sized man with a blonde Van Dyke beard and eyes cold blue like the freezer he spent much of his time in. When he spoke, his voice was not careful or poised. It was always full of surety upon demand. He knew where everything was in his warehouse-size freezer and his voice let you know he knew. In his freezer, he was right. His voice, outside the cold of those four frost-covered walls, was something slightly else.

His office was on the other side of the building from Irwin's. One day, as I was crossing the building to drop off some paper-work, Irwin came out of the shadows to me. "Where're you going?"

I kept to myself pretty much although I knew I frightened him without knowing why. The longer I was with JilSom, the more his voice gained accusation.

"Receiving."

"Tell Jones I want to see him."

"Okay."

Outside the Civic Center people shout at me. They are waving signs and brandishing banners.

I stare wide-eyed. "Hot damn! We're their protest!"

The police keep people back but a man, woman, and child thrust through the barricade and lie on the ground in front of us.

Beriah looks at the man, says, "Thank you," and steps on the man as if he were a stone in the street, doing nothing other than what he'd done before: walk.

The man's eyes go wide. He doesn't expect this. He exhales sharply and convulses trying to protect himself from being used for what he offered himself. "They're not like us!"

Jenreel, is a step behind Beriah. "Thank you."

He takes his step.

Cetaf is about to step on the woman. Her brow creases and her eyes, I notice, are an icy blue. "You monster! you'll kill me!"

His pace never changes. "You saw me walking. You didn't stop me. You could rise up and join me. Instead you offered yourself as part of my path. I hope it will be better for you next time. Thank you."

His foot comes down and the woman is crushed.

The man protects his broken ribs and rasps at the protesters. "I told you, they're not like us!"

Beriah, Jenreel, and Cetaf stop at the child. Each leans over him.

Cetaf, the Walking Wall whom I've come to realize is the gentlest of the three, offers the child a finger. "Do you want to be here?"

The boy, lying on the ground but looking around him and working his face as he fights to understand, whispers. "No. I'm scared."

Beriah's great frog eyes blink. "Perhaps you wouldn't be scared if you were with your friends."

"I...I don't have any friends. Margaret and Bruce won't allow it."

I turn to the man on the ground protecting his ribs. "Your name 'Bruce'?

He wraps his arms around himself as if embracing a loved one and stands. The pain of breathing whitens his face. "Don't kill my child." His eyes, which I thought also blue, I now realize are hazel, a slight bluish green.

Slight Earth rotation: I know what you mean. I'm looking for my own, as well.

Beriah blinks again at the child. "May I pick you up? Give you a piggyback to that officer over there?"

I look to see who he's pointing to. It's our old friend Distasio radioing for an ambulance.

The boy nods and up he goes, laughing and afraid to laugh as Beriah tickles him while they walk towards Distasio.

Bruce coughs up blood. "Stop them! They're kidnapping my child! Abuse by the state!"

We continue to walk on, past the protesters and those who watch the protest. Blood dribbles down Bruce's chin. "They're not like us!"

I walk back to him. "Damn right. And thank god they're not."

Beriah hands the little boy to Distasio, who takes the child and nods, and rejoins us. "Does this happen often?"

"What, the protesting?"

Beriah's hands move to his head and lie flat where ears should be. "Protesting? No, the shouting. They shout their own needs. They need you to accept their beliefs, their thoughts, their ways as true. Anything else is a threat they are false. Rather than accept you as you are, rather than accept themselves as they are, they shout their needs in an attempt to make you needy."

I laugh. "Oh, that. Yeah, that happens a lot down here." I don't know where they're from, saw them walk towards me from wherever they came, and still unconsciously assume a linear, God-sent-them-to-save-us direction.

Jones the warehouse-knowing Santa Claus-man walked back with me like a man eyeing the gallows. Halfway through the plant, some meatcutters gathered around him like Nazguls around Frodo, blades in their belts like swords in their scabbards. Irwin descended from the darkness like a Serpent seeking another's skin. "What the fuck's going on back there, Jonesy? I spent twenty-five minutes going up and down my freezer and I can't find shit."

Irwin stood directly in front of him, his guardians encircling the Santa Claus-man, Irwin standing like a baseball manager who disagrees with the umpire's call. "I can't find shit, Jonesy." He pulled the manifest from behind his back. "I don't know what any of this means." He tore page after page from the log, crushed each in his hand then threw each to the floor. "You don't either, Jonesy. You dumb fuck. I know you don't. Because you're a flunkie, just like all the rest of them."

Flunkie.

Irwin loved that word.

None of the Santa Claus-man's log was left, but paper remained. "Now this is how I want the freezer set up. I want it done now. I don't care if you have to stay here freezing your balls off all weekend long, and I'm not authorizing any overtime for your men so you'll probably have to do it all yourself, but I god-damn want it done the way I want it and you're going to god-damn do it. It's either that or you can kiss your ass out of here because it's good-bye." Irwin's eyes bulged from his face and spittle gathered on his chin, a technique to be seen on any playground in any part of the world.

Irwin was slightly taller than Jones as inches are measured. Now he towered over him in the way small men tower over those whose fear makes them smaller still. Santa Claus folded, redfaced, sputtering and stuttering, almost in tears. "Of course, Irwin."

Irwin arched even more. The Nazgul circle grew tighter.

Santa Claus Jones swallowed. "Mr. Goldfarb."

It was amazing Jones could swallow, actually. His throat was tighter than a bagpiper at the end of a medley and tears ran down his cheeks. "Of course. No problem. I'll take care of it tonight."

Irwin's eyes receded, he smiled and nodded and walked away. Santa Claus watched him go. Santa Claus never talked with me after that.

When we ask anyone to share our reality, we ask them to join our hallucination. If they awake before we do, we die.

CHAPTER 12

PRAYING

Stop me if you've heard this one before:

A man is caught in a flood. At first the water's up to his ankles. A car drives by and the driver says, "Get in, I'm driving up into the mountains."

The man says, "No, I'll pray and God will take care of me."

Soon the water is up to his hips. A man in a boat comes by, says, "Get in."

The man in the water says, "No, I'll pray and God will take care of me."

Soon the man is sitting on the roof of his house and the water is still rising. A helicopter comes by and the pilot lowers a ladder. "Get in, I'll fly you out of here."

The man hollers back, "No thanks. I'll pray and God will take care of me."

The man drowns and goes to heaven. He meets God and says, "What happened? I prayed and you still let me drown."

God says, "Hey, I sent you a car, a boat, and a helicopter. What more am I supposed to do?"

Sounds of the city. Manhattan is never silent. Most places fall silent 3 to 5AM, not Manhattan. The city seems to sigh only once a week, early Sunday morning, from 4:45 to 5, maybe 5:15AM. It is then you hear it catch its breath, relax, wipe its brow and shake off its sweat, sit back and inventory itself before the next week's business begins.

There are always the sounds of subways, elevated trains, cars, trucks, buses, bridges cracking with the cold, exploding with the heat, swaying with the strains of tons of travel over them.

And people. There are sounds of people, ten-thousands of them, everywhere all the time and without exception. Buildings pulse with the life within them, elevators climb up and down like hearts pumping in some sixty story life form.

A west-blowing breeze dampens us with a 4:52AM, Sunday morning slickness. It rises like a dragon's mane on the mists coming in from the East River as we walk down Peter Cooper Road. The sunrise is glorious. The city almost smells sweet and clean, smells I've never noticed before.

A Federal Express truck stops in front of us. "You Ben Matthews?" the driver asks me.

"Yes."

"Sign this, please?"

"What is it?"

"I just deliver 'em, friend."

I want to ask, "You guys normally deliver this early? On a Sunday, no less?"

It's a letter from the Indiana Church of the Triple Saviors. "We're being asked to go to Indiana to teach them how to pray."

Jenreel frowns. "Pray?"

"Yes, to a god or gods, maybe. You know, to ask for something from some being greater than yourself."

Cetaf looks from Jenreel to the letter to me. "We can't teach what we don't know how to do."

Jenreel joins Cetaf's perusal of the letter. "The truest way to discover your own ignorance is to teach it to others."

Frog Lips joins our inspection. "Only those who don't realize their own ignorance attempt to teach what they themselves don't know."

"They've offered to pay. Pay for the trip, pay for our lodging, even says they'll put something in our pockets." What I really want to know is when did they learn to read? But I don't ask because the answer will be obvious and I'll feel like an idiot for asking.

Jenreel taps his robe. "We don't have any pockets."

Cetaf helps Jenreel check for pockets. "Asking a question doesn't ensure receiving the desired answer. All it ensures is receiving an answer. Even no answer is an answer."

"Come to think of it, I've never seen you three pray."

"You have, you didn't recognize it as such."

"When?"

"Right now," answers Beriah. "We pray constantly."

"Elephant Toes just said you don't know how to."

"Which is why we do it constantly; every step, every breath, every thought is a prayer. You don't need to know how to do it to do it. Often the purest form of doing something is when you don't realize you're doing it."

I skip that last part. "What do you pray for? Who do you pray to?"

Beriah stares at me and blinks. You haven't lived 'til a six-foot tall, red, frog-eyed creature blinks at you. "I pray for you, Ben, and for my other brothers here. I pray to myself."

"No, I mean what do you pray for yourself?"

"I don't."

Jenreel echoes, "Nor do I."

Cetaf echoes and adds a bit more. "Neither I. Praying for the self is self-limiting. Why not pray for all that is around you? Your prayer then touches as much of your world as exists for you."

Beriah walks again and we all move with him. "You are part of everything around you. Prayers should not be limited by you when the whole universe touches you."

We've not gone five steps when I replay the part I skipped. "Wait a second. You pray to yourself? All of you?"

Echo Canyon starts up again with Jenreel. "I pray to myself." Then Cetaf. "I pray to myself."

Step step step.

My hands shoots up as if I'm in grade school and have to wee. "Because?"

Beriah answers, the others nod. "Because to pray to something outside yourself is to deny responsibility for yourself and your actions, which is to deny your right to choose for yourself what actions to take, what actions to avoid, what actions in others to stop, which means you don't care enough about yourself to participate in your life."

Step step step.

"Ultimately, anything you pray to must live within or your prayers are wasted."

The part of that story which really fouls me up is the guy still goes to heaven.

I mean, he must, right?

He's talking *with* God.

CHAPTER 13
MOON OVER MANHATTAN

I t is night. A full moon rises over Manhattan. It casts the skyscrapers in silhouettes such that I expect to hear Ralph and Alice and Norton and Trixie. Behind us is the North River. Across that, New Jersey. We are watching the city slide under Umbra from the docking beds between Bloomfield and Gansevoor streets. I think of all the women in my life and ache for Medea or perhaps some androgynous Morpheus to hold me.

Beriah's eyes look straight up. He doesn't need to tilt his head back or lean backwards. "You seldom see the stars here."

Cetaf does tilt his head back. It's like watching the top floor of a skyscraper about to fall. "Is it like this everywhere on your world, Ben?"

"No. There are places where you can see all the stars in the sky, I'm told. In the high mountains and in the deserts. Middle of the ocean. At the poles. Some islands, no doubt. I saw lots more up in the woods. They're tough to see here because of the lights and the buildings."

Jenreel stares at me, not at the sky. "Are you sure they're there?"

I wonder if some quiz is coming. "Well, yeah. Pretty sure. I mean, I can't see them, but I saw them once. Lots more when I was a kid, so I believe they're there."

He reaches over his head and stretches. I hear things pop and crack in his arms and back as if some galactic chiropractor is at work in him.

I glance at Cetaf and Beriah. "Is he okay?"

Cetaf looks at Jenreel for a moment as if checking his alignment. "Jenreel, are you okay?"

Jenreel's arms come down. "I'm fine. I appreciate your concern." He looks at the sky then at me. "It must be difficult to know where you are and what you are if you can't see the stars. You could look to the oceans, but they wouldn't tell."

I point down. "But we're here." I wave my arms around us. "In New York," I point west, "just east of New Jersey." I stamp my foot. "Planet Earth." Tap the pavement. "North America. Terra." I point to where the sun will rise in the morning. "Sol." I want to add, "You know all that" but realize I'm not really sure anymore. Especially about that last part. Or any of it, really.

I mean, I'm wandering Manhattan with three creatures who walked in over a non-existent desert, right?

We went over all this before, didn't we?

Or aren't you paying attention?

Jenreel shakes his head and shrugs. "You find your place by finding what is around you."

"Of course. How do you do it?"

"By remembering I am the center of the process. By believing I'm the most important part of the process."

CHAPTER 14
THE BORDER BETWEEN SELFISH AND SELFLESS

We walk north on Mulberry and become something of a tourist attraction. Mothers and fathers bring daughters and sons, tourists bring vendors and hawkers, and hookers and sharps bring police on horseback and foot. The streets are still clear and I wait for confetti to fall. Both sidewalks are demarcated by yellow police barrier ribbons, behind them walk people in walkers and others push strollers and some just stand eating apples or pretzels while others sip tonics and sodas. I wonder if anyone is selling tours of my office or home.

An evenly tanned, thin, bleached blond, oriental youth (if only he was tall, fat, and red-haired! But George Carlin passed away, so it didn't happen) wearing cutoff painters' pants, Keds Hightops with red and green laces, a bowler hat, deep blue wraparound shades, a leather vest and nothing else shows some tourists how to play Three-Card-Monte.

Jenreel walks over to the youth and people make way. The police, content to let the game go on with out-of-towners, now show concern. A man holding a dachshund grabs a little boy's hand and says, "Come on, son, let's get Tippy some water." The dachshund licks the man's face as they move out from the crowd. One news crew, a camera man, a sound man, and a woman whom I've previously only seen on the Weather Channel, remain. The sound man nudges the camera man who nudges the woman who drops her soda and shouts, "Damn it, Henry, I told you to keep your hands off -" then looks at Jenreel and the youth standing over the cards and asks, "How's my hair? Do I look alright?"

A car comes around Hester onto Mulberry and straight at us. I think it is intentional. How can someone be driving anywhere in Manhattan and not know where we are?

The car swerves and jumps the sidewalk, crushing the man and his little boy but spares the dachshund because the man throws it back towards us as the car bears down on them. The dog scampers to its masters only to be crushed by the crowds running away from the still revving but now unmoving car.

Cetaf starts crying. Not weeping or sobbing, but great wracking wailing tears of agony for something he didn't do and had no real part in and couldn't have stopped if he'd wanted to.

I am confused. "I thought Cetaf cried only for his own pain."

Beriah nods agreement. "He does."

"Then why is he crying now? He didn't get hit. Or are you linked to everything around you somehow? Is that it? Cetaf is feeling the pain of them dying?"

"Cetaf can only cry for his own pain. Right now his own pain is great. He is crying because he will never know them, and that is a great loss."

"Wait a minute. People are dying all the time, people he doesn't know. He doesn't cry all the time, does he?"

"He can only cry for what he knows. It would be unwise to take on tears for what you know not."

"But he doesn't know them. Why is he crying?"

"When someone falls, your choices are to walk on or help them up. Help them up and now two stand where once there was one. Walk on and you walk alone. Cetaf cries because he will never help them up."

"There will be others, won't there?"

"Perhaps, but now those two will never help Cetaf up, as well."

"I don't understand."

"Does their death sadden you?"

"Yes, of course it does. How could it not? They were human beings, just like me, and their death was meaningless."

"You are sad because they, who you never knew, are dead and you will never know them."

"No, not exactly."

"You are sad at the loss of all people you don't know."

"No, that's not it, either."

"True, you can't be affected by what you don't know, only what you know. Therefore their changes don't affect you, only your own knowledge of change, and that some changes are irreversible."

At this time on my journey I still find argument easier than acceptance. "So he cries out of selfishness?"

"Yes."

"Many of us are selfish, but we don't think of it as a virtue."

"There is a line. Cetaf can be selfish because he first learned to be self-less. The boundary where you stop and he begins is the border between selfless and selfish. When he cries, it is in his own land, for himself, and is selfish. But those tears have no bearing on you, anyone, or anything else. They are his and his alone, and he is selfish with them, giving them to no one and sharing them with none."

"I see, I think."

"Yes, and that is all. What you see is someone who will give you blood but not bleed to death. There is no crime in selfishness. The crime is in not knowing how to be selfless, where others end and you begin."

CHAPTER 15

MOURNING WHAT IS, MOVING TOWARDS WHAT IS NOT

Central Park. That's all I need say and you already have the picture, from movies, from postcards, from television, newspapers, the news. Someone has been raped and murdered. I was about to say "Nobody special" but can no longer lie about such things. There are police everywhere, the mayor is interviewed, and we are politely ignored. Two months into the city and no longer even news. Shorter wars have been spotlit more.

A policeman separates himself from the crowd and approaches us. As he gets closer, I recognize him as Distasio. I hold out my hand and he pulls off surgical gloves before taking it. "Ben, good to see you. Seat-half, Burria, Genteel, how're you all?"

He never did get their names right.

"I've been trying to keep up with where you folks are. It's kind of tough. You're not news anymore."

Whenever Distasio was on patrol, if we were in his precinct or near it, he would drive past and wave, sometimes bringing us stuff he felt we might need.

Until the Commissioner called him on it.

I have a lot of respect for Distasio. Despite all the money and who knows what else he'd been offered, he consistently refused to do a book or anything on us.

"We're not news but this is. We're not news and this still happens." I'm sure of what I'm feeling. It is anger, but at the act, the foolishness of the act, the sheer stupidity of the violence. What did this woman have that her attacker wanted?

Distasio laughs. "Come on, Ben. You been hanging with the brothers too long?" he nods at the Healers. "You guys are good. Who wants to hear about good? This," he nods at the police cars and yellow barrier tape behind him, "this is bad, this is evil. People don't want to know about good. They want to know about bad and evil. That way they can stand up a little prouder of themselves and say 'Ha, see? I'm better than that.'" Somebody calls him. "Hey, gotta go. Coffee break's over. Take care, you guys."

Jenreel stares. "A finite game, for all players."

"A finite game? How can you say that?" My anger, unfocused, now focuses on him. "Finite in that one person is dead? Yeah, I guess that's pretty damn finite."

Cetaf begins to cry.

"Oh, gee, did I hurt your feelings? But you can't do anything. You can't bring her back to life, can you? And if you could, could you heal the damage that other bastard's done?"

Cetaf's red rimmed eyes meet mine. "I know," he says. "I'm angry, too."

Yes. I'm angry and I don't know what to do about it. Somehow Cetaf's admission stills much of my rage. "Why are you angry?"

"Because Jenreel is correct. It is a finite game. Now there is nothing to do, there are no moves left to play."

I look at Jenreel. "Games and moves. Is that how you see this?"

"The game is finite because only one player wins. As in all finite games, one wins at the expense of another. Finite games always have a victor and a vanquished, they always come to an end, always with the vanquished forfeiting something both valued."

"What did she have her attacker valued? He didn't rob her, he raped her and killed her. Are you telling me he wanted her life?

"I don't know," says Jenreel. "I'm not the attacker. Still, the attacker took her life, among other things. Perhaps the attacker took her life because that was something the attacker lacked."

I start crying, realizing how they are affecting me and realizing I want them to.

But right now I opt to use my selfishness as a defense. "What about her body?"

"Perhaps the attacker lacked that, too, and needed to see the victim's fear and pain to define their own."

I give my defense one, last try. "This is wicked. It is evil. It is bad."

Beriah frowns at me, although not in judgment. It would berate them to ever say they judge. He simply doesn't understand. "I don't think this is 'evil' or 'bad', Ben. I only think this is. That's all, this is."

I flashback to sitting on our back porch, a porch my father built because he wanted some privacy, except the porch overlooked our postage stamp backyard into our neighbor's postage stamp back-yard. I remember wanting to get up, go to a corner of our postage stamp backyard, to the fence my father put up so no one could get in and no one could get out. One day our neighbor watered his postage stamp backyard and some of the water defied the fence and fell in on our yard. My father fumed at the kitchen window for a minute then stamped out to that self same corner and yelled at our neighbor to shut off his sprinkler, that he considered our neigh-bor's water defying the fence an act of aggression, and he would retaliate.

Our neighbor stared at my father's waving hands and spittle covered chin and lips. "All you had to do was ask."

I wanted to go to that corner and pee because then my piss would leak through the fence. At least then my piss would be free. Instead I stayed on our back porch overlooking our postage stamp backyard and cried over what was and longing for what was not.

CHAPTER 16
THE INDIANA CHURCH OF
THE TRIPLE SAVIORS

When I was, oh, about twenty, some great aunt died. I went to the wake with my parents. At the time, my first time through college, I thought I wanted to be a minister.

At the wake, I got into a discussion with an aunt about God, Christianity, religion; the usual stuff. I was a newly "born again" Christian, and these concepts were odd to my aunt who believed pretty much as I did with the exception of her not having some uniquely identifiable "born again" experience.

My uncle Tony was listening. At one point, when my aunt and I were talking, he stood in front of me, dropped to his knees, grabbed my hands and put them on his head, and loudly, laughingly, said, "Ben, oh, Ben. Give me some of that religion you got, boy. I'm such a sinner and I need your healing love."

Sometimes it is no fun being a saint.

A delegation of the Indiana Church of the Triple Saviors comes to us while we sit in Grand Central Station.

I can't tell how many are men and how many are women

because they all make themselves up to look like one of the Healers. Some came by it naturally, some cosmetically, some stopped short of the face and extremities but have the bodies down cold. On either side of them are others dressed in white. Pure white. Whitened hair, bleached white skin, white togas, white socks, white Nikes. The only thing about them which isn't white are the sunglasses each wears. All their sunglasses have black leather rims, stems, and earpieces, but each set of lenses is a color of one of the Healers. Each of these people in white - novitiates perhaps - holds a sack in their right hand. As the procession approaches, they run along either side of the worshipers whose colors their eyeglasses match, reach into their sacks with their left hands, and throw a mixture of bleached sand and those little tiny stars I used to get on my papers in grade school in front of the worshipers as they walk.

I am confused a little because each bag contains all different colored stars. I think the stars should match the color of the respective retinue's Healer.

One of the worshipers, altered to look like Cetaf, comes over to me and says, "You're Ben Matthews, aren't you?"

I nod.

The worshiper tears off clothing and I see it is a she. "You must have me!" She falls backwards onto Grand Central Station's never completely clean floor and spreads herself to me, lost between a frenzy and a fugue.

Why would a woman want to look like Cetaf? "No, I... thank you. No."

She is still writhing on the ground when another worshiper, one of Jenreel's, comes up and disrobes. "Take me, Saint Benjamin."

"No, I'm sorry. I can't."

She does not fall. She simply turns, her face more drawn than I thought possible, perhaps crushed or saddened, and walks away.

One of Beriah's worshipers approaches.

"No," I scream. "Can't you get the message? No!"

"But I am different, Ben."

Before I say anything, he shrugs off his clothing and kneels before me.

I am suddenly ill. As my stomach rushes up to greet him, I push him down and away, trip over him as I run to find a barrel or can, which I never do because something at the end of their procession caught my eye.

Behind them, hidden only because they are so many, is a man whose body is painted in thirds, each third the color of a Healer. One third from the tip of his head down front and back along his right side to his navel and coursing to his hip red, one third from the tip of his head down front and back along his left side to his navel and coursing to his left hip blue, from his navel down front and back to the tips of his toes yellow. If he wears anything, it is jockey shorts.

Good thing they come in summer.

He walks up to Cetaf, Jenreel, and Beriah. "This man," he points at me, "is evil and does not worship you. He refuses the sacrifice of your church. We ask you destroy him."

The Healers laugh, genuinely laugh. Beriah points at me. "This man is Ben. He refuses the sacrifice of your church. We will not fulfill your request. You must ask him if he worships us."

Someone, someone not affiliated with this church, offers me a roll of paper towels and I wipe my mouth of vomit and my face of sweat. Our train is coming and I let them know it is time to leave. As we descend deeper, I hear the one I think is a priest shrieking, "He is evil! He is not good! He doesn't deserve your peace! He is evil!" over and over again. The worshipers chant something I can't quite catch.

I lean towards Beriah. "I'm glad you don't think I'm evil."

"No, Ben. We think you are not evil."

"Yeah, it's nice to know somebody thinks I'm good."

"No, Ben. We think you are not evil. There's a difference."

Do I want to hear this? Does it matter whether I want to hear it or not? Is it something I need to know?

"What's the difference?"

He points. "That individual back there is evil because he demands all others believe as he does regardless of their needs or wants."

Cetaf watches the man and his acolytes. "He thinks what he's doing is good. Often that is the way of evil. To define one's good as the good for all is evil. Evil is the shadow cast by good."

"So then what I did, resisting them, is good then, right?"

"There is no need to resist evil. Evil is resisted by the existence of not-evil. Your life is your resistance. Your life cannot be complacence or tolerance. The existence of not-evil spreads until evil cannot survive. That is the resistance. Existence of not-evil is an active process."

Uncle Tony laughed and got up. Lots of my other aunts and uncles laughed, as well. I don't know the expression on my face, but my aunt quickly tried to get my attention back to our discussion. I could feel the heat rushing up inside me. My anger confused me because I'd been told Christians weren't supposed to get angry but were to pray for those who offended them.

I remember saying a bitter prayer for my family's souls.

When we were about to leave, Uncle Tony grabbed my hand and shook it vigorously. He said, "It was good to see you again, Ben. Good luck to you." But he never looked me in the eye. As a matter of fact, he had his face turned slightly away and his eyes cast down when he took my hand. I didn't think of it then, but now, in memory, can only compare his movements to those of a blind man searching for a hand to shake and ears to hear.

To this day, I don't know who was the bigger fool.

CHAPTER 17

THE FREEDOM OF THE SKIES

woke up one fallish August morning to find a parakeet at the bird feeder along with the nuthatches and grosbeaks. At first I wasn't sure what it was, thinking it only a strange bird because the tail seemed wrong and far too blue for the birds I saw coming and going most days. As the wind blew and the feeder whirled, I saw that distinctive bird version of a bulldog's face.

There were thousands of loose parakeets in New York City. I was sure of it. Why had I never noticed one before?

I raised the window and waited. Once the birds returned, I slowly placed my hand outside. All the birds flew except the blue parakeet with the ruffled black on white flight feathers and louder than most tweet tweet voice. It waited until my hand was a few inches away then flew away, as if judging my sincerity or perhaps weighing the comfort of a human hand - regular food, nice cage, warm house, loving attention - with the freedom of the skies.

I thought no more about it because I didn't see or hear the parakeet for a few days. Then I awoke early and realized there was nothing I could do for the bird. Yes, I could trap it, take it inside, give it a cage, confine it for its own safety - it could never survive the winter no matter how much seed I placed in the feeders - or I could let it enjoy the skies for the time it had them. To house it for the winter and let it fly free again next summer would only repeat my indecisions in the future.

It is a bird. It is meant to fly, as high and free as it can. If it knew no other life than a confining but loving cage, a friendly human hand, my decision would have been other. But this parakeet, when I reached for it, seemed to remember the life it had and took flight, knowing the life it has and more content with its new life than any I could give it.

I remember crying, knowing it would die.

We are leaving SoHo along Bowery. There are throngs along the sidewalks on either side of us and some police are working crowd control. The people are an even mix of race and color, although all seem to be under thirty and many appear to have been in hiding since Woodstock.

People are returning to the city. They do not fear us less, they fear their jobs more. Cetaf looks over the crowd, stops, and cries.

"What is it?" I ask, aware of the crowds' eyes and thoughts on me and growing uncomfortable and anxious at the attention on top of attention I'm already receiving. I'm barely comfortable with the attention of being with the Healers. Being the center of the center of attention is a challenge for me.

One of the crowd, a boy not dressed like the rest, wearing leather toughs and gloves with the fingers, thumbs, and palms removed and no shirt, his back and chest scarred and his arms tattooed with demons and dragons and skulls, bursts from the people like an infection rupturing the skin and shouts at Cetaf, "Whats-a-matter? A house fall on your sister?"

He raises his hands and turns to the crowd, smiling and cheering himself on. They look at him and moan his deed. He gives them the finger on both hands. "Hey, fuck you all." He lowers his right and punches straight up into the air. "Yeah, that's right. All of you." He laughs and adds a Tiny Tim line. "Each and every one."

He heads down the street and occasionally pushes someone who isn't in his way.

Cetaf shudders as some deep emotion rocks him like an earthquake rumbling a mountain. "No. One of my lovers leaves."

I stare at them. Lovers? They're not monogamous? Or at least serially monogamous?

Maybe I should ask their pronouns. Seems to be what serves as a chat up line these days.

Then I wonder, how come no one else has asked them their preferred pronouns?

I don't know what to say so go with the obvious, "I'm sorry." I nudge Beriah. "What does he mean?"

"He knows one less is in this life."

"Oh, you mean his wife died." I place a hand on Cetaf's huge shoulder. "I am sorry, Cetaf. I didn't even know you guys had wives."

I wait, unable to express my sorrow yet I feel it fill me until it squeezes from me like puss from a wound, an anger seeking direction. "Wait a minute. How do you know who's dying? Frog Eyes and the Wisp seem fine."

Cetaf rests a gentle hand on my shoulder. "He is not here, my lover. He waits for me, now, at the next time."

The Healers are Gay? Bisexual? Trisexual? Polysexual (because I don't know what's underneath their robes)?

Definitely have to ask them their pronouns.

I hesitate, unable to find the word. "Are there others on the world where Cetaf comes from?"

"Many."

"No, I mean like here, we have men and women, male and female. Two sexes necessary for procreation. Do they have that on his world?"

Jenreel comforts the sobbing monolith and I join him. "You have two sexes. Your kind does. Not everything on this world does. Each method of procreation is as worthy as the next. There is no merit system by which life comes from death."

"What?"

"Whenever new life occurs, it occurs because old life ceases."

I feel more than see CNN's shotgun mikes aiming at us. "I'm not sure that answers my question."

"On Cetaf's world, there is no differentiation between partners. All are hes and all are shes. The greatest creation is a mixture of two things you call 'love' and 'respect,' both directed first at the self. Without these, no lives truly exist. When you have love and respect, what you're doing is celebrating the other's life."

Someone in the crowd yells, "Christ, they're bisexual up there." The police work harder.

I ask without knowing why, "Is he...are you...bisexual?"

Cetaf dries his tears. "True bisexuality has nothing to do with sexuality. It happens when someone isn't polarized as male or female. Bisexuality is when whoever you are loves whoever they are. Procreation is not a necessitate for love. Bi-, homo-, and hetero-sexuality are proactions from within when they are true, reactions from without when they are not. Only here is there great concern for how choices are made."

Some people throw things at us and everything misses. The police close ranks on us and try to move us up Bowery to Fourth.

Jenreel breaks ranks and faces the crowd. "As long as we are safe, you are safe."

Oh, Christ. Was that a threat?

The crowd's arms grow slack.

"Jenreel! What did you do to them?"

"I did nothing to them. My need to be safe went out to them and they felt safe, too. There is no need to attack when you are safe."

Beriah comes forward. "I do not like fearing I will be attacked. Fear of attack is a horrible feeling, don't you think?"

The crowd moves away, dropping bottles and cans and pieces of stone and brick as they go.

I turn to Beriah. "What did you do?"

"I told them I feared their attack."

"And they stopped?"

"The opposite of love is fear, but what is all-encompassing can have no opposite. They attack because they fear. Telling them I, too, fear offers them love."

Too much is happening too fast, too soon. I both don't and don't want to understand. I point to Cetaf, still on the ground, still weeping. "How can he know his partner is dying? Is part of him there? Are you telepathic or something like that?"

"Cetaf cries because one of his mates dies. You believe his mate is nowhere near him. You don't understand how he could know his mate dies even though his mate is far away and you believe no messages come to him."

I nod. This is obvious.

"You ask if we are telepathic. We are not, nor are any of those we know. Telepathy, when it occurs, requires like minds. Where there are like minds there are no individuals. If two think exactly alike, one is useless."

"So what's the answer?"

"Perhaps it is you and not Cetaf who is far away from Cetaf's mate."

Jenreel looks into the crowd. "Consciousness is never experienced in the plural, only the singular. We are made to be different, not separate. Your people work very hard to be separate, not different."

Cetaf rises. "Individuation occurs when differentiation occurs. You spend a lot of time societalizing, training yourselves you are somebody and defining your existence by what is around you. This somebody, this existence, is a separate entity from who you really are. It is this somebody who can die and who is afraid of dying. The real you can never die." His sobbing stops, his pain released. "Although at times I wonder if you're not already dead. You all spend so much time learning not to share who you truly are, to be invulnerable to each other."

I'm angry again and begin to realize my anger is a defense, is not a true anger, not a sense of dignity, but a hostility because I feel myself invaded, unbounded, released and yet confined. "What the hell are you talking about?"

"When you lost your son, you got angry. Is that what you really wanted to do?"

I remembered the fear of Jiminy being crushed, drowned, of not being in control of where and what he was, of not being able to keep him safe. I thought all of these things and despite myself, despite the pain behind my eyes which felt as if it were a sledge driving ten-penny spikes, despite the constriction in my throat which ached as if a giant's hands slowly closed upon it, I let myself cry and in so doing, the pain in my throat and the ache behind my eyes quickly went away, my sadness and fear realized.

"Is what you do now what you wanted to do then? Are you feeling now what you started to feel then?"

I let myself rest on the street. There is no one around us now, not even the police. The crowd has quickly dispersed. "Yes."

They let me cry and I don't know how long. They don't interrupt, they don't hasten, chasten, or sigh. They stand and wait and touch me lightly when my sobs grow strong.

"You must think me a fool, you three."

Beriah answers and I know the answer is for all of them. "Our job is to appreciate, not to judge."

I feel the sun's work on the asphalt of the street under me as I sit there. I begin to wonder about Jiminy, about Gayle, about the three creatures who walk with me and about a little bird I once knew, wondering what has become of them and what will become of me. I feel myself start to cry again.

Jenreel kneels beside me. "Your people must enjoy the pains you put themselves through. You spend much time agonizing over what has been or what will be."

My tears stop and I don't know why. Cetaf holds his hand out to me and I take it, rising to my feet effortlessly now that my fear and rage have passed. "There is no past or present or future, Ben. There is only now and absent."

I don't know what he means, now. Perhaps I will understand when I am absent.

Word came today my mother is on a machine. Braindead. Not for past, not for future, only for now. I've ordered the machinery stopped.

The Healers continue to travel up Fourth and I follow.

"...the dying pray at the last not 'please' but 'thank you', as a guest thanks his host at the door..." - Anne Dillard

CHAPTER 18
NATIVE AMERICAN REGALIA

"I have learned that the head does not feel anything until the heart has listened. And what the heart knows today, the head will understand tomorrow." - James Stephens

There is a man dressed in Native American regalia standing on the corner of 14th St. and 8th Ave. He looks Native American. He's playing a flute of some kind. His eyes are closed. At different times he takes another instrument which is tied in a sling about his neck and blows through it. It is piercing and, although it doesn't make a musical sound, its sound fits perfectly with what the man is doing. There are times when, his eyes still closed, he chants something in Lakotah. There are no hats, no cups, no open cases, no signs, no requests, no nothing around him except his music and his chant. Some people throw coins down on the street around him, dollar bills float up the sidewalk, bump into his footwear - moccasins? - then continue onward. No one takes up the money for him, nor do any take the money from him.

Beriah, alone, walks up to him, stands beside him, and closing his eyes, weeps as his body accepts and follows the motions of the player. The player opens his eyes and, seeing Beriah, smiles. He hands Beriah his pipes, even taking the lariat from his own neck and placing it around Beriah's.

Beriah spreads his arms wide, then hands the pipes back, including the one around his neck.

The player scowls, then laughs. He laughs hard and Beriah laughs with him. The player breaks his pipes and crushes the one around his neck beneath his heel, laughing harder as he does, his face relaxing as tears pour from his eyes.

Beriah and the player laugh and cry, hug each other long and hard, then the player walks away, taking his regalia and tossing it into the air one piece at a time until he is naked, making his way down 14th St.

I watch him walk away. "What is he doing?"

Jenreel also watches. "He is finding out who he is." He turns to me. "Where were you, Ben?"

"Huh?"

Jenreel repeats his question differently. "Where do you go when you do that, Ben?"

"When I do what?"

"When you stop seeing what's in front of you. When you stop hearing what's around you. It must be a wonderful place to go to. Many of your people do it so often." Beriah and Cetaf come up behind him. "Could you take us with you the next time you go?" Beriah and Cetaf nod vigorously.

Cetaf leans over and stars down at me. Have you ever seen a walking wall beg? It's not pretty. "Or could you teach us, Ben? It must be such a wonderful place, could you teach us how to go there?"

"No," I tell them. "It's not a wonderful place."

The three pull back. Visibly pull back. They turn to each other and huddle. The huddle breaks and Cetaf and Beriah nudge Jenreel forward. He drew the short straw, he pulled the low card, his camel can't be healed. "You keep returning because...?"

How come they never ask idiotic, obvious, *Duh!* questions?

Why do I keep returning to a place I spent weeks at LakeShore learning to leave, from which I fought to escape? Am I some kind of emotional salmon who needs to return to pain in order to spawn?

Spawn what?

Is that why most people you see walking down the street look so vacant, so empty, or so determined all the time, because we're all so stressed out and don't know how to heal? Is healing something Eve$_2$ and Eve$_3$ understood and didn't get a chance to share when their lines died out?

These visitors from the Rainbow Tribe teach me something I could not learn there. I realize now I wasn't ready, it wasn't time, or perhaps LakeShore laid the groundwork on which they build: one's history must inform, it must not guide. To do so robs you of the moment, denies you a better future, mires you in the past.

Our history uniquely shapes our present, but it does not define our present.

But one's past is the basis for one's future.

Until one realizes it doesn't have to be.

CHAPTER 19
HOME RUNS

Weehawken Street.
What are we hawking?
What are we hocking?

Well, I've seen a wee hawken. Show me a big hawken.

Weehawken, yes-in-deed, weehawken, 'bout-you-and-me, weehawken, 'till-you-come-back-to-me.

I feel we've traversed this island enough to qualify for an inner-city summer-time slalom gold medal. Heading northwest, Weehawken levels where it meets West 10th and some kids are playing stickball. It is the first time we've seen a group of pure, unadulterated kids playing by themselves and enjoying it, settling their disputes and laughing at their game. I want to join them.

Beriah smiles at them. "The young ones."

The Healers stop and watch, not doing anything other than smiling. As the game goes on, there are some minor scrapes and bruises, but no problems, no complaints which last more than a minute, no anger or aggression.

One boy. No, one youth, Jiminy's age and build and color and complexion, slightly smaller than most of those playing the game, takes his turn at bat. The ball comes at him and one of the older boys shouts, "Come on, boy, hit it!"

He does. A powerful blow which sends the ball skyward and over the reach of all but Cetaf who lets it get away. The kids are cheering and screaming as the boy runs the bases. Both teams cheer him on. The older boy who called the runner "boy" calls to Cetaf, "Hey, mister, can you get us our ball?" and Cetaf runs down the hill all smiles and rumbles as the buildings quake with his footfalls.

I walk up to that boy, the one who called the younger child "boy" and take his arm to make him face me. "Why did you call him 'boy'?"

The older boy's face shows fear and I'm glad. "That's his name, mister, Boyd."

I let go. "Boyd," I repeat in a world gone silent. "Boyd. I'm...sorry."

The older boy and the others surround me, fear gone, concern and compassion firmly in place. The older boy calls out to me, "That's okay, mister. Hey, you wanna play?" The other children nod me on. Cetaf tosses the ball and it bounces off my head. All the children laugh and, after a moment, so do I. Cetaf is covering his mouth with his right hand, his eyes are wide in an expression of surprise and laughter. "Oops."

The Healers watch, listen, and encourage all the children, all of us, as I sweat and remember and am taught this childhood game. I try to enforce rules but am usually voted down, a congress of progress if ever there was one. We play until dark, until the children are called home.

Walking up West 10th as streetlights come on, Beriah asks, "Did you find your little boy?"

"No, no. I told you before, he's safe. He's with my probably by now ex-wife. Is that what you mean?"

Cetaf doesn't answer. At least, I don't think he answers. He watches the children and smiles. "The young ones, the ones who teach us. Those who are capable of living in the instant while being in touch with eternity."

Beriah stands beside him. His gaze goes from where I played with the children to me and back. "You can't ask others to respect what you can't respect yourself."

"What are you talking about?"

"It doesn't matter what you're called. That doesn't make you what you are. It is what you reference yourself as that makes you what you are."

Ah, yes. Boyd. "Listen, I spent my childhood being told I would grow up to be a 'colored man', the early years of manhood learning not to be 'Colored' but to be 'Black'. Then I was 'African-American' for a while and then I was 'Black' again. I was a 'Black Man' for about a week and now they're telling me I'm not 'Black' or even a 'Black man' but I'm 'a man of color'. Is that what you're talking about? Because I thought that kid called the other kid a 'boy'? Is that what you mean?"

"If it is, let that young boy work it out. If it's not, then what about you, Ben? You have to decide if other people's labels apply."

Another game of stickball is forming under the streetlights. The older boy comes out with a box of sandwiches, fruit, and Kool-Aid. He places it at our feet and says, "Here, my mom said you guys were probably hungry. We're gonna start another game soon. You guys wanna play?"

I nod and pick up a sandwich. "Soon as I finish. Thanks."

The boy smiles and runs back to the others. "Hey, he's gonna play again." They start arguing about whose team I'll be on.

Beriah offers me one of the napkins from the box. "Well, Ben?"

I wipe my mouth and wash down the sandwich with a big draught of watermelon pink Kool-Aid. "The hell with you all," I shout to the city. "I've got enough to do just to be me." I run into the game surrounded by echoes of my laughter.

In this life we are allowed to know three things about others; 1) what they've been, 2) who they are, and 3) where they'd like to be.

The first gives a Why to the second. The first and second give a

Why and How to the third. The only ones we can never know are When and If. When and If are two sides of the same coin. "If" because everything changes, "When" because we never know when change will occur.

How others stand and carry themselves, their physical message and sense of self-presence in the world, tells you what they've been. How they interact with you and others - how they change from when you spy them alone to when they're communicating, when and how they work a crowd - tells you who they are. Knowing what's happened in their lives can help you understand why they are who they are. How they treat themselves and you when they interact with you - how they behave and honor themselves and others when they're communicating - tells where they'd like to be. If you know what they've been and who they are, it can explain why they chose to go where they chose to go and the path they chose to get there.

I've marked the passing of my life in portraits of pain and sorrow. The gravitational pull of my past has disallowed me flight, kept the ship close to shore for fear the seas are darker, deeper than could be imagined.

But I am learning to laugh.

It is the ability to laugh at one's past, not be victim to it, which truly sets us free.

CHAPTER 20
FRIENDS WISER THAN I

Two young boys are fighting on the playground across from Knickerbocker Village. Young boys. Too young to know why they are fighting. They fight without gloves, without protection, spitting and kicking and rolling in the dirt, each trying to figure out how to hurt the other and both lacking enough knowledge of their own bodies to know how to hurt anyone including themselves. These boys are young enough to still be shocked by the discovery that hot water burns. There are rings of onlookers around them, all ages. Faces are like seats in the Coliseum, the older ringing the young, older eyes looking over younger heads, allowing the age of the onlookers to be determined as if the crowd were the growth rings of some ancient tree. Further back I see the fathers of these two boys. The fathers stand on a park bench, their eyes over the heads of the oldest in the crowd, their voices cheering on their sons as if this were compassionate stickball instead of some infanticidic brain death. They make bets with each other as to whose son will survive the fight.

In first and second grade, my mother's light-skinned in-laws moved two streets away. My light-skinned cousins Paul and Rosemary, each two school grades my senior, pointed me out to the local KKK-in-training kids, also in my grade, on the playground. Each and every day.

Perhaps, being able to swim in two ponds, as it were, they wanted to beat the black off me to help me.

Not likely. They stood and laughed while the local KKK-in-training kids swung their little fists into my little face, at my little head. I never fought back. I tried once. Paul and Rosemary held my arms so the locals could batter me unimpeded.

It must have been great fun, watching little boys beat one other little boy up.

I have to thank cousins Paul and Rosemary for a lot. For many, many years, the thought of feeling their delicate, soft-fleshed, light-skinned throats crushing under my darkening grip made me happy and proud.

I sense my cousins Paul and Rosemary here, in this crowd around me, but don't see them here. I suddenly wonder who held Paul and Rosemary's arms, who's holding these boys' fathers' arms, who's holding the arms of the people gathering around me.

And just as suddenly know it doesn't matter.

I rush forward, break through the crowd, separate the little boys from each other. They punch and kick my legs in an attempt to reach each other. Beside me I hear the snaps of spring steel and clicks of safeties released. One of the men in the crowd tells his peers, "Watch that blue one, man. I saw him on the news, man. He does some kind of magic."

I no longer see what is around me, no longer hear the young boys' cries and the crowd's screams, no longer feel my feet on the dirt beneath them, the air on my skin around me, and the sun on my head above.

I stop. I realize spontaneous communication has been made. It lasts a moment and is gone.

The Healers walk up to me as the crowd absorbs them, some fistula absorbed into an amoeba. They divide me into thirds with the two children on either side. Beriah stands in front but off center, a little to my right, a hand on each child's head. Cetaf is to my right and a little behind, each child's head under one of his hands. Jenreel is to my left and a little forward, touching each child's head with his hands.

Beriah closes his eyes. "Everything in life is a mirror, everything in life is an echo. If we don't like what we see or hear, either don't look - "

Beriah opens his eyes and Cetaf closes his "- or cast a better reflection, don't listen - "

Cetaf opens his eyes and Jenreel closes his "- or talk more clearly. There are no other options."

They let go of the children. Beriah faces the crowd but speaks to me. "We look the same to you because we don't look like you."

"What are you talking about?

He nods at the crowd. "They look the same to you because they don't look like you."

I look, and this time, I see. There are two groups: Hispanic and Asian. I didn't notice because there were no obvious blacks kids there.

Jenreel faces the crowd and speaks to me. "Are all people from South and Central America Hispanic?"

Cetaf follows. "Are all people from Asia Asians?"

They turn to me, wait.

"Are all Blacks obvious?"

We walk on. I don't want to know what happens when the amoeba releases us, moves on, forgets us.

Over time, over life, I realize each moment is a choice, and I have all the time in the world to make my choices.

Not so light-skinned cousins Paul and Rosemary. One day their swimming-in-the-other-pond friends saw them brushing ash off their arms.

Their swimming-in-the-other-pond friends had no idea what ash was and asked Rosemary and Paul what they were doing.

And I crossed the playground laughing my ass off as my cousins Rosemary and Paul looked at their arms aghast, fear painting their faces an even lighter shade of pale, and exclaimed, "Oh my god. We have no idea. We must be sick!"

Rosemary and Paul made a single choice long ago. I hope it's served them well.

We judge others by ourselves. If I am a thief, you must steal.

And I, at that moment, in that intersection of me and you and we and they and us and them, I understand why my three traveling companions never ask idiotic, obvious, *Duh!* questions.

They don't ask questions they already know the answer to.

CHAPTER 21
RELATIVISTIC RELIGIONS

"The force of the mind is its ability to persist through various states of consciousness.

The degree to which an individual mind extends itself into the world is its way of showing itself unique and separate from the world." - Liebniz

We enter Fordham University from Columbus Ave and walk up. Voices come down the hall to us and we follow them to an amphitheater. A gathering of professors not seen since the 1950's science fiction classic *The Day The Earth Stood Still* fills the hall. I recognize some of the people in the audience. The equations on the board describe situational probability densities. A debate goes on between the man at the board and a man in the audience.

In a chair in the top last row of the auditorium's seats is a man in a turban and heavy blue suit. The man smells of musk cologne and is light skinned. He turns and smiles at us and I note he has a blonde mustache. His left canine is gold and his eyes are bright blue. Under the heavy blue jacket, which he removes and folds neatly then places on the chair beside him, he wears a white silk shirt with a lace collar and string tie. He wears a leather pouch on his left side and it hangs like an old, weathered scrotum. *Lawrence of Arabia*'s Peter O'Toole he ain't.

His notebook is open in front of him. There are equations and notes, neither of which pertain to what is discussed at the board. I understand the forms but not the symbols of his equations. At the top of the first page, headlining the rest and boxed in red ink, is:

As Quantum Mechanics resolves to Newtonian Mechanics under special conditions, is there some universal concept of 'life' which resolves to the various religious belief systems under some set of conditions special to each belief system?

I feel Lawrence of Arabia's throat tighten and stomach tense until reason overrides emotion and he flatly, unequivocally, and unarguably says, "No," and I laugh.

Beriah, ever quick, turns to me. "You laugh."

I wave at the board's equations. "Yes, there was a time when this was important to me. Very important. Probably more important than life itself."

"It gave you something, then."

"Yes to that, too. It let me escape and travel without having to go anywhere. There was a certain sense of travel, of escapism, of adventure in so totally devoting myself to my equations. Whenever things got too difficult in this world, I would take out a pencil and paper and go into the next. That world had just as much if not more reality than this, perhaps a greater reality because there I was known, in control, my decisions were recognized, had merit, made a difference, answered questions, revealed possibilities, created pathways which didn't exist before."

"Escape and travel. It is a theme of many of you. You always come back, though."

I laugh again. "Yeah, I guess."

"Perhaps you travelled where you didn't need to go. Where would you like to go?"

I think for a moment. "Hawaii. Yeah, that would be good. Hawaii."

Two rows down two women turn, so common is our appearance that we cause little stir. One is Gayle, the other is familiar. Gayle mouths, "I thought I'd find you here."

Jenreel walks down to the board. The man hands him the marker, flips the board over, and stands to the side.

Beriah, Cetaf, and I are still at the back of the auditorium. Beriah says, "Let's go to Hawaii, Ben."

"What? That's half the world away. How we going to get there?"

"Would you like to learn how we travel?"

The other woman stands up and barks an order. "Quiet! They're going to talk about how they travel." I recognize her by her voice. It's Harley, the Army colonel who handed me the mobile what seems long, long ago. But she's not in fatigues. Has she left the military?

"Travel," starts Jenreel, "is a matter of Universal instance versus Common instance." He stands with his arms at his sides as if grasping suspenders. He uses the marker like a prop the way Groucho used a cigar. His voice, I notice, shifts from Jewish to German to Chinese to Afrikaans to Indian to Japanese to Lakotah to French to Portuguese to Russian to Kurdish to Jivaro and on to other accents I've never heard before.

I look at the audience. Gayle, Harley, and Peter O'Toole watch us. Everyone else is listening to and scribbling down everything Jenreel says. Sir Lawrence smiles his gold-toothed smile. His enthusiasm is palpable. He nods towards Jenreel without looking at him. "Go on, go. I'll give you my notes when they're done." Gayle watches me intently, perhaps wondering what I'll do.

I turn to Beriah. "Okay. How?"

"First, you must believe the place you're traveling to exists."

Class begins.

Jenreel tugs on invisible suspenders like Fredric March as

Matthew Harrison Brady in *Inherit the Wind* while simultaneously flashing his marker cum cigar like Obi Wan teaching young Skywalker how to use a light saber. "Even though not clearly defined as such, all travel is an occurrence of identity-relational models.

"Begin with the concept of uniformity. This uniformity takes the form such that each place in the universe is governed by the same laws of reality. Remove the actual spaceo-temporal reference points which comprise any two places in the universe, make those two places adjacent, and what remains is identical and indistinguishable one from the other because each place only holds identical amounts and types of information. Note what I said: the amount and type. The actual data can vary widely, it must only be of the correct amount and type. Each place consists of space, time, energy, mass, and so on. Further, all the space, time, energy, mass, etc., in any one place are related to every other place by being in the same universe. By what was stated before, each place has a range of attributes associated with that place. Thus we have

$$R\{A_1, A_2, A_3,...\}$$

I whisper to Beriah. "Okay, got it. Hawaii."

He doesn't whisper back, doesn't care who listens. "Second, you must know why you want to go there."

Jenreel writes on the board. "A_n is an attribute for a given place. Each attribute has a domain associated with it. Thus, we also have

$$A_1\{D_1, D_2, D_3,...\}$$
$$A_2\{D_1, D_2, D_3,...\}$$
$$A_3\{D_1, D_2, D_3,...\}$$
$$....$$
$$....$$
$$....$$
$$A_i\{D_1, D_2, D_3,...\}$$

This can also be written as dom(A_i).

"These D_m's are arbitrary, non-empty, and are either finite in number or countably infinite. They are arbitrary because they are defined by the place they represent. They are non-empty because defining a place creates a non-empty domain. They are either finite - we could define a singularity - or countably infinite - the universe as a whole. Each domain, of course, has its own Gödel number, ditto the sum of these domains, represented as

$$\mathbf{D} = \sum_{A=1}^{A=i} D_1 + \sum_{A=1}^{A=i} D_2 + \sum_{A=1}^{A=i} D_3 + ... + + \sum_{A=1}^{A=i} D_n"$$

Beriah keeps my attention focused. "Third, you got to answer the why."

"How?"

"No, not how, why. You must know the why of your journey, the how is unimportant."

"But this is just something I'm imagining."

"Close your eyes, Ben. Listen to and feel your heartbeat, relax until you feel the floor holding you up and not the strain of your legs balancing you as you stand, breathe without straining and feel your whole body fill with breath. See and hear and feel and taste and smell Hawaii and go. Anything perfectly imagined is real."

Am I just told this world, these ills, the social problems, the conflicts from playground pushing to border skirmishes to nuclear threats are something imagined?

Holy Jesus Fuck! If this is the place we've imagined, what's it like in the world from which we started?

Holy Jesus Fuck Squared! Not "we." Me!

I do as he instructs. "I see it!" My own words surprise me because I hear them over the surf of a warm, white-sand shore. I open my eyes and point. "There's a hut on a beach with a thatched straw and bamboo chair on the porch." I enter it. There's a bed, a vanity complete with mirror, a table and galley kitchen.

Something shifts deep inside of me. I hear over a great distance two women shriek. The feeling of Beriah's presence fades from my existence. I feel the bamboo chair under me and smell a fruit-laced drink, lick my lips and taste pineapple mixed with sweat. The ocean is loud and pounding and the sun is comfortably hot.

I know this is Hawaii. How did I get here?

Jenreel points to the board. "Any relation, f, on a place, R, can be considered as a finite set of mappings $\{t_1, t_2, t_3,...t_x\}$ from R into **D** such that

$$t \in f \mid t(A_i) \in D_i$$

"In other worlds, the mapping of any relation from one place to another can only occur if the mapping of the attributes in the two places occurs within the established domains of those attributes.

"Call these mappings 'conformations'. All relations between places exist in a new space, conformation-space, created by the existence of the relations, relations causing relations simply by their existence.

"What is this conformation-space? It is the place where the attributes of where you were intersect with the attributes of where you're going, of who you were intersecting with who you will be. When you travel - and know movement along any single dimension constitutes a 'distance' - conformation-space is where you are. Your origin and your destination are real. When they get together, it is only in conformation-space and, because conformation-space only exists during intersections, anything created there only has reality while conformation-space exists."

Something happens. My Hawaii shifts, shimmers, changes. I feel another twist, this one in my head and not in my gut.

I'm no longer in my body on the bamboo chair. The skin lightens, the body grows beefier and healthier. A mustache forms.

People raise their hands. Jenreel holds up his palm out. "Patience. All will be revealed." Hands lower. Jenreel continues. "So far we've only discussed homogeneous conformations. A common homogeneous conformation is something like traveling between two places in the same universe.

"What if we want to travel to a totally different universe, one with a totally different reality, one where the laws of our previous existence are in conflict with the laws of our new existence? We can bring enough of our reality with us to ensure a compatible, if temporary, existence. What if we aren't satisfied with a temporary existence? The first can be thought of as an extension of Linear Algebraic forms. We must include in our mapping something like

$$F(place_1)$$

where F() symbolizes some translation of reality existing in both the origin and the destination."

I feel Beriah beside me again and hear Gayle's excited voice as I rise, enter the hut, see my reflection in the mirror and stop. "It's not me anymore, Beriah. I'm still here, but now it's Tom Selleck and not me. It's not me, Beriah. It's not me. And it's not really Hawaii. I was imagining it all, wasn't I?"

"I don't know who Tom Selleck is. Who isn't important. Why is important. Why Tom Selleck, Ben?"

Jenreel keeps the audience's attention focused on the board. His marker flies across its surface. Equations appear as if by magic. "This is working with subconformations and makes it necessary to treat the meta-universe and its realities as a single entity. In other words, we don't work with something which represents a universal instance - the universe doesn't tell us just one thing for all instances. We work with something which can represent any common instance in a universal scheme - the universe tells us lots of individual things for any given instance, and that given instance varies depending on how we perform our mappings - how we form relations which create the conformation-space. What if we want to travel to a place only existing in conformation-space, having no reality except as an entity in conformation-space, and knowing that this conformation-space entity changes depending on what conformations are active?

"For example and thanks to Heisenberg, by our very entering it?"

I'm back in the amphitheater. "I don't know, Beriah."

I see the man in the turban writing notes. Gayle's face shows shock and pain. Harley's moved to the front of the auditorium. She is signaling up towards us and several people approach with instruments I've never seen before.

"Perhaps Hawaii wasn't the place you needed to go, Ben."

"Why?"

"You must ask yourself that."

I look around the auditorium, hear the voices, see the recorders, hear the scribbling of pens and pencils and ruffling of pages, the tappings on tablets, the clicking of phones, and see Jenreel pointing at the board.

Gayle has turned away from me, her shoulders shaking and I hear her sobs. "Perhaps because I don't want the chair on the porch, I want the glamour and excitement. Although I probably need the chair on the porch more."

"Do your wants always get in the way of meeting your needs?"

Jenreel fixes his gaze on me. "Because if we enter a reality we cannot accept exists, we must leave it before it rejects us." He looks down, turns back to his board, and shakes his head as he lifts his marker. "Sadly, few do, and down that path lies madness."

He turns back, once again all smiles. "And now we are overwhelmed by a Blinding Flash of the Obvious: travel is relations performed on a single entity because we perform our mappings and generate conformation-space as necessary."

Everyone nods.

"Can this model of travel include travel between two points that isn't done in conformation-space? Yes. An example of this occurred when my friends and I first came to this world. Our relational model works with the universal scheme, one finite part of which is the universal instance. Indeed, when you create a specific conformation-space, and for however long that individual conformation-space exists and is traversed, you've traveled from the origin to the destination without conformation-space."

And again.

"Fortunately, this is a one-way street. The universal instance can disguise itself as a common instance, but a common instance can't disguise itself as a universal instance."

Notes are being scribbled so quickly notebook pages flip like those flip-page animations I drew in childhood.

"More succinctly, you can't go back the way you came. More correctly, you can't go back, only forward, which is also fortunate. Entropy no longer exists once one realizes the past is not as beatific as one believes. Until then, trees will make seeds but not become them again and again."

I wonder why they're all taking notes. Do they hope to understand? Do they think there *is* something to understand?

Does being from some other world automatically mean he's correct? Did Klaatu just explain to Professor Barnhardt how to solve the three-body problem?

"Entropy can reverse, but the Universe cannot, and knowing the difference is the difference that makes the difference, a Second Order Difference of Reality, if you will."

They're all leaning forward. Maybe Jenreel carries the Third Tablet and I never noticed?

"And now I'll answer my second question; if we're not satisfied with a temporary existence in a different reality then don't bother to bring your preceding reality with you at all. Change yourself to fit the new reality.

"This, beyond far, is the easier of the two to do."

"I finish with two items which make all I've said possible. First, if you believe anything, you can do anything."

The audience grows uneasy in under a microsecond. Jenreel frowns, shakes his head at them. "What? You have minds powerful enough to conceive of such mappings but are unwilling to perform them yourself?"

The contempt becomes palpable. I worry for our safety.

"Because the more explanations can't be proven by direct observation the less you accept the mathematics which make the explanation real?"

Notebooks are slammed shut. Pens and pencils are thrown to the floor. People start erasing recordings.

"Then let's have a proof."

The amphitheater is gone. Everyone save Peter O'Toole is sitting on white sand stretching to the horizon in all directions. Lawrence is still in a stadium chair, looking around, taking notes.

The only ones standing are the Healers, myself, and Gayle. A hot wind blows sand in people's faces. Many stand up; the desert's surface so hot I feel it through my shoes. People are shrieking, screaming, running in all directions. Harley commands everyone to remain calm then begins screaming herself. She reaches for a sidearm I didn't realize she had and blows her head off.

Jenreel's eyes go from one to the other, to the looks on their faces, to the disbelief, the fear, in their eyes. "All your senses are doorways to other worlds, other realities." He turns and points back over the desert to what looks like a tunnel leading to a darkened room filled with stadium chairs, a whiteboard - the amphitheater? "Why do you constrain yourselves to only this one?"

Gayle walks up to me, reaches for me, touches me. "How do we get home, Ben?"

I've learned. "By wanting to be there more than we want to be here and making there our reality, by abandoning this reality because it's not healthy for us, by accepting it as a learning, not a sentence."

We're back in the amphitheater. Gayle sits alone, the auditorium deserted save Lawrence who now closes his notebook.

Jenreel caps his marker. "Second," and then the Healers say simultaneously, "Understanding requires more than four dimensions."

Jenreel erases the board. "Someday your mathematics will be sophisticated enough to conceive the inconceivable." He brushes his palms against each other as if finishing a good day's work. "Until then, your perception will always be limited."

I turn to Beriah. "Did I just do what Jenreel is talking about?"

"Yes, you did, then as proof, and so Jenreel could feel safe, all the people here did. I gave you the same information Jenreel gave the people here. I simply left out the unimportant stuff."

"Will they return?"

Jenreel wipes his hands on each other as if indicating a task well-done. "Those who truly believe the mathematics they've based their lives on, yes. The others will follow the other path. When confronted with the impossible one can either grow with the wonder or die in the chaos. Pity. I never got to the most important part."

"The most important part?"

Gayle walks up to me, looks at me, and her eyes go wide. She continues past me and out the door. I open my mouth to speak but decide against it. Cetaf taps my shoulder. "Those who don't ask for what they want deserve what they get."

I follow her and call out, "I'd like a lock of your hair, Gayle, for when I sleep."

She stops, faces me, stares, then backs away as if I'm alien or foreign although now I'm more me than I've ever been before. "Your ears, Ben."

"I'm sorry, what?"

"Your ears. They're pointed."

I never saw Gayle again. Jiminy, yes. Children, it seems, have understanding when we allow it. I asked for a lock of hair and thought of memorials and pasts and eventually, when it came, discarded it.

The parts of Gayle I loved and the parts of Gayle I hated are not dead. I can go to her anytime. All I have to do is believe.

And know why.

MIDTOWN

CHAPTER 22
HUNGRY UNIVERSES

The air coming up the steps of Penn Station to Fashion Ave is crawling with urine, feces, sweat, vomit, dirt, colognes, and perfumes which gather and thicken to a cloying, invading miasma as one passes by. There is a man at the top of the steps. He sits there in yesteryear's clothes, his own fashion statement perhaps, neither begging nor playing, just sitting and smiling as people pass by. His eyes are covered by cataracts and, as we near, I hear a surprisingly clear voice carrying over the hurried others, over the clack of metal-tipped shoes and stiletto heels, over the earth-deep roar of moving trains:

"If I swallow anything evil
put your finger down my throat
If I shiver
Please give me a blanket
If I'm cold keep me warm
let me wear your coat."

The man is singing. He has no cup, no hat to catch coins in. Jenreel, who is carrying two apples and half a stick of french bread, walks over and gives them to the man. The man grabs Jenreel's sleeve and, in the same musical tones of the song and without breaking the rhythm *The Who* intended, sings:

"Thank you so much my blue-skinned brother
for the apples and the bread
I'll eat my fill
then find me some others
Share with them from what's left
If alive not dead."

My pockets are empty. The city, the state, the government, no one gives us food. Factions within The Indiana Church of the Triple Saviors denounce us and tell their faithful of others who'll come. "That's all the food we have left, damn it." I turn Beriah to face me. "Why did Jenreel give that man the last of our food?"

"How can Jenreel feed him if Jenreel is hungry?"

"I'm not worried about Jenreel. I'm worried about me."

"Good. That's good."

"I mean, what about when I get hungry."

"Are you hungry now?"

I hadn't stopped to notice. "No, I...I guess not."

"Then you don't need the food now."

"But what about later?"

"It isn't later. It's now."

"I don't have any money left to buy food, damn it."

"Then it's your pockets which are empty, not your stomach. I didn't understand that your pockets were your concern."

The singing stops. The man busies himself with an apple and some of the bread.

"Would you have let the man starve?"

"Certainly not!"

"Then why not afford yourself the same generosity you would afford the stranger?"

Crowds no longer even form around us, so common has become

our existence. It doesn't matter. We had far more than our allotted fifteen minutes. "Okay, okay, okay. How did Jenreel know that man was hungry? Is he telepathic or something? You told me and he told me he tends only to his own needs. That makes him pretty self-centered, if you ask me."

For some reason, two women stop and watch us. One is a woman dressed for Wall Street, her three-piece suit accenting yet confining. Her figure is full and strong. She takes care of herself. The other is dressed for Fashion Ave. Her figure is neither full nor strong. The former stares at us, the other does not. The former then turns to the latter and says, "My clock's running out."

"That might be true," Beriah says, suddenly facing the woman, and I'm not sure who the comment is for. He returns to me. "Another explanation is that he's a centered-self. He's simply aware of what goes on around him."

"How?"

"Each of us is responsible for our individual universes. If we are responsible for them, we must be aware of what goes on in them. Responsibility to one's own worldview means a betterment, any betterment in a single worldview cascades into betterment for all worldviews. It is possible to be a centered-self without being self-centered."

More people stop and a crowd forms. A woman with a baby pushes through the crowd and stops inside the ring formed around us. She turns, realizing what is happening, and tries to move back away. The crowd will not allow her back. I feel her discomfort echoed within me and try to score a point with the onlookers. "What you're saying, then, is that your universe is real small because you can't possibly know everything that goes on in it. If nothing exists until or unless you know it, I guess not much exists."

"No, my universe covers all of known space and time. It must. I'm in it."

The crowd applauds Beriah's logic as the woman with child slips away.

"Ben," says Beriah, "there once was a wiseman and a fool. One climbed to the top of a mountain to see the other. When they met, the one asked the other to place a sign on his back, 'Do not disturb' in order that he might meditate upon the panorama in peace. Instead, the other placed a sign on the one's back which read, 'Kick Me'. Over the years, several people who climbed the mountain saw the sign and did. Years later, the wiseman and fool met again upon the high mountaintop. 'Thank you,' said the one. 'I've been able to see the wonders about me without anyone bothering me all these many years.' The other said, 'You fool, this is the sign I placed on your back!' and tore off the sign to show the one the words on the sign. 'I don't know about that,' said the one. 'All I know is no one disturbed me all these years.'"

"Yeah, so?"

"So the only wounds which won't heal are those we need to remember."

The crowd begins to dissolve.

"What?"

Jenreel picks up a sign discarded in the street. "The only hurts we have are those we accept."

The onlookers have completely gruntled away. As the sea parts, I see the music man sharing his bread and half his other apple with a female with quite the same fashion sense.

Cetaf smiles and bows as we pass them on our way north and cross town. "They sing well together."

I stop walking. "Wait a minute, who was the wiseman and who was the fool?"

I am learning to travel anywhere I wish, and all distances can collapse to zero with the correct transforms.

Which universe will I choose as my reality?

Or will I choose to always be hungry?

I hold both the wiseman's and the fool's signs but no longer know where to place them.

Is it possible to reach my own back?

CHAPTER 23

THE WORLD EQUATION REVEALED IN THE COLLISION OF BUMPER CARS

There is a carnival going on in the park on the east side of where Franklin meets LaFayette. We walk through while Cetaf stays on LaFayette because Jenreel is fascinated by cotton candy. He doesn't have the right idea, I think, because he places it on his head like sticky pink hair with a white paper dunce cap on top.

Cetaf, crossing and recrossing LaFayette, has discovered that certain stickers on cars indicate the car has a burglar alarm. He takes great pleasure in finding these cars and setting off the alarms, laughing his high, windful laugh, and moving onto the next one. He reminds me of the drunk who went up and down the street placing quarters in parking meter after parking meter and screaming after each one, "I love this outdoor gambling!"

We pass an enclosure of bumper cars. They are not bumper cars as I remember. These are motorized tricycles, each large enough for at most a light nine- or ten-year-old, each wrapped around with a large truck-tire's inner tube. Each driver is strapped into the tricycle, some of the younger drivers barely able to see over their inner-tube sanctorum.

At the far end and coming fast is a black man with a full beard and rumply clothes. He is awkward and uncomfortable on the tricycle. It teeters and totters as he makes course corrections, bearing down upon a nine-year-old boy.

I didn't like bumper cars when I was a child. No; correctly, I didn't like them when my father was around. The cars back then were cars, metal and fiberglass, running on little electric wheels with antennae-like cables scraping the ceiling, like diesel-electric buses moving on a city street. My father would force me into the car, tie me in and get into a car of his own. Then there would be a succession of bams. Bam Bam BAMBAMBAMBAMBAM as Daddy rammed me from side to side to side to side finally forcing me into a corner of the corral and pummeling me there, using something far heavier than his hands.

The satisfaction he must have felt.

One time he tied me in and I tried to get out. He yelled at me, threatened to punch me, right in front of all the people. "You get in that god-damned car, Ben. You get in that god-damned car and stay there until we're done."

I'm ready to leap the rail and get that child out of the tricycle before the large black man bams him. I reach for the railing and the man swerves and hits his brakes.

I didn't know such things could have brakes.

He hollers, "Yo!" and his son, struggling with the wheel and pedals, turns and putter putter putter bumps into his father's car. The man snaps his shoulders and his car rocks from his movement twice over what it received from the boy's impact. "You got me, son!"

The boy is bubbles and laughter.

"Watch it, Jerry. I'm coming for you again!" The man rides off again. The little boy follows. The man stops abruptly and looks over his shoulder. When his son reaches him and putter putter taps him, he pantomimes being thrown from the car. "Ow! You little fart! You got me again! Where is that boy? I'm gonna get him."

The man waves at a woman standing outside the railings. She's holding a huge green stuffed tyrannosaur, a clown-shaped balloon, a coloring book and two very drippy ice cream cones which she works evenly, uncaring her tongue smears peppermint on pistachio and vice versa.

"I don't know about this boy of ours, Molly," he yells at her. "I can't beat him. I can't find him. I don't know that boy." She nods slightly as putter putter putter bump Jerry taps his father's car and dad rocks his body with the impact. Jerry giggles and putters in a too large circle, bearing down on his father again.

Beriah catches my hand on the rail. "What is it, Ben?"

"Bad memories."

He waits. I don't want to explain, but I do, which means I wanted to explain all along, so I do and finish with "...I've often fantasized about forcing my father to stay in a bumper car the way he did to me."

"Can you separate the fact from the feeling?"

"Huh?"

"What you describe sounds painful. Too painful. I wish I were Cetaf so I could cry. Your impressions of the event are an agony. I merely ask if you can separate the events from your agony over them, if you can remember the experience without reliving the experience."

"Okay." I relate the events of my past.

"Do you think your father knew how much you disliked what happened?"

"Yeah, I think so." Where is this leading and do I want to go?

"Then it might be that you were quite a threat to your father."

"What?"

"You describe a situation where your father inflicted definite emotional, mental, spiritual, and physical damage upon you. You believe he knew this damage was occurring. You believe he was doing this to you. We do not."

"What? Are you calling me a liar? Do you think I'm nuts or something?"

Cetaf joins us. Behind him a block of LaFayette sounds like the shrieks coming from an automotive insane asylum. "No. We believe everything happened just as you described. We accept your feelings about it, as well."

"Then what don't you believe?"

Jenreel's eyes move from the wailing automobiles to me. "That he did it to you. People do nothing to you, they do something for them. The former assumes you are the center of their universe. Such a universe could not survive."

Beriah wipes a tear from his eye. "You were the object of his sentence, neither subject nor verb. You were what he acted on, neither the cause of the act nor the act itself. It was important to him that he attack you. Rather than understand why such attacks were important, he found his safety, his worth, his identity in perpetuating the attacks. You were there, you were available, you were safe, he could rage free of penalty or retaliation."

Cetaf gently runs a monstrous digit under Beriah's eye, lifts the digit to his eye and stares at the moisture there. "Whenever we place ourselves as the object of something - for good or ill - we are the victim of it. Your destruction became the center of his universe. Now you must let him die."

"He died years ago."

"No, you're keeping him alive."

"No, I need to know why he did it. I need to understand."

"Is that what you need to know, to understand?"

I can't stop myself. "Will you enlighten me, O' Great Frog of the Desert?"

The three of them chuckle. Genuinely chuckle. How come they're incorporating earth behaviors faster than I incorporate theirs?

Beriah writes in the air. "Since you asked - " Cetaf and Jenreel sing a quiet, two-part, Simon&Garfunkel harmony of Judy Collins' *Since you asked* - "You left out 'to me'. The full statement is 'I need to know why he did it *to me*. I need to understand why he did it *to me*.' Your phrasing left the preposition and its object unspoken, hence unrecognized and unanswerable."

"What is this, a Steven Fry *QI* grammar lesson?"

"Your grammar is fine, your question isn't. It is incomplete."

I roll my eyes and shake my head. Which when you think about it is more difficult than moving your foot in a counter-clockwise circle and drawing a six in the air with your hand. "Are we going to have another lecture on completeness?"

"Your father sought to destroy in you what he could not destroy in himself. Unable to destroy it, he sought to destroy the memory of it. That memory was you, hence he had to destroy you. Your existence perpetuated a memory he could not face, so he sought to destroy what he believed was its source rather than learn its true source and heal himself."

Have you ever been around someone who's right all the time?

Have you ever been around someone who's right all the time and not egotistical or vain or smug about it?

Have you ever been around someone who's right all the time and genuinely wants to help you learn to be right all the time, to know your truth all the time and know it's independent of their truth, and that that mutual independence is a good and healthy thing?

Beriah faces me. Cetaf and Jenreel's quiet chorus grows to silence with Beriah's next truth. "You, Ben, sought to learn your pain's source and heal. You refuse your inheritance: your father's rage at what he could not accept in himself. That's what all your work is about."

I stare at him and shake my head. I so want to hurt him.

But I can't be my father. "Sorry about that Great Frog of the Desert line."

"You hold your father too close. An attempt to control the past."

"Guess I'm a controlling - " and I stop.

Because I can't be my father.

Jenreel offers me his cotton-candy dunce cap. "What would happen if you discovered there was no reason? What would happen if you found out there is nothing to understand? As long as you seek an explanation, you remain an object, a victim."

Beriah's cheeks dry. "And if there was no reason? What if he did it simply to do it?"

I wonder how much Earth's literature they're aware of. "C.S. Lewis wrote a book, *Perelandra* - "

"You will tell us of Professor Weston killing the Perelandrian creatures simply because he could and that's how Ransom realized Weston was evil, pure evil?"

I grab him, wanting to shake him, wanting to crush him. Cetaf wraps his arms around me, making me a child sobbing into his great chest. "It's not fair."

Cetaf cries with me. "No, it's not."

Jenreel watches our bodies quake. "The goal of understanding is the World Formula."

My sobs end as if controlled by a spigot. "The World Formula?"

"Yes, the most important part I mentioned when we returned from the desert between the worlds. The base, disruptive equation without which no other exists."

Am I about to discover how to unify the fields? "Such an equation exists?"

"Of course. Understand it, use it, and you have an explanation of everything that has ever or will ever happen. Life approaches it asymptotically."

The Unified Field Theory deals with life? Okay, I suppose it would as all natural forces affect us.

He shapes a dying curve in the air. "Trying to understand everything that happens is too limiting. We never attain all knowledge. We can jump to the other side of all knowledge, though. As soon as we are aware of the World Formula, we violate it by observing it from somewhere off of it, usually the other side or close to on this." He waves his hand and the curve disappears, dies completely, vanishes if it ever existed at all. "You don't need all knowledge to have perfect awareness."

I can tell my face is so scrunched I could crack walnuts between my brow and cheekbones. "Perhaps you could show me the World Formula?"

Beriah writes in the air. How come they can do this on my world and I can't?

$$A + B = C$$

"Huh?"

CHAPTER 24
SPIRITUAL IDENTITY DEMONSTRATED AS SEXUAL CHOICE

There was a girl, Jan Kuzko, in my high school chemistry class. She went to the Junior Prom with Rick Gamazi. Rick was a swimmer and weightlifter. Powerful arms and chest. He wasn't the smartest guy I ever met.

Let me correct that. He was a bit of an ass.

Jan Kuzko was white. Polish white. Her skin was so soft to look at and so pure that I wanted to lick her cheek just to see if she tasted real. I told her that once and she laughed.

She was easily the most beautiful girl in high school. She was thin, but not model thin. She had a figure. Nothing fancy, but enough to let you know there was something under the clothes she wore. And she had legs. Legs that started just under her throat and went all the way to the ground and back. To this day I think of those legs in seamed hose and a tear comes to my eye.

Even back then, Jan Kuzko knew she was a lesbian. She knew it and she was comfortable with her choice. She never saw anyone, at least not that I knew.

Who the hell am I kidding? None of us were comfortable with her choice. Back then society told us what roles to play and "high school lesbian" wasn't in the game plan.

She went to the prom with Rick. She didn't come to school the next week. When she finally came back, she wouldn't talk to anyone. Anyone. She wore sunglasses for two more weeks. Six months later she left school.

———

We walk up Broadway in the low 800's. All the stores here are six feet wide and nine feet deep, just barely big enough for Cetaf to fall down in.

There is a man talking to another man. They hug and the first man kisses the second on the lips. They hug again and the first man enters the subway. The second man looks at us, smiles, and walks away.

I evaluate off-handedly, dismissively. "He's gay."

Beriah nods after the man. "Yes, he seems happy."

"No, I mean he's queer."

The Healers stare at each other, then at me, then at the man as he walks down the street, then at each other again. Beriah cocks his head as much as a neckless creature can. "He appears to be just as you."

"No, you don't understand. He's...different. He...," I fumbled. How can I explain this to them?

"We agree that he's different, just like you."

"I'm not gay," I shout, then hang my head because people turn. A gay in New York isn't new, but to be the first queen of spades tour guide to three distinctly different tourists I don't like.

"True. You rarely seem happy."

"Listen. He's a guy who likes guys. He doesn't like women. What do you call that kind of person?"

"A human being."

Cetaf wipes his eyes. "What do I care what form it takes so long as the spirit is the one I seek?"

Beriah points to a vintage portable black and white TV in a pawn shop window. "I heard someone on TV say about us, 'If you do not say what you mean, you'll never mean what you say'."

My anger flees before my shame. Still, it makes one more valiant attempt to demonstrate my stupidity. "I always say what I mean."

Jenreel nods. "Exactly, Ben. You always say what you mean. If another doesn't know what you mean, and if they wish to understand, they must take the responsibility to do so."

Cetaf watches the TV. "And sometimes what you say is mean."

I see Beriah smile. I heard a statement. They offered a question and an observation.

Semioticists' favorite joke is "Which came first, the chicken or the egg?" That's also the punch line because the question "Which came first, the chicken or the egg?" demonstrates a lack of comprehension of the nature of the solution. The egg had to come first because until the first time someone pointed at what hatched and said, "Look! A chicken!" whatever laid the egg wasn't a chicken.

It is I who must pay attention.

Who is the hatcher and what will be hatched?

———

Beauty and the Beast, only this time the beast was us in the form of one strong boy thinking he was a man. I arranged for Jan to go out with Rick. I picked them up - he in a tux he'd purchased "Because it's a sign of class, Ben" with a hard slap on the back. He did look good in it. She looked like she belonged on some Paris runway modeling fashions fit for real women - and dropped them off. I don't know why I did it. Everyone knew she was gay. I found out later I was the only one she'd ever told.

Evidently Rick knew, too, although I doubt he had the processing ability to determine what her being gay meant.

Again, none of us did.

She slept with him. He said willingly and I wasn't sure, but she confirmed it and Jan never lied. The blows to her face were from her mother, whom Jan told, and who beat her daughter for doubly cursing her sweet Polish life. If you're black and gay you're lucky. You don't have to tell your mother you're black.

> Dear Mom,
> Just wanted to let you know everything's fine. I'm seventeen, pregnant, and gay.
> Say hi to dad.
> Thanks for everything (thwack! thwack!).
> I love you.
> Bye.

She told me she slept with him because that's what incredibly white skinned Polish girls with good figures and heart-numbing legs and lips so naturally red and full they call out "Forget me not" do when everything in their lives tells them they're not supposed to be gay.

And I was the only one she ever really told.

I'm sorry, Jan.

CHAPTER 25
PLACK PASTITS

A policeman comes upon a black man beating the shit out of an old Yiddish guy. The policeman pulls the black off the old guy. "What are you doing that for?"

The black guy points at the old Yiddish man, "He called me a black bastard."

The cop looks at the old Yiddish man. "You did?"

The old man says in a thick Yiddish accent, "Vy tshould I tsay tsuch ay t'ing? Tsuch ay fine hyoung man I vould never."

The cop still has a hand on the black guy. "Then what happened?"

The old man replies, "He hasks me vhere de VyHmTseeHay his. I told him he's ay plack pastit."

A block north of Union Square and I understand arguments are unnecessary detours on my path. Beriah tells me this is good. "When we learn to accept others as the universe brings them to us, we stop externalizing our enemies. Our enemies are already inside us."

If he says more it goes unheard because two beat-up pickup

trucks smash into each other, each racing the lights, at the intersection of 18th and Broadway. They are not going fast but each is carrying cases of foodstuffs and those cases go flying, spraying the streets with a rock doves' holiday. The intersection and a little beyond are a buffet of produce, potatoes, thick sausages, and salamis.

A Hispanic man jumps from the truck carrying the produce and a German man from the potato, sausage, and salami truck. The former begins yelling in hispain, the latter in germain. It quickly becomes obvious neither speaks englain. They are yelling at each other in their native languages. Beriah comes between them and, speaking English to both, tells each what the other is saying. They start to calm.

Is it his presence or the service he provides? To let each know he is heard, if not by the other, at least by he who stands between them?

The Hispanic is newly arrived in this country with his wife and four children. He used some of his money to rent a room for a month. He is not stupid and is taking English lessons at night. As a matter of fact, doesn't this German man look familiar?

The German is also newly arrived. He has some English, and he, too, spent some money to get himself a room. He is working hard to save enough to bring his wife and son over as soon as possible. Mrs. Hinga's Class For Non-English Speaking Persons? Is that where I've seen you before?

Hispanic: I'm scared. We have green cards but this country isn't exactly what others told me. I'm afraid I might have to go home. There isn't much to do in Honduras. I'm a smart man and want to make it here.

German: I'm scared, too. My English isn't too good and you know how people look at a person with an accent not wearing a St.James suit? I don't want to go home but I'm not sure when my family will follow. There are people here from my village, but this country changes them and I'm worried I might change, too.

Beriah still stands between them and faces the Hispanic gentleman. His hands touch each other palm to palm in front of him like he's about to do some isometrics. "So your rage is really a frustration you might not be able to feed your family in this new land."

The Hispanic nods.

Beriah turns slightly to face the German gentleman. "Your rage is really a frustration you might fail your family, shatter their dreams to come to this new land."

The German nods.

"Your feelings aren't much different, if they are different at all."

The two men look around Beriah at each other. Like children caught quarreling, they lower their heads and nod, slowly then vigorously. The Hispanic moves back to his truck, to one of the cases which didn't arc into the street, lifts it and places it in the German's truck. The German, his eyes wide with anger or perhaps fear, lifts a case of sausage from his truck and gives it to the Hispanic.

Slowly, without them knowing, Beriah backs away.

The German reaches for the Hispanic's arm. The Hispanic whirls, reaching to his side for something, perhaps a gun or knife. The German puts his hands up and pulls back. "*Nein, Nein. Seine Kinder? Ya? Nein. Kinde,* Childs?" He nods excitedly. "*Richtig, ya.* Childs. Have childs?"

The Hispanic doesn't understand. The German starts to sign and the Hispanic picks up the signs and adds some of his own, the two of them building a language based on the immediate reality of the situation, based on the immediate acceptance of each other, simultaneously and spontaneously.

I am witnessing what I study firsthand, in the moment, possibly the first to ever do so. The only other spontaneous language known is the Nicaraguan Deaf-Child language. Without help, coaching, guidance, intervention, a group of deaf children from different families in one small village created a sign language only they understand. They can teach it but learning requires forgetting how most people are trained to think.

In essence, to become new in that moment of learning.

The Hispanic and German continue.

Yes, I have children.

Wait, I have some milk in the truck. It is for me, but it's too much for me to drink. You take it.

Your family isn't here? Who feeds you?

I eat when I can, sleep, too. I have to work when I find it.

From now on, until your wife and son come to be with you, you'll eat with us. You come for breakfast and supper. We'll make sure you have something for lunch, too.

That's kind. Too kind. I can't.

Hey. You help me and I help you. Maybe sooner your wife and son come here. That's good. You need friends when you come some place strange.

You're right. Okay. What about our trucks?

We do the same work. We only need one.

And so it went until they drove off, plans made for dinner and for a partnership where before there was hunger and loneliness.

I stand where Beriah and the two gentlemen stood as if the spot is a holy site and I'm waiting for a miracle to happen. "That was incredible."

The Healers continue north, turn as a group, and look at me, the asphalt I stand on, then back at me. Beriah offers me his hand, a parent letting a child know it's time to move on. "There are no universally accepted operational definitions - no satisfactory rules of correspondence - for feelings, memories, moods, desires, hopes, volitions; all these things which make up a life, these things you call 'semantic blanks'. It is these things which make us unique, mark us as individuals, each separate and distinct and with a wonderfully self-aligned belief in the world. When these things are denied or rejected, you have felt the cleft of a bloodied axe."

I stop arguing and begin understanding. Spontaneous languages are the languages of immediate reality.

. . .

Of course, what the old man says first is, "Why should I say such a thing? Such a fine young man I would never," and second, "He asks me where the YMCA is. I told him he's a *block past it*."

To understand anything, you first have to stop being part of whatever it is you're trying to understand.

Capital *U*nderstanding requires an acceptance, a willingness to be in this moment, this here, this now.

Heisenberg was incorrect. Uncertainty only exists if you remain a part of what you want to understand; General Relativity becomes Special Relativity because you've pre-determined the universe is fixed, bonded by the rules you place on it so you can be comfortable with it.

In college, I was taught no direct link exists between quantum mechanics and relativity.

Of course a direct link exists. People are unwilling to accept it, to accept what the necessary change in rules tells them about the universe, about themselves.

The universe unfolds itself only as far as you're willing to be aware of its unfolding. Any more and you've traveled to a desert with Jenreel as your tour guide but missed the bus for the ride back.

CHAPTER 26
CHESS LESSONS

Uncle Freddie taught me how to play chess when I was about nine or ten.

Sorry, that's not true. He taught me some chess strategy. A kid by the name of Andrew LaVin taught me the moves. He taught me the moves this way: learn enough to be able to move pieces across the board, don't teach subtleties of movement (castling, en passant, etc.). He makes a subtlety which I duplicate and am told, no, wrong, you can't do that. Teach me the subtleties. Don't teach me any piece can be regained simply by advancing a pawn across the board. Teach me the subtleties. Let me capture his queen on his seventh row because he's going to regain her with his pawn in the next move, thereby placing my king in mate.

When I got a book on beginner's chess and beat him in a game, he refused to play with me for two weeks. I later found out that his older brother, Martin, went to the library and looked in all the chess books until he found the one I'd signed out, then spent two hours each night coaching Andrew until Andrew knew each strategy and counter-strategy in the book. After that, Andrew was once again willing to play.

Enter my dad's brother, Uncle Freddie. I remember Uncle

Freddie best for four things: patiently and kindly teaching me chess strategies, taking twenty years to finish his bachelor's degree while he supported his wife and growing family, letting his infant son cry himself to sleep in a dark room each night because that's what you were supposed to do with little boychilds to make them grow up strong, and boasting at our dinner table that just as soon as he got his wife who'd separated from him back in bed by Christ she'd take him back.

CR-iced.

That's the way he said it.

He spent an evening with me teaching me how to play. I don't know what brought the subject up, perhaps I mentioned that I liked to play, and we got the board out. He taught me strategy by teaching me to think before, during, and after the move, asking me to defend each of my moves with an explanation and a goal, and how did my move move me closer to my goal.

He even let me win.

We come to a street off Mulberry in Little Italy. Some children are playing volleyball with clothesline strung between two first story apartments, one on either side of the street, and a soccer ball. I wonder why Italians would be using a soccer ball for volleyball then see there are Blacks, Indians, Orientals, and others in the group. I think the oldest child is ten, perhaps more, a little over Jiminy's age. On the sides and acting as referees are some city social workers and police. Behind them are clothing racks. I see Colors hanging from racks; one, two, three, four, maybe more gangs represented in this game. At our approach, the children stop and gather around us.

Some - bolder? more curious than the others? or simply not afraid - reach up for the Healers' hands or touch their clothing. Everyone seems to have their favorite. Beriah spreads his fingers and lets the children run their hands over his palms and skin.

He smiles and looks to where they play. "What is this you do?"

One of the children pulls back and frowns. "It's volleyball, man. Ain't they got volleyball where you come from?"

Cetaf's eyes open bright. "May we play?"

The children unanimously think this is a great idea. I begin to walk over to sit on the stairs and Cetaf gently pulls me back. "You, too, please, Ben."

The children show the Healers the moves of the game. The ball goes back and forth over the clothesline. Eventually one player doesn't return a volley. The Healers start playing. The ball stays up in the air. A lot. The Healers don't hog, don't force, don't rush, don't spike, don't curse, don't favor each other over others in the game. They are the epitome of teamwork, even though Jenreel and Cetaf are on one side and Beriah and I are on the other, it is obvious they are aware of each other and work to keep the ball aloft.

One child, Nathan, a small, thin white boy with a thin face and deep eyes, his hair punked out using his mother's mousse, a slight overbite and not much of a smile, drops the ball. Cetaf smiles, hands him the ball and motions for him to continue.

One of the social worker referees trots over to me. "Wait a second. Can you explain to your friends here what we're doing here?"

"I give up. What are we doing here?"

She keeps her eyes on the volleyballing children. "Yeah, okay, that's fair. We're trying to teach them peaceful ways to resolve their conflicts. What they're learning here is to play a game and the winner of the game wins the conflict, rather than have a gang war. We figure if we catch them young, we can get them to transfer the concept of game refs to the concept of arbiters and eventually to the judicial system."

The game continues as she speaks to me. A boy near me, Danny, a boy who I think is too young to wear any Colors other than those of a stickball team, with ruddy blond hair and fair skin, wide, curious eyes and a look of concentration, drops the ball. Before Beriah can get to him, Danny picks the ball up, laughs, and whaps it to the other side. It goes wide and one of the other children, hesitating only a moment, runs out of bounds to return it. The Healers laugh and squeal with the rest of the children.

Another ref blows his whistle but no one listens. Not the children, not the Healers, not me. The game no longer cloisters around the clothesline but processes up and down the street as the two teams become a single force to keep the ball aloft.

The monitoring adults begin to move towards the children and are intercepted by Cetaf's outstretched arms. He hugs each of them in turn, "Thank you for allowing us to share our games." The adults fall away and are greeted by Jenreel's arms. The adults regroup and are met by Beriah's too-wide smile and arms.

"Don't you get it?" The woman who spoke to me screams at the Healers as the children sweep and flurry around them like a whirl-wind of multicolored flesh.

One of the children backs up to give Cetaf a clear shot. "Getitgetitgetit!"

Cetaf dives for the ball and up it goes.

The woman focuses her wide-eyed, throbbing neck veined, spittle spraying demands at Beriah because, evidently, I'm not help-ful. "We don't want them to fight anymore: we're trying to teach them peaceful resolutions to their conflicts, dammit." The phrase comes out ritualistically, like part of a pagan ceremony. Say it enough and it will happen.

The children hustle but no one shoves. In the space between the woman and Beriah, the ball descends. It bounces once, twice, between them.

Beriah picks it up. "Good. We teach them peace. Co-operation and peace. Teach them these, they will have no conflicts." He hands the woman the ball.

Red faced with spittle seeping from the corners of her mouth, she throws the ball over her shoulder. The crush of children explodes into dozens of arms and legs and laughter as they join to keep the ball up.

It's time for us to go. I know this. We start walking away, the adults trying to regain control and the children oblivious.

Jenreel takes one more look. "A finite game becomes infinite."

Cetaf doesn't look, only sighs. "Children don't care about victory. They care about enjoying the game."

I was so glad and grateful that Uncle Freddie taught me chess. Gladder still that I had been able to beat him in a few games. It gave me confidence regarding Andrew.

Later that night, when I was supposed to be asleep and was still listening intently to the adults' conversation two rooms away, I heard Uncle Freddie tell my mother why he'd taken the time to teach me chess. "No Matthews is going to be beat by some white jewboy as long as I'm around. Not at chess, not at nothing. I don't care what it takes."

My uncle wasn't teaching me chess. He was teaching me hatred. Probably not much different than Martin taught Andrew. No matter what we teach - piano, chess, basketball, mathematics, physics, cooking, painting - we teach both the thing and the energy we put into what we teach. If we have a core anger when we teach, we teach playing piano, chess, basketball, whatever, is done with anger if done properly. Have joy about when we teach and piano, chess, basketball is taught as an act of joy.

Gayle got me one of those Kasparov chess computers. I played it for about a week, once a day, losing every game until one game ended in a draw. I won the next three days in a row and put it away. I hadn't learned chess. I learned the computer's game.

We even design our machines to not enjoy the game.

Jenreel gently takes my arm as we walk. "None of us are machines, Ben. Especially if we wish to learn joy."

CHAPTER 27
REFLECTIONS IN SOCIETY'S MIRROR

The goal is to die with memories, not dreams.

There is a trash-strewn playground diagonally across from the Cabrini Medical Center. It is late afternoon and the Medical Center is busy telling children who should be laughing in the playground they can't have abortions because the government won't pay for it. This is being done outside the building because the staff can't even say the word "abortion" inside the building or they'll have their federal aid rescinded.

Police lift limp bodies, protestors from both sides of a public debate on personal choice, and the sounds of arriving and leaving patrol wagons fill the air like a flightless airline terminal.

An Indonesian boy about Jiminy's age stands inside the fence of the playground, at the closest corner, Second Ave and East 20th. He's wearing cutoffs, red hightops, a black leather vest, a top hat, a red neckerchief, a roll of bills as thick as his thigh in his left hand and a gun as long as his forearm in his belt. He smiles a fulsome proud-toothed smile as he sees me but his face goes shallow as the

Healers appear behind me. Around him but outside the fence are various girls. There is a girl who I believe can't even be his age made up as if she's going for the cover of *Cosmo*, some who look older but probably aren't. He turns and I see a black fanny pack. He pulls a bunch of needles from it and the girls swarm like piranha around a hapless pygmy, their arms flailing through the fence with such force they knock him off balance. What had been quiet at our approach now glistens with a thousand screaming children's voices.

He pulls the gun and the girls scatter, most who grabbed needles not moving more than fifteen, maybe twenty feet away before they fall and jiggly sigh, needles in arms, in thighs, under fingernails, in thumbs, between toes, under the tongue; I see one girl lift up her eyelid and another sit on the ground and spread herself as if inserting a tampon.

The boy fires and it is close, splintering the brick facade only inches above my head.

Beriah stares directly at him, I think into him, and the boy runs, now shooting up in the air, into the sky, into the night sliding over the buildings to the east.

At the far end of the playground from us he turns, stands as proud and tall as he can, turns the gun on himself and fires. His body stands for perhaps three or four more seconds before the muscles discover the commands to stand are no more.

I blink, shake my head, list possibilities, shake my head again. Nothing I'm coming up with satisfies the equation.

Beriah comes up beside me. "Give yourself time, Ben. Go slow. Travel the desert."

I frown, look at him, look at the boy's body, look back at him. "You didn't stop him."

"Because?"

"Because he didn't need you to?"

"Is that the first question?"

This is another new thing to me: a first question. I suppose if there's an equation which solves all others, a first, a primary equation, there's a first question which leads to all answers. "I guess not or you wouldn't have asked."

Jenreel comes up on my other side. "Did he want to be stopped?"

"He fired at us."

"At this distance, if he meant to harm us, he could have done so, therefore he didn't mean to cause us pain or harm. What did he want?"

I feel like both John Daly and the panelists on the old *What's my Line?* quiz show when he says, "We're going to toss over all the cards,,," but doesn't add "...because our panelists don't have a clue." I give up. "What did he want?"

Cetaf's shadow envelopes us. "He wanted others to feel the pain he felt. He knew no other way to share his pain than by wounding the physical."

I hear children cry, their voices carried to me by a sudden wind. It is the voices of the girls who surrounded him. They scramble over his body like hungry crabs, tearing his fanny pack from him and moving away.

"What he needed were witnesses to his solution."

I pull back. "Shooting himself was his solution? To what?"

Cetaf watches the girls' needs overwhelm them. "People who commit suicide don't want to end their lives. They want to end their pain. He wanted witnesses to accept his solution. We do. We did. It was the best solution he could come up with in that moment."

"Not much of a solution."

"He was being the best person he could be in that moment. He'd spent many years coming up with the best solutions he could to problems facing him, surrounding him, enveloping him."

"I still don't think of suicide as a reasonable solution, regardless of the moment."

The Healers turn and move on. Beriah turns first. "Doesn't your world have martyrs? Aren't there people who intentionally self-immolate, willingly stand in the path of trucks, trains, busses, tanks? There are none here who sacrifice themselves for their beliefs or the betterment of others?"

"Well, yes, of course. Most religions have a martyr figure as their root. All world mythologies have a hero figure who sacrifices themself for the good of their people."

Jenreel turns next. "They all believed their acts were the best solutions available at the time. How is he different? What does it tell us about a group, a tribe, a culture, a nation, which so limits solutions available to its people that death is a reasonable option?"

Cetaf turns last. "He mirrored the society which limited him. Any mirror can only reflect what is there, instant by instant, moment by moment. If lies are projected, lies are reflected. But sometimes when lies are projected, truth is reflected." Sirens trumpet the arrival of police cars. "We reflected his truth, not society's, and realizing this, his solution was to no longer be society's mirror. Sometimes submission is as good as resistance."

I feel a sad smile crease my face. "Especially if you don't realize you have a choice."

CHAPTER 28

VERD DOESN'T SING OPERA ANYMORE

Verd Scott is, upon seeing him, a Mr. Rosewater kind of man, someone whom you'd suspect of writing lurid and turgid pornography involving adolescent females who are mindless and totally yielding slaves to his Nerotic, Henryian physique. In truth, with his cat always with him, he writes some of the most visual, emotive, and stunning poetry I've ever heard or read.

For the longest time I knew him he repulsed me. He stands perhaps two or three inches beyond six feet, with thick glasses and even thicker chins. The kind of man who hasn't seen his penis in more years than it has inches and whose thoughts of any one else's interest in it come only at night, late, with the lights out save a flashlight under the covers accompanied by a springy sounding thrum-thrum-thrum. Already in his forties, he lives in his parent's basement. I know. I've been there. It is a cold, damp place, more fitting to mushrooms or things needing to be squished than human life.

Upstairs, in the main house, is a different story. All is light and late fifties deco. There are pictures of Verd all over the place. Verd at One. Verd at Two. Verd at Three, Five, Six, Nine, Ten, Twelve,

Thirteen, Fifteen, Graduation, and there the pictures stop. There are mementoes here and there of life past high school, but no pictures. A beautiful, chubby in a baby fat way baby, Verd grew into a relatively slim and yes, even a handsome youth. But it seems Verd stopped growing once high school was over.

A man is singing opera outside the 30th St. Terminal, on the southwest corner of the W 34th and Eleventh intersection. Not a single opera, a medley, opening with Peri's *Euridice* and progressing through Monteverdi, Rameau, Scarlatti, Pergolesi, Purcell, Handel, Mozart, von Gluck, Beethoven, von Weber, Wagner, Meyerbeer, Bizet, Gounod, Rossini, Donizetti, Bellini, Verdi, Puccini, Tchaikovsky, Moussorgsky, Rimsky-Korsakov, Strauss, Berg, Shoenberg, Britten, Meotti, Barber, Henze, Egk - all the schools and all the thoughts and all the hopes and all the fears from all the operas. He is not a man, he is a machine. No one could keep this catalog straight.

Before he starts each piece he flips a sandwich board. Each panel explains the history of each piece and the status of the world at the time each piece was composed. There is a dog sleeping at his feet, a handsome German shepherd wearing a seeing eye collar, chasing rabbits. Beside the dog is a felt padded hat, the better to avoid the embarrassing tinkle and jingle of coins. At the top of each board panel is a braille engram. We arrive when he sets up. It is morning, just as the rush begins. There is a good breeze coming from the North River, and the sun doesn't look quite as fierce today, a welcome break from the days of sweat and thunder.

We stay until dark, when he's pulling his sandwich board over his head and the dog, all rabbits caught, rises to lead its master home. The man lifts his hat, tips it so that all the money stays in a clump on the sidewalk, then dons his chapeau and starts away.

"You dropped your money, friend."

He stops and turns to us. His face goes red. The muscles in his neck knot and bind, locking the words deep in his throat and pushing them back into his soul, pushing them up through his dark glass-hidden eyes, forcing his head to swell and his feet to ache. "Y-Y-You're th-th-the aliens aliens, ri-ri-right?"

Beriah walks up to him. The man follows Beriah's movements as if he had eyes. An arm's length away, Beriah bows and the man returns his bow mimicking Beriah's movements with micrometer precision.

Just then I hear a sound from behind the buildings and around the shadows. It is different from the other city sounds and adds to this surreal landscape, sounds like scurrying scabrous beetles hunting through the carcass of a bombed out city.

"I-I-I ha-ha-have to g-g-go."

The man and the dog hurry away. They're not out of eyesight when a dozen dozen children come up from the tunnels, down from the roofs, pull out from the shadows and descend on the corner, on the pile of silver and green, like famished hounds at a foxhole.

I run after the man, leaving Beriah, Jenreel, and Cetaf to watch the children. I grab his shoulder and spin him to face me. "Why don't you stutter when you sing? Or is that a lie, too, like your blindness?"

He takes his glasses off. There are no eyes there, not even sockets. Just layered, lumpy flesh, scarred tissue that grew with nowhere else to go. "I-I-I s-s-sing for g-g-God. H-h-he l-l-listens and d-d-doesn't-t l-l-laugh."

He turns and continues away from me. For a moment, just a moment, a memory flickers and I see my father slapping a man on the back. The man was stuttering and my father thought perhaps he was choking, perhaps coughing, perhaps needed someone's large, heavy hand to help him form the words.

Back at the intersection the children scurry back into the night. I rest my back against a building, seeing myself as King Kong walking through the city, perhaps Godzilla, taking a break from movie-making, sliding down to the pavement and hiding my face so I can cry silent tears because I really don't want to climb that damn building again or wipe out Tokyo for yet another Saturday afternoon matinee, but this is what my makers made me and it's too frightening to take on the responsibility of making myself.

The tears come more freely because a great fear comes to me. A great fear that, whether they want me to or not, I will.

If you look at the pictures, hold them close so you can see where the airbrush begins and the camera fails, you'll see in his thirteenth year, a little jowl starts to form, even more in the fifteenth, again lipping the collar at graduation, and there the record stops.

At some point, at some place, somebody needed the memory of Verd's maturation to cease. Somebody - and I don't know who and now realize I never will - needed the maturing boy to return to the baby-fat baby as a man. My guess is this is not what Verd wanted. I guess this because of his poetry. I think that through the onionskin layers is something more like Jenreel or Cetaf and unlike Beriah or myself. I don't know why the visual history of Verd stops where it does. I don't know why his parents' basement is his sullen refuge. I only know that some poetry comes out of there, and that poetry has the power to make me laugh and make me cry.

Often both at once.

CHAPTER 29

THE PATHS WE TAKE

New York University is hosting an international gathering of linguists trying to discover the original human language: the One-Tongue. The invitation - sent by the event organizer, Dr. Ebenezer Blockridge - came before I went walkabout with Frog Lips, Elephant Toes, and The Wisp.

We stand at the side of the Galleria.

Some linguists are of the opinion that the original language was a command form that forced humans to do what the speaker wanted. In other words, the original language was something spoken by others who used it to control people to do the speaker's will. For some reason, they died out, left, whatever. The humans who remained tried to use the language to control each other, hence we try to name things which gives us control over these things, eventually evolving into magick words.

This might also account for the proliferation of "ese"'s such as legalese, medicalese - probably social disease, too, now that I think of it.

The presenter, a woman I recognize by neither name nor face, finishes and asks for questions. Professor Blockridge draws the gathering's attention to us. "Perhaps our guests from...," he pauses.

We smile.

"From...," h p__s_s. He l__ks t_ _s, w__t_ng f_r _s t_ f_ll _t _n. (go ahead. fill in the blanks. you can do it. this is an offering, not a test)

We say nothing, only smile back. "Go on, continue," is implied.

He becomes a conductor. Tip of the baton to the aliens in the third row. Violins and woodwinds are doing their part, why aren't you? "From?"

Cetaf walks up and clips on the mike. "Thank you."

I sit back to watch the language learners work.

"The learned gentlewoman's hypothesis is offered only due to the advent of my fellows and me. Without your acknowledgement of our existence, said hypothesis would be laughed out of this meeting."

I lean against a sidewall with Beriah and Jenreel and fold my arms over my chest. I smile quietly; someone has shown the Emperor has no clothes.

"To change your world, you have to change how you talk about your world, find new ways to lingualize your experience of it to change your experience of it. This relingualization is relevant to this meeting's purpose: to determine what the One-Tongue was, you have to become a people who are creating the language, not merely borrowing from another known tongue or hybridizing your own tongue. Doing so merely demonstrates lingualizing an existing experience. You have to become a people who wish to be understood, to whom being understood is incredibly important, to whom survival depends on mutual understanding. You must use all your existing experience if you wish to create new tools to incorporate new experience, like climbing a ladder: you can't get higher unless you're willing to leave the rung you're on for the next rung. Climbing down - returning to existing experience - is easy. Falling off the ladder will do it. Climbing up - being willing to have new experience and create language to share it - takes work. It demonstrates having gaps in your language which your existing experience cannot fill.

Blockridge moves as if to unclip the microphone. "That sounds like you're judging us." He hesitates, his hands hover but don't touch the giant before him, and he draws them back, the microphone untouched.

"No, not judging. Observing. It is the way of any life; this life, the life of this star, this cloud, who is to say the life of the cosmos itself?"

"It sounds like you are responsible for your own creation," observes Blockridge, simultaneously facing Cetaf and smiling to the crowd. "You use our language to interact with us, to share your observations of us."

"Are we responsible for our own creation? Of course we are, as are you. If for no other reason, would you entrust something as precious as your becoming to something else? To your second statement, perhaps you're so locked into your own experience of us you can't hear us when we use new language to understand this place. Perhaps you are Jerry Lettvin's frogs whose eyes could not see what their brains could not want, except you cannot hear what you would not understand."

Jenreel walks to the podium, accepts the microphone from Cetaf, and Cetaf joins Beriah and me at the side of the Galleria. "Example: Your military texts indicate any war against a unified defender requires a 3-1 ratio of attackers to defenders. Some of your religious texts indicate Lucifer left Heaven with one third of the heavenly host. If these statements are true, did Lucifer really want to win or were you using known language, known concepts and understandings, because lingualizing other possibilities would be too horrible to bear?"

Jenreel and Beriah change places. "Read these texts as originally written and it becomes obvious Lucifer's real crime was expressing anger in a sacred space. But if you be you - with all your emotions, all your desires, all your fears, all your hopes - in your sacred space, where can you get angry? Doesn't your god know how you are? Don't you want your god with you always? Yet you work so hard to separate yourself from your god. Is that because you don't wish to create language which would allow you to become your own god?"

Beriah looks at me. Jenreel and Cetaf gently nudge me from behind. I'm Mikey and I'll do anything.

Okay. Fuck it. It's not like I've got something to lose.

What am I saying? Whatever it is I've got, I hope it's long gone. I trade places with Beriah. "We won't have information until we need to know that information. Somebody asked me 'Do you know how to jump over the library?' I answered 'No, but when I need to jump over the library, if I'm aware, I'll know how to do it. Yet the word *jump* is rather inadequate for such an experience. Perhaps the greater work to understanding how to do it is creating new language in which doing it is so natural as to be understood immediately by all.

"We can have no concept of something existing until we acknowledge it exists." I walk away and realize I've forgotten to unhook the mike. I return to the podium. "It's like George Carlin's routine about the attorney asking the witness to describe what they witnessed by saying 'In your own words...' and the witness countering with 'My own words? Nobody will understand me if I use my own words. Don't you want me to use the same words everybody else uses?"

I unclip the microphone and, to the applause of the Healers, exit.

CHAPTER 30
MORE OR LESS

The crippled man walks through the subway, holding a cup, and announces that he's a vet with pan-handlers papers issued by the city of New York. He says this quite loudly and defiantly. The Healers look at him but say and do nothing, which surprises me. The man continues into the car, holding himself up by leaning into the handrails on top of the seats at the far end of the car, and recites his monologue again. At first I think he's trying to convince himself he has the right to ask for money, then I notice the shine of metal protruding from the side of his head and wonder if he's lost the ability to remember recent events. He is dirty, his clothing a mismatch of dumpster chic, he hasn't shaved in so long things crawl through his stubble, and I am aware I don't want him near me. Attached to the rope belt around his waist is a cup, its metal the same color as that escaping from his head, and attached to the cup is a chain. I follow the chain up to his wrist. It is odd to see the cup attached to the chain attached to his wrist. He reminds me of some vagabond courier, a derelict version of the bonded couriers employed to transport sensitive documents, their accountant cases attached with metal umbilicals to their wrists and their minds.

He starts down the aisle of the subway car, not holding his cup out to anyone in particular.

A black man, sartorially dressed, turns to stare at his reflection in the window and adjusts his tie, holding his face firm, almost rigid, refusing to make eye contact with anyone except his own reflection until the beggar passes. The beggar, coming through the train, says "God Bless you. Thank you," at each clink of copper or silver or flutter of green into his cup. The black man continues his finessing, adjusting collar, lapels, boutonniere, tie, pin, hat, checking his teeth, his hair, grooming his beard and mustache. His sprucing becomes more intense, more obvious, with each step of the beggar. Finally beside him, the beggar empties his cup into the black man's coat pocket and says, "God Bless you, sir. And Thank you."

The beggar comes up beside us and nods. The Healers nod and the man moves on. I feel ashamed that I have nothing to offer except my sympathy.

The black man turns and stares ahead into the direction the car is moving. But now he slumps, his face sags, his shoulders roll forward and the trimness and elegance of youth are gone from him, as if the beggar's coins bought from him all that he thought himself to be. I hear him sigh, and against the brightness of his collar, I see him flush.

"Who is the poorer of the two?" I mumble, forgetting who is there and who will hear. "Who got the greater gift?"

Beriah states it as fact. "The black man, the beggar. The beggar now knows there are those more bereft than he."

Jenreel nods. "It was a fair exchange, in any case."

"How do you know that?"

Cetaf points from one to the other. "The black man did not ask for more nor did the beggar offer less."

CHAPTER 31
LESS OR MORE

"It is our silence that separates us."

Broadway where it hits Times Square. Everything you've heard is true. Probably you haven't heard it all, either.

As we pass a door it opens, revealing an ascending stairway, a young, dark-haired white man in a business suit, and a black woman dressed evocatively. "Five dollars," she says.

"Five dollars?" I laugh. "What could she do for five dollars? Shake his hand?"

Jenreel watches the exchange. "Probably something she values at less and he values at more."

My early life taught me the best route for a little nigger boy-child in a town with only three equally gifted families was silent acceptance. My middle life taught me the best route for a person-of-color was aggression masked as Wokefulness - another person-of-color interrupted a meeting I attended by stating that the rest of us refused to acknowledge his skin color. He looked directly at me for confirmation. I nodded because, unlike the no-longer-seen *Lucky*

Strike commercials, I happily switched rather than fight. Years later Cetaf explained mirroring with "...submission is as good as resistance." and I would learn the meaning of choice versus no choice.

Now I learn a new route. "What do you mean?"

"This place," he waves at our surroundings but I get the idea he means us, people, NYC, the world, "games finite or zero-sum. Whatever she gave, she values at less than the paper received. Whatever he received, he values at more than the paper given."

"What's wrong with that?"

"Nothing, if all agree, which is true because this place," he waves at the surroundings again, "games finite or zero-sum."

Jenreel, I am discovering, is an incredible mathematician. It is how his concepts of mathematics are applied which are new to me. The contrast is similar to *The Living Bible*'s "Multiply and fill the earth and subdue it; you are masters of the fish and birds and all the animals" and the nuevo-aboriginal belief "Learn how it works so you'll know how to fit in without messing it up."

"How do you mean, 'finite or zero-sum'?"

"Exchanges are made for temporary things. That exchange," he nods towards the door the man and woman came from, "is zero-sum. Neither profit because the exchange is made for subjectively placed values. Her sense of less negates his sense of more. Sometime later he will seek a similar exchange and so will she." He walks on. "Your people exchange and merit the temporal and place no value on that which remains. Neither of them knows themself better. She only knows what she is to him. He only knows what he is to her.

Jenreel stops and reaches over my head. I hear something hit the pavement behind me. I refuse to look. I know if I do I'll see a dunce's cap rolling in the wind, its black surface a shadow moving across the slightly dark gray pavement. "You are not valued based on my need of you, Ben."

What am I saying? All of them are probably brilliant mathematicians. Beriah and Cetaf never bring such things up.

CHAPTER 32
NEW MATH IN OLD MINDS

"Language is an act of cooperation." - Rita Mae Brown

The Pierpont Morgan Library's entrance is shaded by London plane trees. It contains one of the most extraordinary collections in the Western World. All the manuscripts are originals, usually in dead languages.

I don't know how the Healers know it is here, yet they move towards it like a Cruise Missile seeking funding for its brothers.

Outside are some homeless and some protestors. The protesters are divided between those wanting to kill the homeless, those wanting to ship the homeless to 'Jersey, those wanting to home the homeless in someone else's home, those wanting to home the homeless in their own homes, those wanting to build the homeless homes, and, in the middle of it all someone's playing George Carlin shouting, "These people aren't homeless, they're placeless. They have a home, they don't have a place."

George goes into and out of his routines, working his humor to get his message heard.

There is another man, someone I think I've seen before. His clothes - jeans, red and yellow on black flannel shirt, work shoes and wool socks - are clean but the man himself smells of too much sun and work. I can't make out his features because his hair and beard obscure them all. He holds one of his shoes in his hand, looking at the sole as if it could tell him where he'd been.

As we pass him, he mumbles, "If you close your eyes, the sun don't stop shining for anybody but you."

Inside, I rest, stretching out on a table as if it were a bed. The Healers do not. I do not know the books they read. I don't want to know. Instead I fall asleep, surrounded by ancient wisdom.

How long I sleep I don't know. I know I wake to a massive tome covering me like a lid, a discussion between people I can't see, and about three days growth of beard.

"Isn't it written in one of your holy books, 'And the light shineth in the darkness; and the darkness comprehended it not.'?" It is Beriah's voice. "Why 'comprehend'? Comprehending leaves the problem still a problem, only understood, perhaps. Instead, it might be written, 'and the light shineth in the darkness; and the darkness accepted it.' Accepting something originally thought foreign allows both to grow until neither is.

"Or older still, 'And the light in the darkness appears, and the darkness it apprehended not.'"

Jenreel joins in. In my hot summer afternoon sleep just waking daze, I don't know who they're talking with. If it is with each other, it is the first time they've done so that I know of. "Yes, and more recently, 'His life is the light that shines through the darkness - and the darkness can never extinguish it.' There's also, 'The light shines in the darkness, and the darkness has not overcome it.'"

Then I hear Cetaf, "What is saddest to us is this: when you encountered those who could accept all beliefs, who could share the darkness and the light, you extinguished them."

Jenreel again, "But even he said whoever is not for me is against me."

"Yes, and he also said the kingdom was within. He never said it was without. Yet that is where so many of you wanted it and still want it to be, never at rest with yourselves. There are no devils, Ben, not in the sense your people think of them. Your devils are yourselves."

Hearing my name, I push the tome off me and rise. "Who're you talking to?"

Cetaf points to Jenreel. "To Ben, Ben."

All I see is Jenreel. "Where, I don't see anybody else here."

"There is nobody else here, Ben. Jenreel is Ben."

"How?"

Jenreel draws two distinct coordinate systems in the air. "By repositioning the co-ordinate system. I, like anyone else, can try the other person on. It is the mapping of an individual's experience, a moving from one co-ordinate system to another, like linear algebra or elementary physics, if you will. You see the picture, now, don't you."

"You going to teach me how to write in the air like that?"

He takes my finger and connects the axis-intersections.

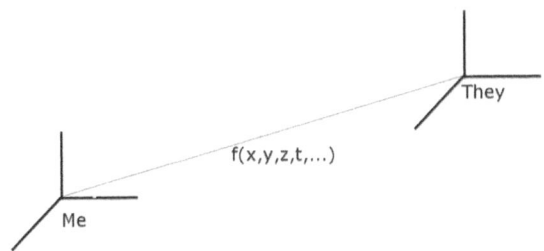

Outside, the crowds have thinned and different players play the game. The man in the jeans is still there. I don't recognize him at first because he doesn't smell. He is clean.

As we pass him, he tosses me a used bar of soap. "Knowledge of what is doesn't open a door directly to what should be, you know. Einstein said that."

"Thanks." My attention is drawn to the crowds. I notice now what I didn't notice then. They are protesting the Pierpont Morgan's collection. How can we keep such things as special, they ask, when there are others hungry and dying?

Jenreel nudges me. "Can you appreciate their question, Ben? Can you appreciate them?"

"Yes. I've learned to be just like them."

He smiles.

My co-ordinates shift. Briefly, instantly out and back, their needs more than this Christ can bear. I say what, from the old co-ordinates, still comes naturally: "The poor you will have with you always."

"You will have the poor with you until you remove the source of their poverty."

"Which is?"

"Your wants exceeding your needs."

Pause.

"So we should sell off these books in the Pierpont to make their lives more comfortable? You think that's a fair exchange?"

"We don't know which shoes the Fisherman wears," answers Beriah. "Your society has to decide which it values more, these books or these people. All exchanges are based on what one values more and the other values less. While you're deciding which is more valuable, if indeed you have to decide, you might teach them to read."

The people don't pay us much attention. "Where do we go from here?"

"We go slowly, breathe, and smile."

Cetaf demonstrates. He inhales, takes a step, smiles. "If you don't change your direction, Ben, you'll get where you're heading. Where you are is obviously where you need to be. Therefore it's up to you to either stay or move on."

Jenreel's blue waif body mimics Cetaf. "The only answer to 'Where are we?' is 'on our way to somewhere else'. The only answer to 'What are we doing?' is 'Exactly'."

My co-ordinates shift. First to Healers, then to the crowd. They stay there. I make them stay. I let them stay. When I'm done, when I have decided which is more valuable, my co-ordinates return to me, which is to say I'm changing and they're changing with me. Or they're moving and I'm moving with them.

"Sometimes I think I'm the last of my kind."

Jenreel, Cetaf, and Beriah laugh and speak as if one. "Perhaps you are the first of many."

1: Start with the different ways in which we function.

$$e \equiv emotional$$
$$s \equiv spiritual$$
$$p \equiv physical$$
$$m \equiv mental$$

2: Whatever we do, whoever we are, we act as a mixture of these four elements, therefore our lives become a function

$$f(e,s,p,m)$$

Which is to say, we are the sum of an infinite series of these functions

$$We = \sum_0^\infty f(e,s,p,m)$$

Or more simply, we respond in the moment with a lifetime of experience.

The best part is, we can change our responses by changing our experiences to suit each moment.

(remember where you saw this. you'll need it later)

CHAPTER 33
PURR-MOTORS

8 30 Fifth Ave is the address of the new Central Park Zoo. As before, it's all happenin' at the zoo, although it has gone through two major changes since Simon and Garfunkel first sang about it.

I wake up violently because Cetaf claims he has gone blind. Beriah, Jenreel and I laugh. As we laugh, a stray tomcat stretches, yawns, and winks at us from atop Cetaf's face. It then makes cushy-cushy between his chin and chest and holds itself like a scarf against his throat. The creature I've called "The Walking Wall" and "Elephant Toes" rolls his muscles in ways no human could and the cat slides up to his shoulder as Cetaf rises to his feet.

Inside the zoo it is feeding time. The cat scampers down Cetaf's back, between the bars of some cages, and comes out with some scraps which are large enough to feed a cat twice its size. It is but one cat out of all the strays we've seen.

"Those beings are not from here," announces Cetaf, watching the animals behind the bars.

"No," I agree.

"This purr-motor" - I can never get them to say 'cat' - "is."

I agree with polarity, "Yes."

"Yet they are fed and he is not."

"Yep."

Jenreel looks around at the homeless. "If they could fit through the bars, they could eat, too."

Beriah agrees. "Yes. That's how it seems."

Sometimes their thoughts hypnotize me and it takes a moment to react. "No, no. That's not how it works."

"We've read of your prisons," says Beriah. "You gather people who aren't from a place and put bars around them to keep them in that place. Then you feed, clothe, and shelter them." He motions towards the homeless, some of whom are now reaching through the bars, risking their limbs to whatever beasts might challenge them within. "Selecting which actions to reward is surely a difficult task."

"Going to prison isn't a reward."

Beriah raises his arms as if to encompass all those around us. "Neither is this."

Jenreel places his hands on the bars. "Besides, the function of a lock isn't to keep everybody out. It's to let certain people in."

A woman screams and people rush towards her. An ape has broken her arm as she reached for some of its fruit. When she pulled back, it threw shit at her which landed in her mouth.

I turn away. "This is just one of society's ills. My society, I know. There are certain evils we've learned to live with."

Cetaf picks up a tomcat and rubs its chin. "I was a prisoner once. It was I who created my own prison. Suffering is mistaken for evil. Suffering is what you've learned to live with. The suffering of others. No one ever learns to live with their own suffering. They deny it, make it into a virtue, or demand others deal with it instead of dealing with it themselves."

Just then a truck groans down Fifth Ave. Its twin stacks spew acrid black exhaust which slides to the ground, never dissipating, never graying. It lands in the street and becomes a puddle of darkness, sticking to clothing and children on bikes and splashing as tires squish through it on their separate ways.

Beriah points at the puddle. "Who is responsible for that?"

"I don't know. I didn't catch the company's name."

"I think it is the driver's responsibility."

"Only if he owns the truck."

"While he drives, he owns the truck. The man driving the truck must be held accountable. He must individually be made to pay because he drives the truck."

"Sure, right. The company will only fire him and find some other guy to drive. You don't understand our way."

"When another is found, and that other drives, then the truck becomes their responsibility. So on, for the next - "

Jenreel echoes, "and the next - "

Cetaf puts the cat down and finishes the chorus. "- and the next." The cat rolls onto its side and lets him scratch it, batting his fingers every once in a while and guiding them to where he should scratch.

Beriah sings lead again. "When enough of this happens, there will be no people to drive trucks such as these. When this transportation method fails, companies will make it a point to find methods that don't fail."

Cetaf scratches as the cat directs. "Responsibility for those trucks, the purr-motors, the people before bars and the animals and people behind them, these are your responsibility, Ben."

I wave my hands in front of me and step back as I shake my head. "I refuse it. I don't want it, and I won't accept it."

"Then don't expect others to assume the responsibility for you, nor be shocked when your problems remain."

"You're not understanding. My responsibility is demonstrated when I vote, that's why there's a Congress and a President and a mayor and a city council and on and on. Those institutions exist so I won't have to deal with such problems individually."

Cetaf takes my hand. He doesn't hurt me, yet I feel myself powerless to resist. He has me scratch the cat. "Feel this purr-motor's ribs? Its narrowness, its loneliness? All it wants is enough. These people. Are they any different? The animals in those cages, the people who are like them, are they any different? All anybody ever wants is enough. Most people learn to be confused about what's enough."

"Tell me what's 'enough'."

Jenreel shakes his head. "No. You decide."

A little girl of perhaps three, all curls and pink, comes into the center of us and picks up the tom. She grabs it under its forelegs, its back against her chest. It starts to slowly slide and she holds it tighter as her three-year old legs trundle towards some adults. "Kitty, Mommy, kitty!"

The mother races forward, alarmed more for the cat than the child. She helps the little girl put it down. It weaves its way through the little girl's legs, a shuttle through a two-legged loom, purring and marking the little girl as its own. "Yes, Jeannie, that's a kitty. I think it belongs to these nice men, though." The little girl is laughing and clapping her hands, trying to catch the kitty.

Cetaf lifts the cat and offers it to the little girl. "I don't know much about the purr-motors. Do you know what they like?"

"Mook! Kitties like mook."

Beriah stares at me. "What is 'mook'?"

"Milk," says her mother. "She means 'milk'."

"Do you have milk?" asks Cetaf.

"Sure, back home."

"Would you like the purr-motor?"

"Do you mind if we take it to the vet? Just to make sure it's had its shots and get it neutered?"

Exasperation lays on me like a rug. "No, please. Go ahead."

The woman picks up the cat. It purrs. They leave. I grab some rags out of the trash and stop traffic. When I leave there is no black striation in the street.

They nod. "Enough."

We walk on.

CHAPTER 34
EXPECTING GOD

Fifth Ave below Washington Square Park isn't. Neither is much else of the gridlike order of the city, which is an indication of where it started if you discount the several thousand years of Native American history which was here before.

A crowd moves with us because it is too hot to stay inside and there's a brown-out which means air-conditioners won't work and we're the cheapest show in town. It is night. City night. Every third streetlight is off and few business signs are on as we walk. Everybody is in t-shirts and gym shorts, including the hookers working the crowd, including the extra-duty police who move along the hookers and also work the crowd.

A pimp begins yelling at a boy but the talk isn't about hooking or pimping at all. The boy is a mule who didn't know he was supposed to save his shit when he came into the city. He crapped away two ponybags - condoms filled with coke or heroin and greased so they can be swallowed, move through the intestinal tract, and passed through the bowels at a later date - and the pimp who evidently deals on the side isn't happy. At all.

Nobody's paying attention to them, not even the cops, and I

wonder if there're any undercover police moving through our throng.

Jenreel walks up to the boy being tussled by the pimp. "You don't know who you are."

The pimp pulls out a large knife and shoves it in Jenreel's face. "You come here to die, motherfucker?"

Jenreel faces the pimp as if the knife isn't aimed at his eye. "I know who I am."

The crowd divides. I don't know how cleanly. Some people quickly move away, others encourage the pimp, others beg Jenreel to do some voodoo-science-bullshit-magic and make the pimp, his stable, the boy, and all affiliated with them go away.

Jenreel doesn't move. Neither does the pimp. A policeman ambles over and places his weapon at the base of the pimp's neck.

The pimp turns his head enough to see the cop standing beside and a little behind him. "Shit."

"Or go blind, asshole. Drop the sticker."

The pimp is cuffed and hauled away. His stable, neighing and whinnying like fillies suddenly dropped in an unbound field, follow close behind. The boy scratches his bottom, his face first thoughtful then broken by a smile as the pimp is taken away. He tips an imaginary hat at Jenreel. "Thanks, Hightop."

Jenreel stares down at him. "You still don't know who you are. I still know who I am." He walks back to us and the boy runs away, avoiding police, us, and the crowd.

"What was that about?"

"I was praying."

"You were?"

"I was, I am."

I'm learning (I hope). "To yourself, correct?"

"Praying to an unknown, unexperienced thing and expecting an outcome is at best an act of bravery and at worst an act of stupidity or foolishness. Faith is knowing something's happened once, twice, ten, ten million times before and expecting the previous outcomes to repeat. Knowledge is recognizing the expected outcome didn't occur this time. Wisdom is understanding what caused the difference and learning from it."

"What was your prayer?"

"When I don't know who I am, I serve you. When I know who I am, I am you."

"That's a prayer?"

"For me, for then, yes. It reminds me part of me shares a part of everyone else. If I don't know who I am I have to look for parts of me in everyone else."

CHAPTER 35
ACTING VERSUS ACTIONS

here is a riot going on on the UN Plaza. We can see it across 42nd St from Tudor City. Cetaf is in profile against the UN building and reminds me of *The Colossus of New York*. There are as many police, National Guard, and other services as there were at our arrival and I wonder if I can recognize anyone. Ambulances pull up 42nd Street as I scan for warriors I know, especially Distasio. I worry for his safety and, as I shape the thought, Jenreel smiles.

Today is the day the WHO decides if food shipments will be made to countries which don't encourage voluntary birth control.

"Encourage voluntary"? It doesn't make sense and I say so.

Cetaf turns to me, his brow furrowed. "Perhaps your em-PHA-sis is on the wrong syl-LA-ble."

A police car is overturned. Four preachers, one dressed in white, one in red, one in black, one in yellow mount four horses painted similar colors. Each preacher carries a sign; one reads "DESTRUCTION", another "WAR", another "FAMINE", and the last "DEATH". The preachers wave swords and, like Assyrian generals, direct their troops into the UN.

From the main doors people swarm onto the plaza. Four groups form as if to do battle, one group per general's army. One group carries a sign reading "SPEECH", another "EXPRESSION", another "WORSHIP", and the last "FEAR & WANT".

Police fire gas into the crowds. The horses panic and people start going down. Someone in the crowd flashes a gun. The police, in riot gear, their tasers and riot sticks aloft and squeezed between their shields, move forward. Automatic weapons fire and the UN Plaza becomes Hanoi, Dublin, Moscow, Managua, Beijing, Lima, Jerusalem.

We watch. A man drags a girl towards us without seeing us. He throws her up against a wall and she slides down. The man is the preacher wearing yellow. The girl has "F&W" embroidered on her shirt. She is pregnant, perhaps six or seven months so. Also, she is young. I think perhaps sixteen, although it is difficult to say. She wears clothes typical of a teenager who has been on the street, in a shelter, fostered and again out on her own: dirty, patched, and ill-fitting. Her face is also dirty, with stringy blonde hair and cloudy blue eyes, although there is a mindless, beatific smile on her face and she licks her lips with her tongue, extending it so much my throat aches to watch.

The man is older, much older, her father or grandfather in comparison. Beneath the yellow smock is a black robe. He not only wears a black robe, but I see his clothes are severely cut and are black on white, no other colors show. His shoes are black, heavy-soled Knapp work shoes. His face reminds me of a glacial moraine, so heavily creased and cragged is it that I see myself scaling it, hanging with ropes and pitons and crampons as I swing an ice-ax into his nostril or perhaps his eye. His hair is black. Greasy boot-stamp black, as if polished with the same wax he uses on his shoes. His eyes are clear in contrast to hers, but where there is no life in hers neither is there life in his.

"There's life in your belly, girl. Respect it. Let it live!" he orders.

On the ground, on the paver, her body pressed into the crevice where wall and sidewalk meet, the pregnant, dirty teenager punches her belly and chants to her blinding god. "You bastard, you bastard, you bastard."

The man kicks her hand away and drools out the words, "If I can't save the world then God give me strength I'll save you."

I stand before the man and push him away from the girl. He lunges at me and I turn into his charge. He cracks his skull against the wall and collapses beside the girl.

The paramedics closest to us open their doors but do nothing else. I lift up the girl. She folds onto me as if she is a cat and I am the pillow where her mistress rests and I help the paramedics place her on a stretcher. Before they transfer the stretcher into the ambulance, I've returned with the man. "If they don't have any insurance, you know where to find me."

The driver nods and they're off.

Cetaf watches the ambulance pull away. "There is a difference between the acting of the faith and the actions of that faith."

CHAPTER 36
A PART OF THE WHOLE

Somewhere between sophomore and junior years in high school, I became the guy to know.

As I think about it now, I wonder if somehow they found out I was black. I mean, *The Cosby Show*, *In Living Color*, and *The Fresh Prince of Bel-Air* were must-watch shows on TV, at least one if not all three (the more you watched, the more sensitive you were to the plight of your black brothers, of course). If you didn't know somebody Black, you just didn't belong. You had nothing to talk about.

You were *kuhl*, and no teenager would risk their social worth by being un*kuhl*.

It doesn't matter. I went from twelve years of being the kid to kick, verbally if not physically, to the kid everybody had to say hello to in order to be cool. I remember my first day of junior year, everybody - and I mean 'everybody!' - greeting me with a big smile and, in some cases, a handshake. I spent several days wondering when the hammer would fall, probably directly on my head, and spent that first day sweating in cold fear because I'd learned at home and elsewhere that when someone is openly your friend they're looking to drive ten penny spikes up your butt as sure as not.

And everybody was my friend. I thought and sometimes still think that perhaps some high school committee was formed over summer and it was voted that, yes, by Christ, Ben Matthews had had enough, let's find some other poor dumb bastard shit and fuck him over for the next two years but let's let Matthews have a break, Christ he needs it.

Even people I didn't know knew me. You simply didn't *belong* unless you were Ben Matthews' friend. The only kids who didn't partake were Tina Kolas, Steve Chamber, Brian Amora, Heidi whose last name I can't remember, and Raven McCloud. These five, of all those who knew me before I oozed cool and after, treated me the same no matter what the invisible committee said. Tina still gave me grief, although it took me several years to find out why, Steve still treated me as Ben Matthews whom he was talking with today and who cared about yesterday or tomorrow, Brian Amora who was always friendly and a good listener and openly took notes on everything everyone said and did because he was going to be an author some day, Heidi was still quiet but was quiet with every-body, and Raven didn't care what anybody said as long as I didn't give her cause to be otherwise, was going to be my friend.

It didn't help that I was already working hard towards becoming a teenage alcoholic by this time. I followed the patterns passed on to me as well as I could. Sarah, the girl I dated I treated like shit - god, when I think about what I said to her, what I did. I fucked lots of others including right on my desk after school Mrs. Johnson, a pencil thin English teacher who was having marriage problems, and Ms. Kiriakoutsis, another English teacher with tits so huge anything she wore made her look like a skirted guernsey and some of the mothers (and Mrs. Betz, in particular) who loved to scream and claw - I didn't mind. The black garters were kind of a trip. Oh, to be *plack* in the nineties - or the girls who, up until the year I oozed cool, wouldn't admit knowing anything about me during the day.

I kind of got off - pardon the pun - duking a girl's mom when the girl wouldn't even look at me during school.

Those last two years, though.

Yeah.

Of all the compliments I've ever received in my life, the three which meant the most came from Tina Kolas, Jenny MacInery, and Jodi Liezenstein. In my senior year, Tina Kolas told me I looked good. She was sitting on the radiator outside of the boy's locker room and more fitting a picture I couldn't give. If she wasn't drying out the receipt she was keeping it warm to collect the rent. I came up the stairs and, seeing her, started back down, thought better of it, and continued around the corner and down the hall.

I hoped to blunt the inevitable attack and fired the first volley. "Hi, Tina."

"Hey, Matthews, you look good."

I tightened my gut.

I didn't say anything, just stopped walking and turned to face her.

"You do, you know. You look good."

I spun as if I were on a runway and someone were detailing my sartoriation. "You really think so?"

"Yep. Wouldn't say it unless it were so."

Which was true. Tina never bullshit anyone.

"Would you go out with me?" It was a stupid question, then and now, but was the only way I could relate to any attention back then.

"Well, let's not go nuts about this. I said you look good. We'll talk about the rest later."

When you're a Jet you know you're a Jet.

We've come upon our first gang war and I am frightened.

Simon and Garfunkel sung about this place and, like the Zoo, it has changed. A group of young men, I don't know their number, undulates under the Roosevelt Island Tramway like a spider testing her web. Close by and in the shadows beneath the Queensboro

Bridge is another pack of youths spreading like a Prince Charles Sound oilslick, slow and steady. The only thing separating one group from the other is the color of their clothes. Each huddles, slithers, and breathes in the shadows of early morning rain and a cold wind kicks up spray from the Harlem River and leaves for the far-wested Park. Sitting on a buttress halfway up one of the tram supports is someone, I can't tell if it's woman or a man, with a gray blanket around them. Their only distinctive element is a brilliantly scarlet carnival mask and I point at it. "Who's behind the Pimpernel's mask?"

Beriah pauses, frowns, then smiles. "Every reader in the world."

We walk between the two groups, between the bridge and the tram, and I am afraid.

The group on our right calls us as we pass, "Hey, cuz, you better come over this side you want be safe." From our left come words in a language I don't understand. It sounds like a mix of Vietnamese and Haitian. I don't know the words but their actions make it clear they feel we would be safer with them.

The two groups start shouting at each other and Beriah looks from one to the other. Another frown levies his face. "These people do not like each other."

Evidently that is a cue. The two groups race towards each other with pipes, chains, knives, nunchukus, sais, automatic and single-shot weapons.

Across the intersection of 60th and First a lone cruiser sits, two police inside. Its lights are off and the car idles. Inside, windows rolled up against the chill, the officers sip coffee and eat donuts, a cliche made real by its sympathy. They have not lifted a mike to call for support, nor do they seem concerned, more like tourists seeing a smalltown football game, curious but uninterested, not so much enthused as intrigued that the rivalry exists.

Beriah continues walking. "Objectivity is intersubjectivity. It is agreement amongst observers."

"What?"

He points to the police, to the first group then to the second. "If everyone agrees a thing exists, then it exists because there is agreement."

"The Emperor's New Clothes? Or the elephant in the living room?"

A boy from the first group runs up behind Cetaf and uses him as a shield, not because he is Cetaf so much as because he is big and he's there.

Again, reflexes faster than I feel they should be, Cetaf turns to the comparative mite before him. "What have I stolen from you?"

A path forms in one section of the melee and the youth runs into it, a game of Stratego where everyone wears a flag.

"What did you mean, 'What have I stolen from you'?"

"He wished to make me dependent for his survival."

"Kind of. He was using you as a shield."

"If he wishes to become dependent on me, I must have stolen something from him, something he wishes to regain. I didn't want him dependent on me and didn't know what of his I had stolen, so I asked. Tell me what it is and I will give it back."

The elephant has taken up residence in the living room. Instead I look at the teenagers, children from age ten to youths of nineteen. "I was never part of a group like that. Any group, for that matter."

"You have always been part of a group, Ben."

Jenreel rubs my back. "Several."

There is a heat to his hand I've never felt before. Not hot, more like warming. A glow. I feel it in my heart as well as on my back.

It is acceptance.

"For a long time one group didn't know you existed."

"For an even longer time you refused to be part of one other group."

The only group I know I exist in is the three men (did you catch that? You can't let things like that slip away) I now walk with. "You mean I'm only here because you three want me here?"

Cetaf's hand replaces Jenreel's. Same feeling, only different. Again, my heart understands while my mind does not: he touches me with compassion. "Oh, no, Ben," Cetaf answers me. "Without Hope the Universe has no meaning."

Pay attention, goddammit!

Jenreel's hand raises to the back of my head and cradles it. He gently turns me and smiles down on me except it is not Jenreel I see; it is a mother looking lovingly at her child. "Did you, Ben, ever doubt *we* would be here?"

Car doors slam and the police walk halfway towards us. One holds his hands up, palms out and towards us as if holding us back. "Don't get involved. This goes as far back as far back goes."

The other looks to the battlefield and places a hand on his holster. "These two hate each other so much they took vows on it. It's special."

Jenreel looks at the police then at the rivaling throngs. "A special relationship is anything outside of us which we imagine to have power over us."

No shots have been fired yet there are two piles of bodies forming where each gang drops their dead.

Beriah follows my gaze. "They could get up and walk away."

"Who, the dead?"

"No, the living. The dead already have."

I started to walk away and Tina, quietly but not so quietly I couldn't hear, only quietly so no one else, no one in the pissing on trees camaraderie of the boy's locker room, could hear, said, "I'd go out with you."

I heard that team mates often urinated on each other when psyching themselves up for a game. In the locker room. Often with the coach either watching or planning strategies in his office, not ten feet away.

Probably has something to do with the sense of smell being our most primitive and wanting to mark your tribe so you wouldn't rip their heads off by accident when you were blinded by 'roid rage.

This is Kant via Henry Margenau via Ben Matthews because it's important to our concept of communication and languages:

Immediate sense impressions are "primary" impressions and are "P-experiences". Because all sense impressions are how the mind is aware of the world, we are not directly aware of the world, but only get information through the filter of our impressions.

Because these sensory Primary impressions are not true reality, one might think of a plane between reality and our mind upon which these impressions occur. We communicate with one side of the plane, reality communicates with the other of this plane. The plane itself can be labeled the "P-plane" because it is our Primary reference to reality. All primary P-experiences can then be mapped onto this P-plane and the P-plane becomes the totality of our experience.

In order for me to communicate "car" to you I need a way of sharing my concept of "car", not my impression, because it doesn't matter if my sensory impression of "car" is your sensory impression of "car", it only matters that we both agree whatever's causing those sensory impressions is "car" regardless of our individual impressions of it {thus, true reality is already one level removed from who we are}. This communication of concept requires some means of measuring the source of our impressions, hence I communicate that something is in the domain of all four-wheeled transportation vehicles and in the range of four-wheeled non-mass transit transportation vehicles, regardless of my impression and you agree regardless of your impression because we share the same concept.

These concepts by which we measure and categorize our P-experiences can be called the "C-field" for "Concept-field".

The means of linking observation to immediate experience - linking concepts to primary impressions - can be called P-C relations and thought of as "rules of correspondence".

Because concepts are usually defined by our P-experiences, anything we observe is a construct of our P-C relations.

Standing on the shoulders of giants I offer the following definitions:

Phenomenon - a set of sensory data, a P-experience
Noumenon - an objective interpretation suggested by data but
not necessarily one that corresponds to a particular
phenomenon; a construct before it is verified
Transcendental object - the verified construct corresponding to
a particular phenomenon
Thing-in-itself - the unknowable factor behind experience
which accounts in a mysterious way for the thus-ness of
particular objects

In my teens, Tina said I looked nice. In my twenties, Jodi said I had a nice cock. In my thirties, Jenny told me it was a little bigger than average and she, I knew, had been as inclusive as Gallup in her poll. Funny how we define ourselves at times.

At times.

Tina said I looked nice and, yes, she'd go out with me. Years later I understood.

CHAPTER 37

THE ELEPHANTS ARE HERDING IN THE LIVING ROOM

I was sitting in my mother-in-law's family room reading a magazine and the buzzer on the stove went off. Gayle and her mother were on the porch with the door closed. After a few minutes of listening to the buzzer, I decided they couldn't hear it, opened the door and pointed toward the kitchen.

My mother-in-law raced in and picked up the phone. "Hello? Hello?" With the buzzer still sounding, she said, "What's wrong, Ben, there's nobody on the phone."

"I didn't say the phone was ringing."

She then heard the stove buzzer and took the pot off the stove.

Gayle said, "You said, 'The phone'."

Sometimes I'm not sure of what I do. This time I was. "No, I didn't. I just pointed into the kitchen."

"You pointed at the phone."

"No, I pointed towards the kitchen."

"Then why didn't you say what was wrong?"

"Couldn't you hear the buzzer?"

My mother-in-law, her face tense and voice terse and trying hard to deny both to everyone around her, said, "However."

. . .

The New York Public Library is at the southwest corner of 5th Ave and 42nd Street, in the 460s block and next to Bryant Park, where 42nd Street divides into East and West as 5th Ave spines the island, and is guarded by the great stone lions, Patience and Fortitude, resting but raising their heads in smug judgment of all who enter her doors.

Beriah strokes one as if it's a cat wanting a ball of string. "These creatures must be important to you."

Jenreel pets the other. "Yes. They've hunted them almost to extinction."

Inside we go unnoticed except for one security guard, a man of average height and complexion (careful) whose long black hair is tucked up under his cap. He is not powerfully built but stands with his arms square across his chest and stomach pulled in, his shoulders back and pelvis tucked, making himself a pained and awkward parody of strength. He walks up to us as we enter and says "I don't want any trouble in here."

Jenreel walks in without hesitation. "Then cause none."

Few others in the library notice our existence, those who do smile and nod, others look up then down back to whatever holds their interest. In the left corner, behind a pillar, are two Hassids, a Mutt and Jeff pair in black hats and curls. Their conversation grows more animated as we draw near and, as we come abreast of them, they approach us.

Mutt has a high, tall voice that belongs in a high school auditorium. His beard has thin streaks of gray coming from the ends of where a mustache would be. Because his eyes have slight epicanthic folds I see an orthodox Fu Manchu. "My name is Abraham. Today I leave to bring my sister back home."

Jeff's voice is a needling soprano in my ears. "I go with him."

Mutt points to Jeff. "Elijah will burn the place where she stays once we leave."

Jeff nods vigorously. "I will burn it."

"Tell us, how many must we find in order that their camp be spared."

Jenreel and Beriah pull back from these two and I realize they do so to protect themselves from a plague indigenous to Earth: us.

Beriah shakes his head. "None."

Cetaf cries. Is he already infected? God, I hope not (Something important is communicated here. Can you guess what it is?).

Jenreel agrees with his Brother Healer. "Yes, none."

Cetaf reveals the reason for his tears. "Spare it for the sake of none."

Mutt and Jeff flush. They converse tightly and quickly in what I guess is Hebrew or maybe Yiddish. Mutt turns back to us. "That is not the answer we seek."

Beriah turns toward Mutt. "Then ask someone else your question."

Foam flecks the edges of Mutt's mouth. "No." He closes his eyes and seems to calm. "You do not understand. My name is Abraham. I go to return my sister from the camp where her mind has strayed. You three appear as did El Shaddai to the Patriarch. Now you must tell me what I must know."

Cetaf cries and the unmuscular guard begins his approach like a 747 coming in to land, three circles to make sure the runway is clear and the tower knows then it's down to the earth in a glory of thrust.

Cetaf moves his massive frame and blocks the guard's landing. "It is not God's responsibility to appear in a form which is acceptable to you, nor is God responsible for your understanding what God has said. God's only responsibility is to let you know it is God who has appeared, that it is God who has spoken." The guard climbs and circles again as he prepares for another landing.

Beriah blocks the field. "If you're not sure your God has spoken, then you don't know your God. The problem lies within you, not your God. Whatever is inside of you, that is your god."

Altitude, circles, approach.

Jenreel finishes the job his Bother Healers started. "The universe can't present you with a different god. There is no room. You've imagined the perfect god for your goals. You can obey your god's edicts, but don't expect others to join in your revels."

The guard leads us outside. We start down the steps and stop when Cetaf pats one of the stone lions, gently and kindly. The clouds briefly cast a shadow and I see the lion wink.

It would not surprise me to see Cetaf pick the lion up under its forelegs, hold it to his chest with its forelegs stretched out in front, a great fur covered airplane waiting to land, and waddle down the street claiming, "Kitty, mommy, kitty!"

The lion, I am sure, would only smile.

I learned a valuable lesson about communication that day. There's nothing wrong with how I give a message and there's nothing wrong with how someone else receives a message. The problem occurs when the message sent isn't on the frequency of the message received. I understand my universe through my ears, my nose and my hands. Gayle and her mother understand their universe by their eyes and their tongues.

Jenreel quoted First Law of Semiotics blocks ago and I didn't realize it as such: The First Communication Must Be Instructions On How to Build a Receiver. It's how they learned our language walking across a white-sand desert.

I stand at the intersection of yesterday and tomorrow and become the Now-point of Minkowski's Cones.

(Stay tuned. It's important)

How can we ever share our universes when we understand them differently?

Is anybody listening? Can you see me shouting, "Hello?" (Careful. The only way you can is if you know what I'm saying.)

CHAPTER 38
THE GREATEST SIN

Long before the terms "geek", "nerd", and their variants came into language, every school had one. At least one.

In grade school, we had Gary Kutis.

Gary was a twin. I don't remember the twins' name - Greg, I think, was his brother - but I remember Gary.

My first exposure to them was in kindergarten. We were all standing for something, probably that epitome of societilization, "The Pledge of Allegiance", and I wasn't paying attention to whatever it was we were doing as a class. Instead I was looking around at the other kids in the class, already aware that I was different from them but not yet societilized enough to know how, when I saw Gary pick a booger out of his nose, put it in his mouth, then wipe his hands on his pants.

Greg, if that was his name, had already learned to look away.

Many years later I had been societilized to my differences from the other kids by the repeated insults, taunts, and punches. I learned to be on my guard and trust so few people that I can, in memory, effectively say 'none'.

I remember clearly that it was a day near the end of the school year in June, third grade. The playground had an eastern exposure.

The girls' half - we still segregated by sex back then. Hell, we still do, we just don't do it so openly - was barren except for bike racks which ran the length of the building and thus covered both girls' and boys' sides. The boys' half had a pole sticking out of the ground where a playground carousel used to be, and a basketball court shaded by trees from the neighbors' yards. The whole playground was tarred and sloped, at times severely, towards the school building. I suppose this was in the hopes that, if a child was hurt playing, they'd roll into the nurses' office.

What marked this day so differently from all the others wasn't the bright sunshine or the radiance of mid-spring growth or the elegantly high, wispy clouds. It was different in that no one was beating me up on the playground.

I remember realizing this and immediately spinning around to see where they were all hiding, where they were all preparing to leap out at me. What I saw was the usual crowd of kids all huddled in a corner of the playground, behind and under one of the basketball hoops. I also realized that not everyone on the playground took part in my ritual humiliations. There weren't many that did, it turned out. I discovered there weren't that many of them because now I could count them. All of them. They were all beating up Gary, little fists punching little face, little feet kicking little legs, little boys showing how little they would, perhaps, forever be.

I also realized that the majority of people on the playground - teachers, students, volunteer mothers, principal and vice-principal - while not taking part in my punishments also never took part in my salvation. I knew this because, even as I witnessed Gary's tiny face bloodying, I saw all the others turn away.

I ran up to the crowd of apprentice sadists and worked my way into Gary, fighting the others to reach him before he fell and was lost under their little feet. Some made way, others found me as likely a target as I moved upstream to the source.

And when I was close enough, when it was eye to eye and victim to victim, when I saw the look on his face that let me know he knew it was me and that I understood his humiliation, I hit him.

As hard as I could and right in the eye.

"The Silence of The Majority is the greatest sin."

"Huh?" I don't hope for the cure for cancer but am not yet willing to cure myself.

We pass an alley in the Amsterdam Houses. There are screams. Children's screams. This section is middle class and people hang out of their windows, watching the children's game.

Suddenly a little girl screams, louder than the rest, terror adding volume to her voice. My mind blanks and we are across the Island, across the 59th St. Bridge and in Queens. Kew Gardens. Austin Street.

We are in the alley where Kitty Genovese lay bleeding so many years before. Where people just like her sat in windows, watching.

The stains on the pavement and dying lawn stand out as if Harlan Ellison is reciting them from *The Whimper of Whipped Dogs*. "Do you know what happened here?"

Jenreel takes in the scene and I wonder what he's seeing that I'm not. "What is happening here."

I hear screams but there are no voices. I smell blood but see the street sweeper's path clearly leading away. There is a torn dress, blood stained, erupting from the broken concrete sidewalks. Winter snow exhausted to cold coal slush reflects Christmas lights from windows as I gape at the steaming summer pavement. A weight enters my hand and I look to see a knife there, blackening crimson dripping from its tip, the white handle slippery with my sweat. It drops from my hand and falls blade over handle in slow motion as I look up at the smiling faces, crying faces, looking away faces, men's faces and women's faces and hear the cry of children as a mother leaves her window perch to tend them and demands of her husband, "Tell me what's happening down there!" Kitty Genovese becomes Sandra Zahler becomes someone I don't recognize and the screams never stop. Far away and down beneath my feet, the knife I held crashes to the ground and bounces slightly then crashes again, its sound changing the alley from thirty-forty-fifty years ago to today.

"The Silence of the Majority is the Greatest Sin," repeats Jenreel, although I know now that Beriah originally said it.

They walk on. I stand at the face of the alley, the alley in the Amsterdam, surrounded by children, their tiny little hands beating their tiny little breasts.

The next year, when I returned to school, I discovered I was no longer the preferred punching bag. It wasn't always Gary, but more often than not it was. What I discovered was something Fulghum never learned on his playground: as long as I was more often the puncher, I was seldom the punchee. Gary's abuse continued through sixth grade. I never saw him after that. I remember once, in fifth grade, he was offered the same lesson in playground dynamics as I.

Unlike me, he refused and walked away, ensuring his fate as surely as if he'd volunteered to test for sharks by swimming with fresh pork on his butt.

Gary.

If there ever was a kid who had the right to take a rifle into a tower and blow a few hundred-thousand people to pieces, it was Gary.

Greg worked very hard to grow himself away from Gary, getting and working hard at a job in our town's first real big chain grocery store, putting himself through college, going on and far and who knows where he is now.

I'm sorry, Gary.

CHAPTER 39

SOLUTIONS TO TWO BODY PROBLEMS

This guy goes to see his doctor. He says, "Doc, you got to help me."

"What's wrong?"

"I can't get enough sex. I have my wife before we go to sleep and when we get up. Most days I have her before and after dinner. I have my secretary when I get to work, during coffee breaks and during lunch. I get in the elevator with one of the office girls and go at it twice a day. I don't know what's wrong with me, Doc."

The doctor says, "Mr. Jones, you've got to get a hold of yourself!"

The guy answers, "I do, Doc, twice a day, but it's still not enough!"

When I went north for the cure, I was put in a co-ed wing. Sandy roomed next door to me, and I frankly admit I wanted to meet her in the shower at some point. She was a stunning, vibrant, young, curvaceous, auburn-haired, brown-eyed, doe of a woman who had a way of bending over to pick things up that could make you spill your coffee and pull your cigarette clean with one breath. She never dressed to accent but she didn't have to. One look at her and you knew. She was married to a man on his third marriage, twice her age, gave him a son a year earlier and now he didn't want her. He didn't want her so much he was going out drinking and whoring and told her his behavior was her fault. Hence, she was in the Home for Mental Wanderers.

Across from me was Proud Mary, the woman who would give birth to Jesus. She was in her late thirties, early forties. She was a woman who, with little effort, could have been attractive. She had moments of turgid lucidity. The rest of the time she was quoting the Gospel according to Her and awaiting the Spirit so she could have a Virgin Birth. The fact she already had three kids - who were terrified of her by the way - didn't matter. God turned Saul into Paul by knocking him off his ass, so He could just as easily restore her hymen enabling her to offer hers, no problem. Lesser miracles had happened. We'll get back to Proud Mary in a moment.

At the end of the hall was Kitty-Kathryn-Kate. She was nineteen and h-u-g-e. Her body displayed the layers of flesh which start in early childhood and continue, unbridled, into adult life. This picture was only reinforced by her sour smell, the smell of flesh left unwashed because it is too far away to adequately reach with soap and water. I was stunned to find out she had a child. My first reaction to this news was, "How could he find it?" I also remembered, "Roll her around in flour and look for the wet spot." These were quickly followed in rapid succession by "He was drunk" and "It was a mercy killing".

Kitty-Kathryn-Kate's roommate was a mid-twenties gifted pianist with hideous scars running from wrist to elbow, also named Kate. The pianist. Not the elbow. The elbow's name was 'Sid'. It was a good thing Kitty-Kathryn-Kate wouldn't respond unless you used the three word monicker as her name, huh? Gifted-pianist-Kate was average build with blue eyes, wire rim glasses mangled together with paperclips, and long stringy blonde hair. She didn't wash often and only showered when a nurse was with her in the bathroom. She wasn't afraid of being raped. Hell no, she encouraged that. Especially if it meant someone would be in the shower with her. She was afraid of the water. Specifically, the shower. And not as in *Psycho*. It was the water itself that terrified her. You never could tell what was going to reach out of the shower head or faucet and suck you up into the pipes. The difference in size between Kitty-Kathryn-Kate and Gifted-Pianist-Kate caused me to refer to them as Kate-the-Greater and Kate-the-Lesser. I remember looking at Kate-the-Lesser's arms and thinking, "Christ, this woman knows how to do things right."

Down the hall was Elaine, a sack of white hair-topped bones, a woman of puckered angry flesh housing an intentionally failing eighty-three-year-old mind. She had a room to herself because nobody else could stand her.

Nobody except Brian, a seventy-six-year-old man whose children thought The Home for Mental Wanderers the best place for him. In truth, they may have been right. He was a sad man, sad because I don't think he honestly knew what was happening around him or to him. He would sit in a chair, look out a window, and make great, sweeping plans for home and hearth and garden, preparing his snowblower for winter and his tiller for spring. He let people lead him hither and yon never questioning or asking who they were or why. He had succeeded where I failed. He gave up. I never could.

The only time Brian was alive was when he snuck into Elaine's room for the night. Once or twice I woke up to her rages as they pulled Brian from her. They slept together. Slept. Nothing else. There was something in the closeness of a warm body that made them both rational and happy, something no therapy ever could. Brian would mumble and titter, "Sorry," and Elaine would rail their keepers, "What're you doing? Can't a grown woman get any sleep? Leave me alone. Get out of here." Then all would grow quiet as the nightwatch took up their posts at the far end of the ward. It would remain quiet thus for a few minutes, maybe ten. Slowly, quietly, doors would open and bed springs would creak, followed by her heavy sigh then his, and all would be well until they snuck back to their own rooms before wakeup the next morning.

Brian's roommate was Andy. I never learned a lot about Andy. He was a mid-fifties man, balding, heavy, who walked with a cruel intensity. The first night I was there, Andy came out of his room to the public area wearing a beautiful green-on-white striped shirt, smartly accenting paisley print tie, brown vest with spanning gold watchfob and matching jacket, no pants, shoes, socks, or underwear, gushing blood from his groin. He held the wall with his left hand and had a fistful of crimson covered razor blades in his right. He cleared his throat, quietly, and said, "Excuse me. Could somebody help me?"

Welcome to J-ward.

Sandy's roommate was a teenager named Lill, and that brings us to my roommate, a lawyer named Fred. Lill was in because she was about to be married, got pregnant by her fiancee after the wedding was announced, and tried to abort herself before he found out. She was caught by her mother, an overbearing drug addict herself, lying across the kitchen table with a bottle of Clorox on a chair beside her and still undoing a coat-hanger when her mother walked in. Home alone all day and she waited until her mother called to say she was on her way, did they need anything before climbing on to the kitchen table?

Her mother didn't understand and decided her daughter was uncontrollable, so put her away for a while. Did I tell you it was her fiancee's child? Lill was, like any groping teenager, cute in her way, clear white skin, teenage bikini body, moon-pie face with a jet-black lion's mane surrounding it; kind of an anorexic Cowardly Lion from the movie *The Wizard of Oz*.

Fred. Fred was intelligent, genuinely so. He was handsome in a second-generation Italian kind of way. He was a good guitarist. He was a marathoner. He had a good job in a good law office and was destined to become a partner in a short period of time. He had a wife who loved him and was willing to wait until things worked out or he reached a decision. He was living with a woman who loved him and was willing to wait until things worked out or he reached a decision. Within two days of his arrival, he was caught sleeping with Lill in my bed. Lill, who tried to kill herself by making love to a bottle of Clorox, who decided she loved him and was willing to wait until things worked out or he reached a decision.

Give yourself this one. Neither of them were snoring, their eyes were wide open, they were sweating, it wasn't Saturday night and the lights were on.

I know because I found them.

Have you ever noticed that you can't do The Nasty without your legs straightening and your feet pointing? I'm not talking love and honor and respect and someone with whom you have a long, rich, full, and growing history, I'm talking sixteen-inch shells launched from destroyers ten miles from the coast acid-burning fire-in-the-crotch break-down-the-walls I'm-coming-home God-is-that-You sex. Try it sometime.

I said nothing. What could I say? I didn't want to join them and their lives were their own.

Proud Mary discovered that Fred's real name was Alfred Joseph. Joseph. Mary, the mother of Christ, met Joseph in a psychiatric hospital. Anytime he wanted her, she was his.

When I came to the hospital, I was so internally focused that, sitting in a chair in the entrance interview, I bent the arms of my chair in towards me. The first two days I walked about realizing, "Christ, I'm a lot better off than these people," then realizing, "Christ, this is what the rest of the world lumps me with," then realizing, "Christ, I'm sick. That's why I'm here. This ward is where the staff" - and I had a lot of respect for the senior staff - "put me because they think this will help me."

The final realization was the one that worked. I looked at the people around me and knew I had to get better to get out. Not simply tell them what they want to know and fake sanity the best you can but Jesus Christ I've Got To Get Better To Get Out!

. . .

Underneath the 145th Street Bridge for the night, watching the tides push up and pull down the Harlem. It is a cold night. Genuinely cold, the air having gone past chill. One of those freakish midsummer things when there will be rime on the brickwork for a few minutes after the sun comes up before all hoariness is lost.

I want a cup of coffee. I want a cup of coffee, warm socks, and my own bed. None of these things are far from here. Every cabbie in the city knows us. Knows me. In the early days, I could flag a ride, talk to them, and they'd forgo the fare because Bill Maher, Jimmy Kimmel, Steven Colbert, Fallon, Tamryn, Natalie, Whoopie, Larry, Moe, and Curly would give them ten big ones each just to sit and talk for an hour or so. Now it is different.

The *Enquirer*, the *Globe*, and the *Star* no longer pay writers to encapsulate us. We've stopped being the Alien Sex Bizarre Menage á Fourple *du jour*. Sally Burroughs and Georgia Nicols no longer cast our daily horoscopes. Chip Coffey, John Edwards, Sylvia Browne, Theresa Caputo, and Tyler Henry no longer channel Jenreel's father or Cetaf's mother. My - Our - fifteen minutes of fame is gone. Now even the gypsies drive past and, if my hand seems to raise, flip me the bird as they drive on.

Cetaf hangs his feet over the seawall and laughs when the water laps them. He starts playing tag with the waves. I want to kick him. He's being childish.

As if knowing my thoughts, Jenreel and Beriah join him. Their legs are not long enough to reach the water. Cetaf gives them rides on his.

Like a tired parent I yell out, "Stop it, damn it. You're going to get wet. You're going to get cold. You don't have any clean clothes and there aren't any towels to dry you off. Stop acting like children. Stop being so childish."

They don't.

I stamp my foot. "Stop it!"

They don't. They don't even acknowledge me being there.

I decide to use a ploy that got me backhanded as a child: I throw a temper tantrum. "Stop it Stop It STOP IT!" I jump up and down. I want to take my ball and go home.

Suddenly they are around me and, for the first time since South Street Seaport long long ago, I'm afraid. The way they stand, the way they look. They should pull knives or guns or something. Here's my wallet let me live.

Beriah stares into my eyes with concern. I know it's not threat as they've never threatened anyone or anything since they've been here so I'm going with 'concern'. "Who is childlike and who is childish?" he asks.

"What?"

"Who is childlike and who is childish? We are all childlike, we are not childish. Childlike is a way of being. Childish is a way of doing. A child shows maturity not by becoming an adult. All that shows is the death of the child. Maturity is shown through responsibility, not to others, but to the child. An individual is mature when they can take care of their own child and not at the expense of others."

Cetaf squats so he can stare into my eyes as well. "You told us you lost your child when we first met you. How did that happen, and when? We think it happened long before we met you."

I want to holler "Foul!", to call a time-out, but don't even know if there are rules to this game.

Jenreel leans over but not as an adult reprimanding a disobedient offspring, more as a parent helping a nonverbal child understand its own needs. "You want us to stop. What is the cost to you? What is the cost to us?"

I offer an excuse. "I'm...I'm tired. I want to sleep."

They bring me into a huddle. I'm not sure, but I think they expect me to quarterback.

Ben offers me the ball. "Ben, life is lived one way and thought about another way. Life is experienced in the body by feelings. It is thought as conceived in the mind and described with words and language. The intersection of these two events is the current disposition of attention."

Cetaf checks the ball for flaws in workmanship. "What are you about now, Ben?"

"Now?"

Jenreel takes the ball from Cetaf, offers it to me again and whispers. "Yes."

Does he think the other team is listening?

Why do I assume there's another team? Why do I need there to be an adversary, an enemy, an antagonist?

Jenreel holds the ball out. "'Now' is wherever our attention is."

I play the good old HALT strategy I learned up north where I wanted to shower with Sandy in the next room. "Now I'm hungry. I'm angry. I'm lonely, and I'm tired."

"That is your life, your experience right now?"

"Yes."

"What do you choose not to experience, then?"

"What?"

"What would be the difference that makes the difference?"

I try to break from the huddle but am too tired, too lonely, too hungry, and not enough angry. "This is insane. What the fuck are you talking about?"

Beriah claps his hands and the huddle separates. "Exactly. We're all pretending we're sane. Fortunately, most of us do such a good job we have most of the people fooled."

Is this where they show me the zippers in their suits and the good brain-salad-buffet people from up north reveal themselves? Yes, Ben, you've Passed! You're Healthy and Well!

Cetaf picks me up and holds me against him as he lays down. He is warm and I can cush him like a cat softening its mistress' lap before it takes a nap. Shouldn't he be cold? Wasn't he playing in the water? I want to ask but am too tired. Instead what comes out is "Tell me a bedtime story."

He begins, "There once was a man who spoke in nothing but gibberish. No one could understand him. Not his wife, not his children, not his friends. The religious leaders of his country were called and they said he was possessed. The great thinkers of his country were called and they said he was diseased. The great philosophers of his country were called and they said nothing, merely nodding with all the gibberish the man said. It so happened that this man had once done a service for the king and, the king remembering this, offered a reward for anyone who could make the man speak sanely again.

"Many tried and all failed until one day a great wizard came to this country. 'I can make him speak so all can understand' said the wizard and everyone laughed. But the king stood by his promise and said, 'What do you need to make this man speak as do we?' 'I need a full moon's time with him, through waxing and waning, from full to new and back again. Then this man will speak.' The king ordered a chamber set up and thus it was so.

"The wizard and the man entered the chamber and it was sealed. There was no way in and no way out, and only a mirror which hid another room allowed others to see the wizard and the man as they worked and lived. In this other room the king sat, day after day, watching the wizard and the man, waiting for some magic to be performed.

"The first two weeks the wizard sat and watched the man, listening to his gibberish but saying nothing and not moving his hands. 'What wizard is this?' said the king. He wanted to pull them out but the man's wife bid him not.

"The third week the wizard sat and talked with the man, talking the same gibberish the exact same way. They laughed and argued and cried and smiled and wrestled and drank toasts and slept and each day it would begin again, the wizard and the man sharing views and dreams and all in gibberish. 'Gads,' said the king, 'now I have two daft men.'

"At the start of the fourth week, the wizard kept up his gibberish fast and furious. The man, however, did not. As the days progressed, he looked at the wizard more and more as if he were looking upon some stranger, some foreigner, someone sadly different from himself.

"On the last day the king ordered the chamber opened. The man came out and greeted his wife, his children, his family, friends and king in their own tongue, speaking as did they as if nothing strange had occurred. The wizard came out next and spoke as well, as if the month had been but a moment passed between them.

"The king threw a feast, the man on his right and the wizard on his left. Later and well into his cups, the king demanded to know the magic. 'I sat in the next room and watched through the entire moon. No magic did I see,' he declared.

"'You saw none because you watched. If you listened, you would have learned the incantation.'

"'But there was none,' protested the king.

"'Aye, there was,' explained the wizard. 'For two weeks I listened to find out if he thought he spoke words to me. For one week the words he spoke I spoke back. For the last week I gave him words he did not know. He could either follow or go back. The magic was in knowing he didn't want to listen. He only wanted to be heard.'

"The king turned to his friend. 'Is this so?' he asked. 'Yes,' said his friend. 'I needed to know someone could understand me.'

"The king gave the wizard the reward and many think there the story ends. Not so.

"Many years later, long after the king had died and his son sat upon the throne, the wizard was traveling in another, distant country and a minstrel approached him. 'You are the one whose magic brought the gibbering man back, no?' 'Yes, that was I.' 'I was in that village when that month went past,' said the minstrel, 'and recently traveled there again. I met the man whose speech you restored. He gave me this scroll for you.'

"The wizard took the scroll, thanked the minstrel, and gave him a copper for his trouble. The note again thanked the wizard for what he had done and offered mead, meal, and bed should the wizard ever return. All was well and he had prospered a hundred-fold since the wizard left. As he got to the end of the scroll, the wizard laughed. He tossed his hat to the sky and fell to the ground in laughter, and each time he read the note's end he laughed again, for there, at the very end of the note, was a line of gibberish, the exact same gibberish the wizard had learned to speak."

My eyes close and I can't rise because I fall quickly into slumber. Beriah must be close because his voice is a whisper. "The only time 'here' 'where I am' is 'now', Ben."

What struck me more than anything else was the number of people with such diverse backgrounds who acted out sexually. It seemed that no matter what their individual delusions, paranoias, dementias, schizotisms, obsessions or compulsions, the mental energy necessary to establishing and maintaining their worldview found escape by making their bodies behave sexually. Is this something society teaches us? Is it a primal response?

Then, as I watched, I gained information. The information became awareness - for we *must* have information before we have awareness - and the awareness gave me options. It allowed me to decide if I wanted to change.

I discovered that people - at least me - don't act out sexually, necessarily. I, at least, acted out *abusively* - to ourselves or others - taking part in some bizarre, violent, finite game.

What I then needed to do was decide if I or any of us consciously chose those rules? Having done that, I had to decide if I wanted to make myself new rules, decide to play an infinite game.

This was aided by the admission of Debbie. Debbie, whom a visiting friend said, "She's alphabetical, Ben. 'ABC', you know? 'Alcoholic, bisexual, cocaine-addict...'."

Debbie sent five dollars to a convent outside of Montreal each time she sinned. She came to The Home for Mental Wanderers because the convent stopped accepting her IOU's. This visiting friend helped me with an offhand comment: love is what you've been through together.

I wonder if this friend realized she helped me find a path for changing my universe?

The chief psychiatrist of the hospital, a Dr. Santiago, was a brilliant, compassionate man, a handsomely dark Puerto Rican who was willing to teach me how to play the guitar. Back in his home country, he had several number-one radio hits. He confided in me that, during his graduate days, he became "lost" for almost two months. He started studying all the wrong courses, attending all the wrong classes, taking the tests, doing the work, and discussing intelligently the subjects he was "lost" studying. It was the start of a new term and he kept telling the professors his administrative paperwork was on its way. The university being large, they accepted this. He was "lost" taking engineering courses. Advanced engineering courses. He got top grades. One of his professors said his solution to the two-body problem was genius.

He hadn't had math or physics courses since his sophomore undergraduate year. Those he had squeaked through.

He "found" himself when the university refused to post his grades on his midterms. He became a psychiatrist because, with plans already made to become an internist, he needed to know what became of that "lost" knowledge. Days after "finding" himself, he couldn't understand his solutions to a test he'd aced.

Months later I read an article about him. Early in his career he worked in a drug rehab center. He flouted conventional wisdom by getting himself addicted to heroin then getting himself off the addiction so he'd know what it was like and could treat addicts with understanding and compassion.

He would often ask me about my equations, my work, intrigued, awed, and, by his own admission, impressed. I liked him and listened to him.

How can you help me unless you're just like me?

UPTOWN

CHAPTER 40
DANCING WITH DEATH

The Levy-Madison-East 101st-5th Ave rectangle houses the Sinai's. There are other Sinais throughout the City but here is where room is made for all those dying of...pick one. Ever since St. Clare's-Baruch-Johnson Memorial closed in '07, all the world's attention shifted to the Sinai's because young, old, rich, poor, white, black, yellow, blue, green, and gold ended up here dying.

For help.

A sophisticated fiber-optic communications system and a fleet of thirty-year old taxicabs with their rear seat and trunk sections cut and welded into makeshift ambulances ferries people from distant places, from private airfields, from rundown tenements, because Covid, Mpox, Ebola, Swine, Avian, not to mention our thought-long-gone-and-now-returning childhood favorites - polio, measles, whooping cough, ... - if it's contagious and it spreads easily, it's here.

Like a cat turning a corner in midflight, Jenreel's step turns in midstride and we change direction from west up East 101st to up a flight of stairs into Contagion Central.

Why this place is marked as BioHazard 3, 4, or 5 is anybody's guess.

I lived my life neither in a bubble nor safely by many standards, and I don't want to enter. I feel surrounded by twenty-first century lepers as men and women pass me coming and going up the stairs. I want them to carry a sign, ring a bell, and shout at a distance of twenty paces "Unclean! Unclean!" A man and a woman are dancing to some song on the radio as we enter the reception area. Jenreel speaks to the receptionist and I hear the lyrics on the radio.

> There's gonna be a change of season
> Indian summer look around and it's gone
> Why you wanna save the best for last
> We grow up so slowly and grow old so fast

The receptionist hands Jenreel a map and a pass and we follow him through several sets of doors.

I think it's a morgue. It's cold even though the sun screams through the sealed but curtainless windows. It is clean. Aseptic, and smells more like a veterinarian's office than a hospital ward. I feel myself in violation of some trust by being here in clothes worn too long and too long without a bath. The faces on the pillows demonstrate the final state of mankind, oblivious to race, caste, class, history, sex, sexuality, or sexual preference. I am frightened to be here.

The dancers come through. The music follows them.

> What about now
> Forget about tomorrow
> It's too far away
> What about now

The waiting-for-death raise their hands and limply clap. Some laugh and it sounds like a far distant crash in somebody else's subway tunnel. Cetaf, Jenreel, and Beriah, one by one, move through the ward lifting each body enough from their sheets to hold them, hug them, then lay them back down.

To rest.

The dancers come back through the ward.

What about now
Close your eyes
Don't talk of yesterday
It's too far away, too far away
What about now

A doctor and two interns come into the ward. The doctor, a tall, gaunt woman in her late thirties with rings around her eyes and none on her fingers checks the life signs of each individual the Healers embrace. At each bed, she lifts the covers over the faces, writes something briefly on a tag, and hands it to an intern who ties it to the individual's toe.

The dancers come back again.

In the walk of a lifetime
When you know it's the right time
I can't wait until the ship comes in
I can't wait starting all over again
The errors of a wise man
Makes the rules for a fool

There is one empty bed at the end of the ward. Jenreel, Beriah, and Cetaf stop there. One by one, the interns and the doctor take their turns there. Each is hugged and each dies. There is no one to write or tie on their toe-tags.

The spectacle numbs me. I can not move until the second intern has passed, then the spell is released. "What are you doing?"

Beriah arranges the bodies so they're stacked on their sides, lovers playing spoons in bed, and I realize their frames were shallow, weak, not much stronger than those they cared for, so frail the three of them can fit on the bed and leave room for one more. "Releasing their pain."

"What pain?"

Beriah, Cetaf, and Jenreel look at me, turn towards me. Beriah holds a hand out to me and all I can remember is him helping me up at the long ago Seaport. "The deepest wounds are those inside."

Jenreel holds out his hand. "You know that, Ben."

Cetaf holds out his. "If you didn't, we wouldn't have chosen each other."

They stare at me in quiet silence. Beriah, who I once thought my size, now seems to tower over me and I feel myself before the principal as he demands an explanation, why did I play hooky/hit that boy/shout "Hey, Baldy" at Mr. McDonough/throw the grasshoppers out the window of biology class/ask Mrs. Kariakoutsis for a date/offer to do her after class hey I knew your husband's fooling around/quit school.

As if knowing my thoughts, knowing my hesitation, knowing my fear, they speak in a unison Crosby, Stills, and Nash couldn't beat. "I will catch you if you fall."

I gently push aside the bodies of the doctor and two interns, now at peace and rest, and take my place upon the bed.

The Healers smile, then cry, Cetaf loudest of all, and take their places with the dancers.

What about now
Forget about tomorrow
It's too far away
What about now
Close your eyes
Don't talk of yesterday
It's too far away, too far away
What about now

I leap from the bed, from the bodies, fearing they might reach out and touch me, hold me, draw me into their dance of death even as I reach out for life.

I walk up to the dancers and ask for my turn, relieved, smiling, and alive.

But it's too late. The music stops. The dancers cease. The Healers move through the other doors and, before these doors swing shut, I follow, finally aware.

If I don't want to lie in the bed, I have to learn to dance.

CHAPTER 41
IN THE SPIRIT OF DENIAL

Lawrence who is Larry at Columbia is a thin, wiry man with a thin, wiry mind. He wears his thick, black hair long which is cosmetically odd because it offers no contrast to an otherwise handsome but too-long face. His voice comes from high in his throat but not quite from his nose, except when he laughs, at which times you can almost feel his nostrils vibrating with the henh-henh-henh sound, and he meticulously manicures his nails in public, then bites them to the quick uncaring if others watch.

He's his own man, that Larry.

Lawrence said nothing when I was having difficulties with Gayle. He never commented or insinuated or questioned anything although much of what was happening must have been obvious if not directly known by him. Jenny worked in his lab. I worked several doors down. His office was two doors down from mine. Jenny spent much of her free time in my office with the door closed and the radio on loud. The rules were clear and plain. From eight to twelve she is mine. From one to five she is mine. When she is mine she does her work as well as she can. Nothing less will be accepted or tolerated. Any other time, she is yours.

. . .

The Healers and I watch the crows swarming around Rockefeller Center and I wish the Healers could see this in winter. It's fun to watch the pickpockets taking off and putting on their gloves. It kind of makes you want to offer them your wallet; they're working so hard.

A familiar voice calls me and I turn to see Lawrence. He walks directly up to me and between the Healers. "Ben! Christ, man."

The way he says it, I can't tell if he's confused about my identity or simply evaluating some Lockeian existential thought. "Froats isn't going to keep your office open forever. You've got to get back to work."

I stare at him. Manny Froats is the chair of the department I'm partially in. He is more my boss than some others, as my office is in his territorial space.

"I'm surprised they kept my office available this long," I tell him.

"They've got you down on some kind of weird sabbatical shit. I told them they had it all wrong, but they wouldn't listen to me. I told them you were working things out with Gayle but they said no. So what's the story?"

"I need something more to go on, Larry. Which story are you talking about?"

"You coming back, Ben, or what?"

He walks beside me. In front of him is Beriah. To Lawrence's left is Cetaf. Behind me is Jenreel.

"I don't know if I'm coming back. They can box up my stuff, if they want to. I'm sure somebody else can use the space."

"Ben, Jesus Christ, man. What's wrong with you? What are you doing walking around here that's so damn important to you?"

I look up at each of the Healers. They say nothing, just walk, slowly, suredly, each step covering an eternity of space in finite three-quarter time. "I'm kind of busy," I pause, unsure, then add, "with my friends."

"What friends?"

I stop and the Healers stop with me. "These three," again I pause, taking less time, then add, "men."

The Healers again say nothing, their eyes and bodies pointed forward to wherever it is we go.

"Ben, you're all alone out here. There's nobody with you." He takes my arm compassionately. "Why don't you come with me, Ben. I think there's something wrong."

"You can't see this yellow man beside you? You can't see that red man in front of you? You can't see this blue man behind you?" I point at each Healer in turn. Beriah is pressing his palm into a young blonde girl's coloring book. On one page the summer sun has melted a melange of colored waxes together. On the other page is a drawing of him and he makes a palm print, picking up the melted waxes on one page in the creases of his hand then pressing them into the other page. Cetaf is blowing up a big yellow balloon for a vendor whose helium tank is empty. He does each balloon in one breath. They do not float, as if filled with helium, but the vendor, a man I think in his fifties dressed as if he should have a monkey on a chain and not balloons and a tank, ties them and gives them free to children and adults, all of whom seem total strangers. Jenreel is beside a hotdog vendor. He's laughing at himself learning to put hotdogs in buns, adding condiments, and handing them out. The hotdog vendor is laughing, too, as Jenreel doffs the vendor's hat and starts calling out, "GET-cha DOGS, KOSH-ers, FOOT-longs, HOT dogs, ALL kinds."

"Lawrence, have you ever read *The Chronicles of Narnia*? Specifically, *The Last Battle*?"

"No, why?" The look of concern is still obvious on his face and I realize I love him for that.

"There is a point in that book, when the worlds are coming to an end, where Aslan walks into a hut in which all the dwarves have gathered. We know they know it's the end of the world, and we know they're all huddled together in this dark hut where they can't see the end coming and can't hear it, but we know they know it."

He lets go of my arm. We start walking. The little blond girl shows her picture to the balloon vendor. He gives her a balloon. She hands him her picture. She takes the page with the melange of colors and Beriah's palm print to the hotdog vendor and exchanges it for two foot-longs with lots of mustard and ketchup, onions and piccalilli. "Yeah, so?" Lawrence says.

"So Aslan walks into their hut and roars at them to look at him and follow him and he'll make sure they're safe. But they don't. It's obvious they know he's there, but they just say it's the wind beating against the thatching of the hut. Then they say, 'The Dwarves are for the Dwarves' and stay in the hut even as the world ends."

"So what's your point?"

When we had weekly staff meetings, Lawrence questioned nothing other than an individual's scientific method. In that constrained and confined and yes I admit highly important area, he was meticulous and unforgiving, much like the one true vocalist in the small church choir whose clarity of tone and lyric is quietly despised by others.

There were some of us in the department, either because of disposition or research, to whom scientific method didn't mean much. Often, when there are no paradigms, you must give up all that you know in order to know more. It's like that with spontaneous languages. You can only go so far and then you go on hunch, chance, a close-your-eyes type of thing and absolve yourself from the experience you know to the experience you don't.

Lawrence couldn't accept this. If there was no rigorous proof, there was no answer. Lawrence has two paradigms I'm aware of. One is Jerry Lettvin's Frog's Eye Concept, the other is the Mopsus mormon spider when it is presented with a prey-sized frog. Lettvin showed that there are certain things we see clearly which a frog doesn't see at all. To be more precise, the frog's eye doesn't even send data to the frog's brain that certain things exist. The Mopsus mormon spider, when presented with a prey-sized frog, makes no attempt to attack. The frog, evidently, isn't transmitted from spider eye to spider brain as anything, neither food or foe.

"Sometimes," I told him, "you have to know the answer before you can even ask the question."

I found out Lawrence's mother was a medical doctor. I've learned from my time with the Healers that to watch him is to see the family he was raised in. I feel I can say that because we seek out and perform the familiar. It is only with lots of time spent on unfamiliar paths that we attempt anything new. Like mayonnaise and mustard on a sandwich together. I used to hate it and Gayle loved it. I never even tasted it, just knew I'd hate it. The other day the Healers and I stopped at the local Umbrella Room and got tubesteaks, all around. It was a treat to see the Healers finally grappling with something which I was content to let drip and ooze all over my hands. Their tongues twisting and looping, rolling and piping as they dipped them to their tasks, trying to isolate and awaken to the individual flavors of sauerkraut and chili and hot tomato-onion sauce, crushed red pepper and too much salt and Gulden's Spicybrown mustard and pickles and relish and ketchup, one-glass-to-a-gallon-of-beer-steamed dogs and Harlem River steamed buns, all wrapped in paper that by the time you finished your feast contained more of it than you did.

I offer my inner-city expertise to these from way-outta-town tourists. "No. Not like that. You've got to take it all in at once. If you taste everything separately, you'll never know how it fits in with the whole."

Jenreel and Cetaf damn near choked with laughter.

I also got a big soft pretzel, heavily salted, and asked for mustard down one side and mayo down the other.

Beriah smiled.

3: These four elements either do or don't change over time and their interactions constitute our P-C relations, specifically the P-C relations involving how we do who we think we be. Before any event occurs in our individual lives, we are our own *Phenomenon*.

If all four elements don't change we have

$$f(e_k, s_k, p_k, m_k) = K_{espm} \parallel K_{espm} \in \text{some constant}$$

It is possible to learn from an individual who doesn't change, but can someone who never changes ever teach? To learn is to change. Can someone incapable of an act teach that act to you? The most you might be able to learn is enough to change who you are to who that person is.

Likewise, if any number less than four of these elements is fixed and nonmuting, we have

$$\Sigma_i \, f(e, s, p, m)_k = \Sigma_i \, K_i \parallel K_i \in \text{a constant along any one element}$$

It is possible to learn from an individual who changes on less than the four elements yet at least one of them. But again, can this individual teach? They can teach you a great deal in the directions they travel, but only as much in the nonmuting directions as they've traveled.

What if all directions change? Then we have

$$\Sigma_n \, f(e, s_k, p_k, m_k) \, de + \Sigma_n \, f(e_k, s, p_k, m_k) \, ds + \Sigma_n \, f(e_k, s_k, p, m_k) \, dp + \Sigma_n$$
$$f(e_k, s_k, p_k, m) \, dm =$$
$$g(e, s, p, m) \parallel g(e, s, p, m) \ni \text{a function containing all four elements as}$$
$$\text{variables}$$

Which is an interesting development because it's also the base form of the Schroedinger Equation, the basis for much of Quantum Mechanics.

Can we learn from this individual? Probably, as what they can teach us is what they do, which is change in all four directions.

CHAPTER 42
THE INTERSECTION OF MULTIDIMENSIONAL HELIXES

We pass Gracie Mansion heading towards the Fire Boat Station and learning has become addictive. My companions' quiet surety challenges my thoughts, my language, my life. "Tell me about finite games."

Jenreel is the closet mathematician among them, but only because I don't understand he is learning mathematics. "They end."

"Yeah, so?"

"That's all. They end."

"Life is a finite game, then. It ends."

The three of them stop and stare at me.

"My mother's dead and buried. She ended, didn't she?"

"You speak of her, therefore she continues."

"What if no one who remembers her is alive anymore. Then is she ended?"

"I don't know. I do know that she no longer continues here. Life, as far as we know, is an infinite game. It is this place which doesn't want to play it that way. No other world promotes pain and calls it love. Pain is pain, love is love, there is no confusion."

"Yeah, we're stupid."

"Not stupid, only more comfortable in ignorance."

Cetaf's massive hand wipes a tear from his cheek. "Love and pain need no language to express, they only need an observer who is willing to act. Few of your people willingly act. The majority prefer not to, choose to be ignorant of another's need. It is your people's way of being dead-alive."

Dead-alive? Another new term, the words familiar, their usage not. Yet I understand. They are teaching, I am learning. Didn't Wittgenstein say "The limits of my language are the limits of my world"?

"Are your people ever dead-alive?"

Cetaf wipes away another tear. "When we are who we are not."

"When are you alive-alive?"

The Healers speak in turns and I hear an inner-city symphony, their voices distinct and clear and blending with the sounds of the city, of where we've been, where we are, where we have yet to be:

Cetaf: "When you freely cry for your own pain. Denying or ignoring your own pain is to deny yourself to yourself. No being can survive such."

Jenreel: "When you state your own needs clearly, succinctly. Denying or ignoring your own needs is to deny yourself to yourself. No being can survive such."

Beriah: "When you share how you feel. Denying or ignoring how you feel is to deny yourself to yourself. - "

I understand. "No being can survive such."

The Healers nod in unison as my journey continues. "I am the books I've read, the movies I've watched, the people I've spent time with, and the conversations I've engaged in."

Their eyes on the unseen path we follow, I know they wait for me to finish. "I must choose wisely what I feed my mind."

Jenreel the closet mathematician raises a finger and patterns form in the air. "Each is a multidimensional helix mapped mathematically. Consider the variables involved in a simple 'Hello.' How many ways can the message be sent? How many received? And without guarantee the message is the one intended on either side of the conversation? To assume any communication - between people, between species, between realities - exists in 4-space is to force a meaning which may not even exist."

I study the image and blink, suddenly aware I'm seeing in more than four dimensions. I raise a finger and modify the image. "The game doesn't end because I'm no longer aware of their existence or where they exist. To assume so is my limitation. not the games."

We move on.

CHAPTER 43

SOCKS FOR THE FEET, FIREWOOD FOR THE SOUL

A boy and man drive their pickup up and down the alleys which run like varicose veins through Little Italy and behind Center Market Place. They are dressed for Saturday play even though it is early Monday morning. The side of their truck is paneled with 'Firewood for sale/Delivery included/508 621 1419/M. Bennett and Son'.

The boy is perhaps ten. The man is perhaps thirty, although there are lines like rivers on his face that say he's forty or forty-five. It is summer in Manhattan and no one is thinking of firewood.

Neither are they. They are going through the trash bins and I don't want to know what they're looking for.

But I look. I must. We are walking down the alley where they rout.

As we pass, the man smiles and nods as he pulls a pair of wool socks from a bin. They need washing and darning and are too small for him, more his son's size.

He calls his son over. Yes, they would be nice for winter.

There is no shame here. They are seeing to their needs. The father, rough bearded with patched jeans and flannel shirt and fraying suspenders and thrice cobbled shoes, and the son with clean face and good teeth and twinkling eye and a smile which says "Everybody loves me" and is good and right and looking like the younger brother of Scraps.

"We'll have to get some thread. I think I used the last of it on your pants last month," says the father.

A full faced woman, her head framed in a grate-reinforced second story window providing a rent-raising view of the alley and access to a fire escape, taps on the bars of her prison. She wears a bulky sweatshirt with the sleeves cut off at the shoulder and the neck tailored into a modest "V". The sweatshirt is old and faded light brown. Her face is unmakeuped white and her hair is dyed scarf red. Simple clothing, simple colors, which she wears well and also without shame.

Her face is also lined and its tributaries reach out to the man's, I think.

The boy and man look up. "Need firewood, Ma'am?" asks the father.

"I got a brick oven in the basement. I bake bread for some of the shops and families. It uses wood, but it's got to be cut shorter to fit in the stove."

The man nods. "Nice seams on your blouse, Ma'am."

"Thank you."

"You know how to sew, Ma'am?"

"Yep. Sure do."

"My son could use some work on these socks, Ma'am."

She considers this. Her head disappears then emerges a second later followed by the rest of her as she opens the grate. Below her full face is a full body, also in its thirties, early or thereabouts, her body not fat but full, filled out with a mixture of strength from kneading and years of needing. Below the sweatshirt is a peasant dress with bright embroidery and baking stains. She stands on the fire escape a moment longer than she needs to, looking at the boy and man and letting herself be looked at. "What's your name, child?"

The boy's 'Everybody loves me' voice echoes like a choir,

"Tommy." He smiles. His father nudges him, slightly, lovingly, reminding the boy he is good and right. The boy nudges his father back. His face goes "Oops!" and he adds, "Ma'am."

"You hungry, Tommy?"

Tommy looks at his dad. His dad nods, quietly, reminding his son that he is right and good.

"Yes, Ma'am."

"You like fresh bread? Maybe a little soup?"

Tommy doesn't look at his father this time. "Yes, Ma'am."

She lowers the fire escape. "Better have your dad bring those socks when you come up, Tommy."

Tommy scampers as only ten-year-old boys who know everybody loves them can. His father, I think, wants to scamper but the rivers in his face won't let him. The lines in the woman's face tell him it's okay, there is a friend here. He reaches the top of the fire escape. They shake hands and their waters of tears become rivers of joy.

I shrug, amazed at the transaction because what transacted I did not see. "What has more value, a felled tree or a pair of darned socks?"

Jenreel states the obvious because it's obvious who's the booby and what's the prize. "It depends on whether your feet are cold or your stove is empty."

"But if you have the tree, you can fill your stove."

"Oh, I understand. You plan on carrying your stove wherever you go."

CHAPTER 44

THE SCHOOLYARD BULLY'S DEAD

"...man is the result of a purposeless and materialistic process that did not have him in mind. He was not planned. It is, however, a gross misrepresentation to say that he [man] is just an accident *or* nothing *but an animal." - G.G. Simpson, "The Meaning of Evolution"*

A lot of things happened on 19 August 1991. The two locked in my memory are Hurricane Bob and the overthrow of Mikial Gorbachev. One we had some warning about, the other was a devastating surprise.

I remember getting up. My mother was in the kitchen, the radio on and listening to Carl Kassell announce the Soviet Coup as she filled the coffee-maker's reservoir with water. She shut off the water and the radio, went into the living room and turned on the TV. Tom Brokaw was on the *Today Show*.

She kept her eyes on the TV, her brow furrowed and her face tight. "Something's wrong. He's not supposed to be doing the *Today Show*. Not anymore."

I listened to the TV and stared out the window from where I sat beside her on the sofa. There were two bird feeders visible from the window and, listening to Tom relay events in Moscow, I watched the birds fly and flutter and fight for seeds. One of Tom's concerns was a strategic projection regarding the change of power in the Soviet Union. The leaders of the coup were Stalinist hardliners. Did this purvey a return to the Cold War?

I kept a close watch on the birds that morning as I felt the shock wash over me. I knew - a special, innocent part of me knew - that if the birds became suddenly quiet and stayed on the ground, The Bomb had been dropped.

Workers are scrubbing valuable bird guano from the stone benches around the Conservatory Garden. There is one worker, and old Chinaman, who occasionally stops and performs some T'ai Qi.

When he dances, the birds land at his feet and hunt for seeds. Along with his coveralls and tools, he's wearing a fanny pack. Some of his moves bump his hands into the fanny pack and I wonder at his awkwardness. After each bump of his fanny pack, his hands continue, now filled with seeds.

I smile and I'm not sure at what. "In one of our great books, 'The Bible', it says something about God knowing if something so small as a bird falls to the ground, how much more he will be aware of our well-being."

Cetaf watches the birds and the Chinaman. "I don't think the Universe concerns itself with an individual's well-being. I think that is the individual's responsibility. To foist that responsibility onto another is to deny responsibility for self. Denying responsibility for self is to deny responsibility for the universe."

"You make it sound like I'm responsible for what happens in the universe, like there is no God, like there's nothing to look forward to."

A starling lands on Beriah's horny crown and, like a tick bird on a rhinoceros, pecks. "You are responsible for the universe you're in.

You are your own god, and by looking to tomorrow you lose sight of today." He is content with the starling's grooming.

"A lot of people believe we're made in God's image. I don't know how your beliefs coincide."

Jenreel stands and asks the Chinaman to teach him T'ai Qi. "You think your creation was an act of love for you." Each phrase rides on a move's breath. "No, it was not. Your creation is the Universe's gift of love to the universe. The Universe so loved itself that it wanted to share itself with you. Your creation wasn't an act of love towards you, it was an act of love towards self."

The starling lifts from Beriah and he watches it fly away. "Your creation, then, is an act of sharing. By what you say, you choose your God to be separate and distinct from you. You choose not to be with your Divine. Who, then, is rejecting who? And if your Divine is in you, as you say, you are rejecting part of yourself."

Jenreel perfectly mimics the Chinaman's seed grabs but comes up empty. The birds don't seem to mind. "So there is a hole now, inside you, which, without your knowing it exists, you try to fill. You must try to replace that part which you reject because part of you remembers the wholeness of life, but can anything be better for you than your Divine?"

The Chinaman fills Jenreel's hands with seeds.

Cetaf watches his fellow Healers. "Any being so truly delighted in itself will share that sense of self-love with you, letting you know that you, too, can love yourself. Your people do not love themselves. You have filled yourselves with strange gods."

Jenreel, finishes his dance. "And your gods are killing you."

"So you're saying we're God's affect?"

Jenreel offers Beriah some seeds. He sprinkles it in the grooves on his crown. The birds create a feathery, flapping wig with no wind around. "Our beliefs make us an affect. Your beliefs make you an effect."

I look at the Chinaman and Jenreel, wondering what is inside looking out, what is outside looking in.

· · ·

There are four events by which each generation anchors itself in history, define who and what they are. My parents' generation had the Cuban Missile Crisis, Kennedy's assassination, Neil Armstrong's single step, and Woodstock. Other generations have other events. For some the Chicago 7, Neil Armstrong's single step, Nixon's resignation, Fall of Viet Nam. For mine, the Fall of the Wall/Soviet Union, Internet, cell phones, iPod/iPhone. Those which come easily are your generation's anchors. Can't come up with four? Anything more than one will do. Have only one and you don't know - at a deep level - who you are, where you reside in history.

Kennedy came on the TV and said we were blockading Cuba. Walter Kronkite told us what this meant.

And I remember crawling under an end table in my parents' living room at Carl Kassell's announcement because I knew as only a child can know that there, under the end table, it would be safe.

Even then, part of me knew the end table was too close to the exterior wall, too close to the front door, was fairly open and exposed. None of that mattered at the time. A very strong and very real part of me knew down there under the table I would be safe. Perhaps, when I was younger still, I had escaped my father's wrath there and that younger child shouted to the Mikial Gorbachev over-throw child, "Here! Hide Here! They'll never find you here! You'll be okay! You'll be safe! Come here! I know! Hide! Hide! Hide!"

I did not realize my nation's 20th century schoolyard bully, the one which caused Cuban Missile children to hide under other end tables, was dead.

Many times since then I've waited for the birds to become silent and fall and looked for an end table under which to hide.

Hurricane Bob came and went, the only personal damage a fallen tree knocked the bird feeders to the ground. Early in the dark of the next morning I woke and, dressed only in my shorts, stepped outside. Making sure the door remained ajar, making sure the path to the end table was clear, I dragged a stepstool outside and put the feeders back where they belonged.

The sky was full of stars. Power was still out from the storm so there was no ground illumination to interfere. I had never seen so many stars or a sky so clear, so clean, even tasting and smelling different than I had known, as if Bob had scrubbed the sky of all the waste I'd grown used to seeing there. For a moment I wasn't in the city, I was somewhere else. I started to cry because it was so beautiful and, as I cried, finches and bluejays and mourning doves and cardinals, rose-breasted grosbeaks and red-breasted nuthatches and black-capped chickadees, began flying and fluttering and fighting over seeds.

CHAPTER 45
MISTAKEN PSYCHIATRIC CENTERS

My father died in old age after a long, lingering illness and haunted by the mistakes he made.

Interesting word, "mistake."

"Miss take."

You can reach again.

He never did.

He started dying when he was young, perhaps fifty and not near sixty, when he began to realize that all the physical, mental, and emotional pain he had caused his family, all the terror he crushed into us in his fear we might identify and reject the bitterness in him, had succeeded in pushing us far, far away. So far away he succeeded in keeping his littleness from us.

Or so he thought. Seeing him in the last years of his life, I saw him grow smaller and tighter as he worked harder and harder to protect himself from us, even to the point of not telling us when he had to enter the hospital.

It was a quiet day the day my father died. I don't remember much detail. It was mid-summer. I remember that. Late in the day, I think. The sun was in the west and big and red as it slewed over the mountains of his central New Hampshire home, the home in which

I spent the later years of my youth before going angrily out on my own.

There were some clouds, high cirrus clouds, that caught the sunlight and made the sky beautiful when you looked overhead and towards the north, south, or east. You couldn't look directly west yet. I remember rhyming, "Red sky at morning, sailor take warning, red sky at night, sailor's delight." I never knew what that meant. Maybe a red sky at night meant good sailing? I would think something about a storm. I didn't know.

We were in the backyard as a family, the first time in twelve years. I was a failure to him without knowing why. What had I done, as a child, to anger him so?

His anger was never measured or tempered. Suddenly it was there and just as suddenly not. He sat across from me, across a picnic table he'd made and on which I hadn't helped. He was an excellent craftsman and hand-skills were something I refused. I did so to hurt him. He was so talented with his hands, crafting things from houses to dressers to ornate engravings in wood, so patient with wood and brick, so capable of pulling beauty from a pile of sticks or a mortise of stone, that I refused to learn from him. He never tried to teach me. Even if he did, I would have refused to learn.

The picnic table was weathered and needed to be stained. He tried to interest me in how staining was done, how brushes had changed and become synthetic sponge blades and how chemistry now made one coat take the place of primer and lacquer and topcoat, all three rolled into one. I listened, wanting to be interested. We'd never talked about these things before. I'd been forced to help him when I was growing up, and I would rather have kept my nose in a book than my hands in grease from an early age. He knew this, as well.

What was I doing, he asked.

I remembered when I was twelve and asked him the cube root of twenty-seven, just to anger him, to show him as a fool. Why did I do that? "I work for NASA, dad."

"You have anything to do with the ISS?"

"What I do for NASA isn't related to the space station."

He looked at me then and winced. His head bobbed to the left and obscured a garden I had always refused to tend. His right hand reached across the table and clutched mine. His grip wasn't forceful, as I'd remembered. There was a gentility there I barely knew. His left arm pulled into his side and his body, like the sun, slewed across the sky and fell onto the grass.

My mother was up faster than I. "Oh, Joe, oh, Joe," she cried, her feet doing that little desperation dance I remembered from when father would punch me into a corner and she would beg him to stop. Now she called to me, "Oh, Ben, oh, Ben," and once again I was forced to react to a situation I didn't understand.

I stretched him out on the ground and felt first his wrist then his neck for a pulse. "Go call an ambulance. He's had a heart attack."

He lay on the rich green grass. No dandelions, few weeds, and clipped as if this were the eighteenth hole on the last course of the PGA tour. Golf was something he always wanted to try but never could. I opened his mouth with one hand and pinched his nose with the other. He smelled to me then as he always had, when he was angry and when he was not, of Old Spice and El Producto cigars and Captain Black pipe tobacco and cheap wine and sweat. It was a powerful smell to me, climbing the years from childhood until I left home, a powerful, wonderful, evocative, erotic smell; calling up memories that triggered others that triggered others that triggered still more.

Why did my father's smells arouse me?

I put my lips on his and pushed my air into him. I noticed then, as if I'd never noticed before, how small my father really was. I must have been six or seven inches taller than him, but this I judged purely by the size of my head over his and my hands covering his face. He was smaller than I'd ever thought before, a small china doll too easily crushed to be anything but precious and kept hidden or on a shelf, shown to others who knew they shouldn't touch. My mother stood where she was, still frozen to the ground on this too-hot summer's day, her legs losing their piston-like momentum as she perhaps realized their desperation dance pumping would be neither recognized nor honored, wouldn't be accepted by the god of such things, and wouldn't bring father back.

Depending on your politics, we walk north on either Franklin D. Roosevelt Drive or East River Drive. Directly across from the East River are three campuses which have always caused me anxiety: the Manhattan Psychiatric Center, the Kirby-Forensic Psychiatric Center, and, partially hidden by the latter and the Triborough Bridge, the Manhattan Children's Psychiatric Center.

Cetaf looks out to these campuses and starts to weep. No longer arguing, now only questioning, I move to him and place my hand on his great back. "Can I help you?"

"No. Sometimes I am sole witness to a horrible beauty, and alone am blessed to understand the perfection in the suffering."

"I did volunteer work in a county home, once. There was an old woman there, a very old woman, who screamed because she was in so much pain, then screamed all the more when they gave her an injection to ease her suffering, then screamed still more when they left her to rest. She did, eventually. Permanently. I remember the nurse who cared for her was brought up on charges." I stare at the campuses and wonder what he sees that I don't. "I don't know if I've ever witnessed what you are now. But I'm here for you if you need me."

My words shock me.

He cries, looks at me and smiles. "We are the sum of the events in our life. The universe brings events to us. It is how we integrate those events into ourselves that determines the paths of our lives." He takes one more look at the buildings. Does he wonder if I saw something he missed? "Thank you for being here for me. It means a lot."

I feel something move inside me and see a yellow flash.

Somehow, I know Cetaf's words are true; my being there does mean a lot.

I comfort Cetaf and Beriah rests his hand on me. "We are the four elements, Ben, the four elements without which nothing else can exist: mind, body, emotion, spirit."

When my father died, and his brothers and sisters were gathered around him, I saw them, knowing I was to say something, and could only look at them and laugh.

He could not forgive himself the errors of his past, so much so he denied to his death the errors he had made.

Mistake. Miss Take.

Ha!

Ha! I Reach Again!

CHAPTER 46
RELIGIOUS ZEALOTRY AT THE MOVIES

"We are vessels of our experience of the universe, constantly being filled, constantly threatening to spill over, and constantly growing so that neither occurs." - Daskele

T here are two movies you should see/rent/buy/whatever. One is *The Amazing Colossal Man* and the other is *The Front*. They have more in common than just being chemical etchings on celluloid. For one thing, they both take place in the same era in our society.

First, *The Front*. High concept: a mensch fronts TV-scripts for blacklisted writers during the McCarthy Era. Starring Woody Allen as the mensch and several actors who were blacklisted in leading roles.

Skip down to the scene break if you haven't seen *The Front*.

Right before Zero Mostel commits suicide, he tells Woody Allen "The water is full of sharks". He then graciously bids Woody goodnight, checks into a ritzy motel, generously tips the bellhops, gets a big bottle of champagne from which he sips a little, waits till everybody leaves the room, and jumps out the window.

As they say, what was left you could pick up with a sponge. The two scenes go back-to-back because Zero Mostel is told he has to name a name in order to work and if he doesn't he'll never work in this town again.

The only problem is Zero doesn't know any names. His only crime was an abundant libido when he was a kid.

Doesn't matter. To paraphrase *Pippin*'s Charlemagne, the fornicating he got wasn't worth the fornicating he was going to get.

The government gives him an out. Find out something about Woody Allen. Anything. Tell us who he knows, who he sees, what he does, what he likes. He stumbles into Allen's apartment, smashed because that's the only way he can deal with what he's doing, sacks out on the couch and, when Allen is fast asleep, rifles through Allen's personal files.

And tells the FBI what he found. An address book. Names.

He comes back to Allen's apartment a few nights later seeking forgiveness for a crime Allen doesn't know Mostel committed and Mostel can't admit he did. Allen gives him a drink which Mostel downs in one gulp, and explains that he, Mostel, never learned to sip a drink. He used to watch his father, who only drank one shot a day right after some prayer and downed it quick and fast.

So here he is, preparing to die, and he sips his last drink.

"The water is full of sharks."

At the end of the movie, Allen is before some subcommittee looking to bleed him of every drop of humanity and self-respect he's taken the last ninety minutes to gain.

They are pressuring him, threatening him, intimidating him.

He looks out at them and shakes his head. "You can all go fuck yourselves." They stop moving and he walks out. I mean, they stop. Through some miracle of film technology, the actors playing the subcommittee et al freeze in place like it's a snapshot, not even breathing, and Allen's character walks out.

Intense and, like this, no mistake.

Now I will tell you the punchline. Stalinism, Naziism, McCarthyism, Zionism, Fundamentalism, Patriotism, Conservatism, Expansionism, Darwinism, Legalism; only the spelling changes.

What is the malaise which migrates people into demons of their day? I know the world rotates on its axis and revolves around the sun, but how many times do we need to go around this wheel before the lesson sticks?

There are several people with paper bags scurrying about the two hundred block of West 109th Street. They are different colors, different ages, some hair is corn-rowed, others are pulled back. Some run back and forth in technicolor Nikes, others maneuver joysticks which direct their wheelchairs.

Some wear t-shirts with whales or dolphins or tigers or seals, others show Malcolm X or Nelson Mandela. Every once in a while I see a sweatshirt with a tree. There is even one with Mr. T. Some have jackets with church, synagogue, or temple names. Some men hold hands as they walk, as do some women, as do some men and women together. There are even a few people wearing Colors. There are street people and people I'm sure have never seen the street. There are people in collars and people in chains.

The only thing they have in common is they pick up litter as they scurry, slowly moving up the street. I bend over, pick up some papers and ask the person nearest me, "Are you separating by colors and types?"

"Hell, no, man. Everybody's welcome."

Beriah, Cetaf, and Jenreel help as well. We clean two blocks before our path takes us up Morningside and the others continue towards the Park. At the end of their street I see a Finish line, complete with booths and what looks like pitchers of lemonade. Every once in a while somebody stops cleaning, moves to the side and cheers the others on.

I am amazed. Do the Healers understand what's happening here? "That's quite a feat."

Beriah stands. His hands are full of paper cups, plastic bottles, and things I wouldn't care to touch. "Really?"

"Sure. To get that many different people working together to achieve something, damn right."

"They weren't working together. They each worked individually."

"Well, yeah. I mean they were all doing the same thing, trying to clean the street."

"Each of them wanted the street clean."

"Unfortunately, individuals don't always do such things. Things like that usually don't happen unless there's a group."

Jenreel watches the people cheer each other on as they sweep the litter from the street. "Individual goals become mutual goals when the individual recognizes themself as separate and distinct, unique and individuated from all else around themself. Recognizing oneself as separate and distinct allows the individual to recognize a personal good and well-being. That which creates a personal good and sense of well-being - if that is what it truly does and is not a mask of fears - must be good for others, for how can something be good for one and not for all? When this occurs, individual goals become mutual goals."

"There are those who would argue: religious zealotry, vast personal wealth, things like that."

"Any extreme is a cry for help."

Skip to the end of the chapter if you haven't seen *The Amazing Colossal Man*.

In *The Amazing Colossal Man*, they've placed this poor soul in a circus tent because nothing else will house him. He eats whole turkeys the way we might eat corn niblets, and somebody comes in with a newspaper.

Prior to this, and here is what's important I think, is he picked up a Bible - the only thing to read in the tent - and couldn't read it because the print was so small. The Bible itself was like a kid's CrackerJack toy in his hands. But he can read the paper - its headlines are huge - and what he reads sensationalizes him.

We then find out through bold-faced and poorly written plot exposition that his heart isn't growing as fast as the rest of him and he'll probably go insane: "His heart won't be able to carry the load any longer...his mind will go first, then his heart will explode."

When all is stripped away, there is only one thing we came into this world with which we are guaranteed to carry away: our feelings. Our bodies, our homes, our wealth, our minds; all and a lot more are important, but the one thing we'll always have no matter what is our feelings.

And we have them in abundance. We never run out. There is a bottomless well in each of us which creates them like cold in the arctic and no matter how much we give away the more we have.

Why, then, can't we share them?

There is a third movie, *I am the Cheese*. I won't say much about this movie except to note that the clues are so subtle, so well placed, and so delightfully textured, that if you know the ending before it occurs, it is an indication of how you've lived your life.

And that's what this is all about, anyway.

CHAPTER 47

THE WOUNDED GODS WE CARRY CANNOT HEAL US

Cathedral of St. John the Divine is in front of us. In our travels we pass many churches, temples, synagogues, circles, covens, gatherings, and mosques. The Healers read their legends but never stop or question. I walk on only to find them entering the Cathedral's main door.

I rush after them and shout in a whisper. "We shouldn't be in here."

Beriah does not whisper. "This place was built for the Divine?"

People turn and hush us to silence.

"Can the Divine hear you hushed?"

"Let's go outside. We'll talk there."

Somehow the bright sunlight is neither comforting nor convincing. "God can hear because God is inside of us."

Beriah, Cetaf, and Jenreel look around us. There are drunks, derelicts, bag ladies and bag men, whores whose arms are junkied tattoos on tattoos, street kids who hustle their sisters and brothers and mothers and sons.

I follow the Healers' eyes.

"Don't say the money spent on this cathedral could be better spent on the people here on the street. 'The poor you will always have with you'."

"If your God is always with you, what need do you have of a separate place to worship? It doesn't seem like the Divine to tell people, 'Upon this place build a great fortress to separate those who worship from those who don't."

"Some religions call their faithful to be in the world, some to separate themselves from the world."

Beriah stares at me, his big frog eyes reflecting me in front of the cathedral and the several street people laying around.

"And don't say 'What difference does the religion make when all go to the same place?'"

Beriah, Jenreel, and Cetaf walk on. "We can't say that. It isn't true."

I run in front of them. Cetaf is closest. I grab his sleeve and tug him motionless. "What do you mean, it isn't true. Is there a right way to God? Is there a right way to believe? Is there one true God?"

The Healers smile, Cetaf most of all. "Of course there is, Ben. You just told us so." He smiles and cries, a giant whose pain brings him joy. "You said the Universe, the Divine, is inside of you. Your creation is how you love yourself." He waves behind towards the cathedral. "You need to create such things to humble yourself. Evidently it's not possible to humble yourself otherwise."

They walk around me, I gaze at the hungry, cold, vulnerable, damp people outside the Divine but not outside the Universe.

I met a woman at LakeShore. She had a dog and it died. She was a LakeShore inpatient because she couldn't get over her grief.

She told me she learned many things from her dog, and the one she'd never forget was her dog telling her its world consisted of answering five questions: Am I fed? Am I warm? Am I safe? Am I dry?

She paused.

"That's four. What's the fifth?"

She stared me straight in the eye. "Am I loved?"

"Your dog told you this?"

"Without the last one, the first four are meaningless."

"Sorry about your dog. Recent loss, huh?"

"It's been twenty-three years."

I didn't know how to respond. She reminded me of Mr. Bojangles, His dog up and died and after twenty years he still grieved.

People exit the Divine as music from an organ so grand, so majestic professional classical organists book recording time on it. It shakes the cathedral's stained glass windows, drives birds from trees, causes women to tuck their heads and pull their fine fur mufflers up over their ears even in this summer's heat and men light cigars which cost more per stick than most people earn in a day.

I can accept Christ. I just have trouble accepting those who praise him.

CHAPTER 48

THE IMPORTANCE OF SEEING IN THE DARK

n first grade, on my way back from the boys' room where the janitor held the door open for us and the whole Webster School world could see what we were doing, I stood behind Leonard Espinoza waiting to get a drink of water at the fountain.

"Benny, you got a needle or a pin?"

"Needle or a pen?"

"No-no. A pin. Like you stick things with."

"No."

"Can you get me one?"

"I guess. Why?"

"Because if you stick 'em in your eye, you can see in the dark."

We are at the South Campus of CCNY and a streetwise Sam Jaffe of an Einstein impersonator is running after us, perhaps trying to figure who's Klaatu and who's Gort, which shows he never read the original. He calls us but the Healers continue to move. He runs in front of us and stops. As I think Beriah might walk over him, we stop.

He stutters at us in a thick German accent. "I have studied all you've said and done, and I'll have none of it. None of it, do you hear? You will have us believe all is vanity, as said the prophet, and I have charts and diagrams. I can prove it isn't so."

I look to see if people with nets are coming for him and then realize if they come for him they must come for us.

Thankfully, there are none.

Beriah takes the man's hand, shakes it gently and stares into his eyes. *"Ich glaube, dass Sie glauben, dass das, was Sie sagen, wahr ist. Aber das ist alles. Ihr Glaube. Akzeptiere es als solches und wir werden gehen."*

My eyebrows rise so high I feel my nostrils widen (anybody remember Chevy Chase on one of the original Saturday Night Live *Weekend Update* segments? The one where he's supposedly quoting George Wallace? "I don't judge a man by the color of his skin but by the width of his nostrils!"). Beriah speaks German? I don't. "What?"

He repeats to the child standing beside him. "I believe that you believe what you're saying is true. But that's all it is. Your belief. Accept it as such and we will go."

He's so patient with me.

I love him for that.

The man isn't in a loving mood, it seems. "No! You'll have mankind recede to stones and axes. Your talk of harmony and peace. It has been man's dissatisfaction and competitiveness which have led to our technological greatness."

Jenreel leans over him. "Explain your greatness, please."

"We have cars, hospitals, world-wide second-by-second communication, computers, breakthroughs in biology and disease prevention. This is our greatness."

Cetaf leans over Jenreel leaning over the man. "You do have those things. You also have an atmosphere soon to be unbreathable, a system of healing which is optimized according to profit and not according to need, the disintegration of personal freedom in the name of bureaucratic security, the belief that a silicon toggle has more validity than a starving child, biologies which are convenient and diseases only prevented when they are politically expedient.

You have *a* technology, one among several. You can say neither more nor less."

The man points an accusatory finger and sneers at us. "You have faith. All you have is faith."

Beriah stares first at the man's finger, shakes his head, and focuses beyond. "No. There are several technologies. We have yours, and, among several, one of ours. A technology of consciousness. We know."

"How can you know what you've never proven is real?"

Cetaf moves away. "We have proof meet for our knowledge."

"Do you mean experience? Then we know, too."

Beriah follows Cetaf, stops, and addresses the man without facing him. "There is a difference. You have faith, and when that which your faith is directed towards doesn't come to pass, you say you are being tested or you did not ask as you should. Always the burden is yours, the blame is yours, as if the universe holds you accountable for its actions. And always the glory and triumph is another's."

Cetaf stops as well, also not facing the man. "Better to know that the universe provides what is needed and know it is enough. There is no faith. The faith you speak of is a bottomless grave."

The man runs off. He opens his briefcase and hands out pamphlets as he goes.

I walk with them and watch the man go his way as we go ours. "I didn't know science was connected with faith, like you suggest."

Jenreel stops and does face me. "If you can't explain something, but the effect is reproducible, is that science or faith?"

"I don't know."

He smiles. "Good, Ben. Good. Believe in both, as the more you know the more they are the same. Never either-or, always both-and."

In sixth grade, Leonard Espinoza sat across the room from me in Miss McCarthy's class. She was an even-tempered woman who wore her prejudices like a phylactery. Paul Hong, a Chinese-American boy whose father was a neurosurgeon, was always praised and encouraged no matter what he did in class or even if he answered a question wrong because you know how industrious and polite those Chinese people are, right, Paul?

Leonard, who was neither polite nor industrious and often came to school wearing his pajama tops, made the mistake of raising his hand to answer a question one day in class. This was a mistake because Leonard rarely raised his hand even to go to the bathroom and Miss-McCarthy-god-bless-her let him know by god he rarely raised his hand in class by calling on him even when it wasn't raised just to let him know she knew he didn't know where we were or what we were doing or what she was talking about.

But today he raised his hand. Not high, not excitedly, he simply held it up and looked at the arithmetic problem on the board with his usual bland expression on his square-headed, criminally low-browed, dark-complexioned, recessed eye, little Neanderthal-in-training face.

Miss McCarthy was looking towards my side of the room and said, "Go ahead, Leonard, answer the question."

Leonard's little sixth grade face fell. The dark complexion turned pale, the low criminal brow furrowed like a glacially compressed mountain range in the making, his eyes got watery, and he stood up.

"You don't know the answer, do you, Leonard," said Miss McCarthy as we all watched Leonard squirm. "You raised your hand because you didn't think I would call on you and you thought you'd show me up by raising your dirty little hand, isn't that right? Isn't it, Leonard? Why did you raise your hand when you know you don't know the answer?"

Leonard's face grew calm but I saw his body tense. It was a calmness I would come to know many times from those who face death and stop caring, from those who don't know which way to turn and know any direction will cause someone pain. He closed his eyes, said, "Seven-hundred-and-seventeen," and opened them.

Directly on Miss McCarthy.

He hadn't even written the arithmetic problem on his paper. He simply knew it and answered, as she'd asked us to do.

Her face first ashened (with shock, I'm sure) then reddened with rage (I know because she proved it when she hissed). "What is that, Leonard?"

"The answer is seven-hundred-and-seventeen, Miss McCarthy."

I quote Jenreel back at him. "'Never either-or, always both-and'? What does that mean?"

"Are we here?"

"Of course you are."

"Yet there are others who can't see us, others who will not see us, some who will see but not hear, some who will see yet will not hear."

My thought is still the Healers have come here for external change. "And there are some who do see and do hear. You can't deny that."

"What they see and hear is us healing our own wounds. We came here not to heal your world or anything in it. We came here only to heal ourselves."

"No, no, No! You don't give me answers. You never give me answers."

"You couldn't heal if we gave you answers."

"I thought you only healed yourselves."

"Correct. And because we do, we allow others to heal, as well."

I really want to hit something and my frustration comes out in tears. Cetaf wipes them away. "Hearing, seeing, feeling, tasting, touching, knowing, sharing. Do one without the others and you've lost them all."

He holds me while I sob into his landscape of a chest. "Tell me what to do."

"Stay on your path. Your frustration is because you're not satisfied with it, it neither takes you where you want to go nor does it take you fast enough. Frustrated, you get off your path. More frustration follows because where you want to go isn't where you need to be, nor does the speed of your travels allow you time to learn."

Beriah echoes the same thing differently. "Grow."

Jenreel joins the chorus. "Heal."

Cetaf brings the song to a close. "You weren't even sure how this journey started, Ben. Only that it did. Which is more important? That it started or that it did?"

There are times when, no matter what our age or level of sophistication, we know the universe has turned slightly on its spindle.

Miss McCarthy didn't respond. She stared at Leonard for a moment, her eyes tightening and her lips wrestling each other as the class waited for the next question. She never told Leonard to sit down, never said he was right, never said a thing to him again. She continued with the next question and asked Ann Kostakin , a good, delicate, and intelligent Greek girl whose father was a lawyer, to answer, which Ann did and was duly praised for.

That day the universe spun a little for Leonard Espinoza, Miss McCarthy, and me. I wonder if anyone else in the class felt the slippage in the gears.

I would like to say I met Leonard much later and that he had the walk of a man used to labor, proud and at ease, comfortable with his work and glad for it. Instead I have to say the last I heard of Leonard was as a teenager. He ran away from home and his mother ran an ad in the newspaper asking him to come home. He was a severe diabetic who needed a needle a day to live. Andy LaVin said he saw him, wearing a leather jacket and trying to look tough, moving his arms as if he was muscle-bound and shouldn't be toyed with.

Will we never see certain things because we don't want to see them? Or because they don't exist? Or is there some reason in between of which, only over time, we'll become aware? Do we have

Jerry Lettvin's frog's eyes or the Mopsus mormon spider's acuity? Is it a conference table or a battleground where science and faith must meet? I don't know. I do know where the sacrum and innominate bones, literally the "sacred" and "unknown", meet. I wouldn't be surprised if science and faith meet there, as well, someday.

George Carlin says you'll never see a big tall fat Chinaman with red hair, you'll never see a wheelchair with a rollbar, you'll never see Margaret Thatcher strapping on a dildo, and you'll never hear anybody say "Just as soon as I shove this red hot poker up my ass, I'm going to chop my dick off".

And you'll never see four colored men walking up and down the streets of Manhattan, asking answers and offering questions in reply.

Miss McCarthy died shortly after we graduated sixth grade. Four boys, Matthew, Hank, Mike, and Ricky, all of whom Eddie Haskeled her, went to her wake acting like real men about it.

If he's alive, my hope is Leonard learned how to see in the dark sans sticking needles in his eyes.

CHAPTER 49

HORMONE FREE DANCING IN HARLEM

igh up in Harlem we walk along a street where a crowd gathers around twelve black men. The twelve black men are lined up in four rows of three. Some are Rastafarian black, some are West Indian black, some are South American Portuguese West African black, some are dark as dark as night and some fifty years ago could pass and perhaps even they wouldn't know.

The crowd is white and black and Indian and Sufi and men and women. The twelve men move in a dance, their black and not-black sweat-glistening bodies slither and dither, anguine and sanguine, and I am uncomfortable around them without knowing why. The smell of the city mixes with sweat on the bodies and the hints of the bottles the onlookers pass around. The dancers' fingers snap in movements both martial and marital, their bodies enjoying a unification of movement, a simultaneity of expression which is an evocation without invocation.

For the first time in my life, I am aware of what it is to know something is erotic and not be aroused. Their movements call out to me, echoing some harmony surging along my bones, and I feel myself in heat not due to this waning August sun but erupting from me suddenly like sweet-tasting bile that catches in my throat.

There is a sign on the curb:

Black Gay Men
Dance For Dignity

Their dance isn't a dance of racial pride or an indignant shout to others "Beware". It is a celebration of their life, an invitation to understand, to appreciate, not to participate, a demonstration of sexuality without demonstrating sex.

My hormones wonder who I am.

So do I.

I turn to the Healers, more uncomfortable with the growing echo within me, but look up at the laughter of the onlookers and see a fifth row join the other four. Beriah, Cetaf, and Jenreel, their different bodies joining the harmony of the others, moving their moves, stepping their steps, their faces smiles and laughter when they miss a step which grows less and less as they share the celebration of the dance.

A tear mixes with my sweat. How much have I learned? What does it mean to be free?

I take two hands in mine, not knowing if they are male or female, and a sixth line is formed in the dance. I, much more awkward than my partners, until I learn to laugh, to feel the celebration of the dance.

CHAPTER 50
A PENNY OF SELF-AWARENESS

Street vendors turn the Harlem side of 125th into a kaleidoscope with shifting colors and shapes and tourists, locals, and assorted others come and go among their tables and booths and stalls. The vendors' voices rise and fall as prospects go and come.

It's not good customer relations to shout at someone who's standing in front of you with cash in their hands.

Food vendors are mixed in with the others and the scents of Italian and Haitian and Iranian and Chinese and Venezuelan and Argentinian and Congolese and Jamaican delicacies make my mouth water. One enterprising hawker notices the polite attention we draw. "Hey, you guys hungry? Want something to drink? My treat."

The Healers move smoothly through the crowd towards him. I pass a table with vintage cast iron mechanical banks. I smile passing the display, look down, my smile fades, and I stop. My eyes locked on one just right of center, one given no special place of honor, one given no more due than it is one among many and has a price tag on it within a few pennies of other banks of similar era, of similar size and shape.

The bank to the left of my gaze has a cannon which fires upon a fort. Put a penny in the cannon's slot, press the lever down, the penny is "fired" into the fort, a small bell dings. To my gaze's right is Uncle Sam with his hand out (go ahead and laugh). Put a penny in Uncle Sam's hand, press the lever, Uncle Sam lifts the penny to his mouth and in it goes, also with a small bell ding.

The Healers return to me and follow my gaze. Beriah frowns as his gaze goes from one bank to another. "What troubles you, Brother?"

It is not the first time they've addressed me so, it is the first time I am offended by the term, a term they use with sincerity, a term they use as a recognition; I am more like them than not.

I am offended because of the history of the term, a history assigned long before our cross-Manhattan journey began, a term which will probably last long after it ends, and because of the bank holding my focus on the display in front of me.

I point at a bank with a horse being led by a groom, by what we used to call a lawn jockey and I'm sure others still do, towards a barn. Put a penny between the horse's rear legs, press the lever, the horse turns around, kicks his groom in the back, the groom goes down, the penny goes over him into the barn, a small bell dings, then everything returns to its pre-penny self.

"My father had a bank like this one. Might have been this one. He got rid of it one day. At least it wasn't on our mantle anymore." I blink back tears and Cetaf's ready hand gathers them from me. "He'd take it down at least once a week, at least once, put it on the kitchen table, and have it do its thing." I dry the tears Cetaf's gathered. "He would sit by himself, push the lever, and say, 'Pay a penny to see the nigger get it.'"

Jenreel's blue shimmers on my skin. "Do you hate who you are, Ben?"

"No. Sometimes I wonder who I am, though. Is that the same?"

"One creates a pit, the other a ladder out of the pit."

I laugh. "There's a joke about this guy who falls into a deep pit. The walls are smooth, there's no ladder, no way out. A doctor stops by and stares into the pit. 'Hey, Doc. I'm stuck in here. Can you help me out?' The doctor writes a scrip, tosses it in, and walks on. A little while later a priest stops by and stares into the pit. 'Hey, Father, I'm stuck in here. Can you help me out?' The priest throws down a prayer book and walks on.

"Some time has passed and the guy hears another guy he knows singing as he's walking past. 'Hey, Harry! Is that you, Harry? I'm stuck down here in this pit. Can you help me out?'

"Harry comes over to the pit, stares in, sees the guy and jumps into the pit with him. They guy says, 'What the hell did you do that for? Now we're both stuck in here.'

"Harry puts his arm around the guy's shoulder. 'It's okay. I've been here before and know the way out.'"

Beriah puts his arm around my shoulder. "It's okay, Ben."

He backs away and Jenreel takes his place. "We've been there before."

Cetaf replaces Jenreel. How something so big can be so gentle constantly amazes me. "We know the way out."

CHAPTER 51
TREAD MARKS ON MY THIGHS

William Henry Bishop wrote an article about Southern California for an 1882 edition of *Harper's* Magazine. This isn't staggering in itself. He was literate, articulate, there was a southern California and a *Harper's* magazine at the time.

Also what isn't staggering and which should be is what he, a white man, wrote about at that time: he assigns a value to the southern California Hispanic society based on the differences between the White Anglo-Saxon society he's used to in the Northeast and said southern Californian Hispanic society, then implies the cultural difference's assigned value is a fact instead of his opinion.

Seventy Years later, James Baldwin's "Stranger in the Village" appears in a 1953 *Harper's* Magazine. Baldwin writes of the affect and effect of being black in a white society. He notes that the whites expected the adulation of those they came to conquer.

Sometime in the mid-1960's there was a show on TV, ABC, called "TURN ON!", which was only on once. It was on during the time *Laugh-In* was big and I think the same people put it on. Tim Conway was on it, I remember that. In one segment of the show,

Godfrey Cambridge and some beautiful black woman played a husband and wife who were trying to convince the world and especially themselves they weren't black. I remember, in the skit, he comes home and tells her how horrible the day was. While he was riding home on the bus, the woman sitting next to him screamed out, "A nigger!" and he spun his head and shrieked, "Where?". The capstone of the skit was his revealing he'd purchased a watermelon. He felt guilt and shame and his wife the beautiful Negress was apoplectic over this act of obvious infidelity.

I could imagine Negroes - that's what we were back then - everywhere wanting to laugh at this skit but feeling it cut too close to the bone as it was on a white TV show. Humor, as any worthy anthropologist will tell you, is culturally based.

There are some nice restaurants in Harlem. This one, with no stairs but a handicap access ramp, has people who stop us at the door.

I look through the windows and see free tables. "Why can't we eat here?"

The lead stopper holds his hand in front of him, palm out, our entry forbidden. "We don't have the proper facilities."

"What does that mean?"

"Where, well, I mean how. Look, we don't have bathrooms for them."

"Give me a fucking break. They've been on candid camera for the past two months and no one's ever seen them shit, piss, drop their drawers, jerk off, or break a sweat."

"Some of the other patrons might have difficulty getting around them."

I wonder if it's worth arguing.

A man in a wheelchair, the chair's battery almost spent, has trouble getting up the ramp. Cetaf, Jenreel, and Beriah move as one to help him along. He locks his wheels at the top and looks over his shoulder. "Thanks."

I note his footplates dig into the shins of the man denying us ingress. "Thirty years ago I was denied access because ambulatory patrons might trip over the wheelchair. Fifteen years ago I had to piss into a coffee can because my chair couldn't fit into the men's room." He spins his chair quickly, and the man is butted into the doorjamb. "You want tread marks up your thighs or you want to let them in?"

As I say, there are some nice restaurants in Harlem.

Currently Rover and some other Mars missions are mapping the surface with the aid of orbiters fifty miles up directing their path. They're seeking rich ore deposits. This isn't common knowledge.

I've seen some of the mappings. What impresses me the most are all the Earth English American names for things which have existed on the red planet for, perhaps, billions of years.

I didn't know the Martians spoke English.

What does it matter. Perhaps they only spoke gibberish.

CHAPTER 52
AT THE INTERSECTION OF RIVERSIDE PARK AND POLLUTION CONTROL YOU CAN ASK ALICE

As part of my ongoing therapy, I got together once a month with a group of seven other people. These people came from different walks of life and about all we had in common was that we all needed help. One was a banker, one was a writer, one was a magazine editor, I think we had one or two programmers, one was a mother, one was a wannabe with no particular wanna in mind, and then there was me, wanting to be nothing so much as left alone in my self-made hell. There was one major difference between this monthly therapy group and others I've participated in. This one didn't know it was a therapy group.

We had a common goal and there was a strong covert rule that there would be no variations in how that goal was achieved. You played by this rule or you were not allowed to play. You weren't asked to leave, you simply weren't allowed to play, an ostracization without an egress - even Nolan's shipmates afforded him genuine pity and not paternistic mockery. I think the senior members of the group hoped you'd eventually realize what a fool you'd been for not harboring their ideas and return to the fold. Clever thoughts or insights were viewed more as something capricious and not the products of a thinking, reasoning mind.

In any group there will be a pecking order. Put two people together and one will lead, the other follow (I am learning non-exclusively in this. All it has taken is a long walk on a small island). Even the Healers have their roles, although who leads is still unclear to me.

This group had its pecking order, its leader and its followers, as well. Because there were several of us, we could even afford a lieutenant and an acceptable and therefore politically correct dissenting speaker.

Leadership is a strange thing. One can only stay a leader as long as the group accepts that individual's elements of leadership. Like Hitler, all you need do is mimic the childhood family patterns of members of the group to ensure group loyalty no matter what the leader is doing. Like Hitler, all you need do is ensure that members of your group shared similar family patterns. Gas everyone else, or come close. Don't believe me?

Go ask Alice. Miller. Not Carroll's and not Jefferson Airplane's, either.

In this group, Dave was the leader, he was gently and encouragingly grooming Steve to follow him as leader as soon as he felt we were all thinking like him, and he was offering guidance but more freedom of expression to Alexander who was given the dissenting voice. It was Alexander's job to promote group contiguity and harmony by demonstrating that dissenting although just as exactingly intellectual opinions were acknowledged and tolerated.

Yep, that's right. In a group of eight which included three women the leadership was all male.

Each in the group would have their say, state their piece, offer their opinion, then Dave would kindly and lovingly explain to them where they had gone wrong and how to make it right and what should be done so that it never again went wrong but not to worry, he would be there to lead us out of our own individual morass again and again. Often, after Dave had lovingly and concisely corrected us, he would sit back - literally - and allow Steve to elaborate on what he'd just said.

A gentle hurrumph, a clearing of the throat, and you could hear, "What the good Master is saying..."

On those rare occasions when Alexander's opinion was at odds with Dave's, Dave would allow Alexander his way, sitting back and watching Alexander through narrowed eyes and tightened lips. Polarity opinions elicited little response, although parallel were, of course, best. The gauge of how far Alexander's opinion differed from Dave's and therefore the group's was the line of color across Dave's face. Close opinion, say ten degrees off the accepted path, no change, there was hope, perhaps only a minor error in Alexander's judgment and easily corrected if Alexander was in a listening mood. A little further, say thirty degrees, and the line of color stopped just above the eyes, a white forehead and ruddying complexion below. Go to forty-five degrees and the line went from ear to ear and right across the nose. At ninety degrees the situation was hopeless, Dave's leadership was in jeopardy, his entire face became the Phantom's mask, and both he and Steve his lieutenant would socrate Alexander until he fell and order was restored.

Jesus Christ, who kept the script?

It is loud and scary walking under the Henry Hudson along the west side of the island towards the George Washington. North of midtown, we are beside the North River Water Pollution Control Plant and, for lack of funds, it is shut down. This far north, Riverside Park is given over totally to the homeless. It is difficult to know which smell chokes me first, the shut down pollution control plant or the unwashed and unkept bodies of those frying in the sun along the tracks of Riverside Park. The only part of the recreation area still open is a road leading to the Boat Basin, which is guarded by a private security force.

The security guards open the gates for an Audi, a BMW, a rusted and Bondoed Volvo, and a Taurus wagon. I hear the car doors close and then the gate. My name is called.

Dave, Steve, Alexander, and all the others save one call me from the other side of the gate.

Our path shifts slightly as the Healers move with me to the gate.

"Come back to the group," says Dave although I hear it as if spoken by all their voices. They press against the gate, their fingers entwined with the grillwork, their arms reaching out to me. Beside them stand guards in pseudo-police dress, flanking each side of the group, each guard facing his opposite, guns holstered but broad chests, strapping arms, close cropped hair, mirrored aviator eyes, nightsticks and jackboots all on display. Trust me, these pillars are Hercules.

The guards look at neither the group nor us, their mirrored eyes reflecting their partner across the group strewn sea, yin with yin and yang with yang.

The group keeps their eyes on me, their faces tight and strained, as if some taut visual umbilicus exists between us.

"Look, Ben," says Alexander, "we think enough time has passed and that you might benefit by coming back. I know I took some time off and came back. It helped quite a bit."

"I appreciate the offer, but I don't think so. At least not yet."

Their eyes still on me, Alexander recedes and Steve steps forward. Before he speaks, I say, "The way you're all staring at me makes me uncomfortable. Please stop."

Their faces become more tense, more strained. "What else is there to see?" asks Dave. As he speaks, the group moves behind him. He's not near the gate. He stands between the two guards, a moth caught in their coils, as the group backs away. His eyes do not waver from mine, but the color starts to leave his face.

One of the men, Barry, the one who did not call my name, leaves the group and opens the gate. He smiles as he walks past me, then embraces each of the Healers before he leaves, heading up towards Broadway.

Dave's face is white. Behind him is spoken reinforcement, "Nothing else to see" "Might as well go" "His loss not ours", deny even Barry's exodus a moment before.

"Beriah, Cetaf, Jenreel, do you remember that song I taught you?" They nod. "Hit it, boys."

We lock arms and sing, "We-are-family...I've-got-all-my-brothers-with-me..." high-stepping on each beat. They finish and unlock arms, smiling and laughing at the awkwardness of their moves, high- and low-fiving each other and missing most of the time because they haven't got it totally figured yet. I step forward, snap my legs and bow slightly, never taking my eyes from those of the group. I look like Ben Vereen on the cover of *Pippin*. "Doo-dah!"

Beriah claps his four-fingered hands. "That was fun, Ben."

I nod. It is fun. "A little traveling music, Sam." The four of us transform into a technicolor Rockette's chorus line and continue up the Henry Hudson.

When I returned from LakeShore Psychiatric, I had gained many tools for recognizing and reintegrating my emotions and - lofty of lofties - my spirit into what I do. Mind and body were no problem. I was destroying both, and if you're taking the time and effort to destroy something, you're sure as hell not ignoring it.

Of course, no one was spared.

This included the non-therapeutic therapy group. What was wrong, I wanted to know, with arguments and appeals made to other than the intellectual self, and why shouldn't our paths to the mutually agreed upon goals encompass those elements?

I had learned enough about situational dynamics to know better. I tell myself that now. Observing a group which needed a father to lovingly and tenderly chide them and not a group allowing themselves a diversity of opinions, and a leader who needed the perpetuation of himself through others and not friendly challenges which would have allowed him to grow, I should have been smart enough to leave sooner than I did.

I won't nor have I ever discredited their paths. I did and do note their paths in attempting to achieve the mutually agreed upon goals; they only and always appealed to the intellect.

There are four elements to any solution to our ills: the mind, the body, the emotions, and the spirit. One cries for his own pain, one tends to his own needs, one tells you how he feels.

Who, then, am I?

Are there three of them?

No, there are four of us.

4: People who do change tend to do so continually and along all P-C relationships in their lives. Therefore the equation in formula 3 becomes

$$\sum_n \int_0^1 f(e,s,p,m) \, \partial e \, \partial s \, \partial p \, \partial m = g(e,s,p,m)$$

which *is* the form of the Schroedinger equation.

From Item 2 earlier, "$f(e,s,p,m)$" is the equation of a life. Therefore, I've quantified what a teacher is, which is defined by the above equation: A teacher is an individual whose life is changing in all four directions.

What also falls from this is I've also shown what a teacher teaches: a teacher teaches you how they live their life. They may pass information on to you regarding a specific subject, but if you're to learn from them, they must be teaching you how they live their life as the basis for the subject.

CHAPTER 53
THINK, THANK, THUNK

This is what happened -

There were several children playing in the street, along with some adults sitting on stairs or gathered in groups of two and three, smiling and watching the children.

A black male, age seven, held a 22-caliber pistol in something like a firing stance. He shouted, "I'm a policeman! You got to stop, Monasses, you're the burglar."

One of the children, a white male, age seven, crouching behind a shining aluminum trash can and holding a yellow-drawstring kitchen garbage-bag filled with plantain peels, breadfruit rinds, sugarcane husks, pomegranate seeds, corncobs, and leaves over his shoulder, stood up with his hand outstretched in a pistol shape. He shouted, "BANG."

A woman screamed.

There were three clicks as the pistol's hammer fell on the firing pin which in turn punched into empty chambers. While the pistol clicked, the black male shouted back, "Uh-huh, Monasses, I got you first." His words were followed by three small explosions similar to the sound of a 22-caliber pistol firing.

Another woman screamed.

Adults and children fell to the ground. The only people still standing were the black child, a mulatto woman standing behind him, a black man running towards the white child, Cetaf, Jenreel, Beriah, and I.

This is what I think happened -

We started up a street because Jenreel was hungry and there were some kids with a lemonade stand selling cookies about halfway up the block. Next to the kids was a man selling corn. There was a sign hanging from a window on the building behind him, "Fresh Native Corn/Broadway & 153rd", and I laughed. On either side of us were parents and children. Everyone was smiling. This was the Caribbean neighborhood, up around 153rd near Trinity Cemetery. The talk was fast and the music lively, but was neither loud nor offensive.

Twenty feet ahead of us and to our right, a little black boy, his eyes bright and clear, his skin a rich ebony, his teeth strong, and his young body already showing the strength it would contain as a man, ran out from a basement stairwell and threw down his mother's purse. He got into a policeman's firing stance and yelled "I got you, Monasses."

I said, "Geez, that looks like a real gun."

We looked to where he was aiming. A slightly smaller white boy with hair red as if a crayon had buffed his head and eyes dark brown and skin tattooed with freckles down his face and arms and hands awkwardly large for his age smiled an old man's toothless grin and jumped up from behind a sun-shining silvery-new garbage can, a yellow trash bag slung over his shoulder as if filled with childhood gold, held his hand out as if it, too, were a gun, shouted, "Bang!" and laughed, clutching his sides and dropping his gold as if God descended the heavens to tickle this one small child.

A woman looking like the small black boy and wearing a loose-fitting white dress with a yellow flower print came running up the same stairs the African-American boy emerged from, looked around the street, and started screaming, running for the child with the gun.

A woman wearing a man's t-shirt and cutoff jeans buying corn and carrying a pitcher of lemonade turned at the sound of the other woman's scream and started screaming herself.

A man started running down the stairs at the far end of the street, his unbuttoned shirt flying like a cape as he dodged between playing children and shock-faced adults, his strong chest pumping under a white tank top, his black pupils tiny against the white surrounding them, his many-sunned skin going white, his mouth frothing like a stallion's chasing down a mare, his dark, bare feet slapping, slapping, slapping the pavement and his arms outstretched towards the red-haired boy, his own black tightly-curly hair slowly glistening as sweat came through and flew away.

I started running towards the boy with the gun. I opened my mouth to shout just as he started firing.

Nothing happened. I heard the hammer fall and thought the gun was empty. I kept running but now without the urgency I had previously felt.

Something blue moved through me and past me towards the red haired boy.

The pistol fired three shots.

Adults and children fell to the ground.

I stood still and slowly raised my right hand to my face. I touched my cheek, felt the beard and sweat there, and walked back to the Healers.

This is what happened to me -

Three things struck me within seconds of each other. First, I knew there was something different but didn't at first recognize what it was. Second, there were no pimps, pros, pushers, or toughs on the street. Third, I had started sorting by what *is*, not by what is *not*. I had gone from a sense of less to a sense of more, from an awareness of lack to an awareness of abundance.

Upon seeing the gun, I grew angry at the need for toy companies to emulate through play something we fear as adults. "How can this help children learn to live their lives?" I thought.

When I saw some parents panic, I knew it was a real gun and innocence might soon end. I felt their horror move through me and I started running towards the children.

The boy started firing and nothing happened. "The gun is empty," I whispered and felt my lungs fill with air and relief. I felt myself burst into a cold sweat as my terror turned to simple alarm - "Simple alarm"? Put that one beside "meaningless death."

Somehow, I don't know how, I suddenly *knew* the rest of the chambers were not empty and wondered what Jenreel, who tends to his own needs, would do.

The pistol fired three shots.

Just as on TV, just as in a movie, everything got slow. I heard then saw the bullet leave the muzzle, saw it glint in the sun as it crawled through the air, pushing cleanly and leaving little whirl-winds spinning like wide-eyed tourists in Times Square as it moved to the freckled, red-haired boy. People fell to the ground, each trained or training in an urban war never quite forgotten.

The running man and screaming women's voices bounced off the pavement and building facades like great basso profundos, or the denouement of sforzando on the Divine's organ.

I stood, unable to move, waiting for the credits to roll and wondering why I'd wanted to see this movie anyway. My lungs crushed my heart because I wanted to cry but could not. I had given up my terror and mute silence came in its place.

I ran back to Jenreel. As I ran the world picked up its pace and, when I reached him, everything was moving in normal time.

This is what showed on the 11 O'Clock News:

Jenreel held me while I cried. I became so weak with sobbing he literally held me up after a while. "I shouldn't have stopped."

Beriah placed his hand on my shoulder, "You didn't, only your body stopped. The rest of you moved on."

I stared down the street wondering if there was some other magic of the Healers which might take place and saw the crowds moving around the freckle-skinned boy, heard their screams, and knew he was dead.

"What good is that? The boy is still dead," I screamed.

Jenreel answered, "You saw to your own need to help. Your desire to help moved through you and to the boy. Your desire may have helped that boy pass from this life to the next. He has moved on, without your intent, he might have not."

"You mean he might still be alive? Still be able to be a child?"

"Perhaps. Crippled for life, a body without a mind or a mind without a spirit or a spirit without emotions," said Beriah.

Cetaf lifted me from Jenreel's arms and cradled me as a mother might her son. "We offer to help and so help ourselves. It doesn't matter if our offer is accepted or not."

Down the street, the dark muscular man picked up the child and wept. I closed my eyes and did the same.

There are two lessons for me in this. One, the more cloying - I am an unreliable witness to my own life.

The first lesson is I can't separate what happened to me from what happened. I - who have been and am still subjected to covert and overt acts of prejudice - must now confront my own prejudices, prejudices which are meticulously insidious.

This leads into the second lesson and it has to do with role models, choosing your idols carefully and helping them up when they fall.

I think it's better when our idols are our friends. This way we get to see them when they're sick. We get to see them when they're sick, when they eat, when they're drunk, when they're sad, when they're happy, when they're mad, and, most importantly, when they're mad at us. It's tough to keep somebody on a pedestal when you see them naked. They can be completely clothed when you see them naked.

I found out I was a role model for a friend and one of my idols was my role model. My friend told me, when certain situations arise, he filters things by pulling back slightly and thinking, "How would Ben react to this?"

He stayed with me, on the phone and in my life, when I was having trouble. He told me the truth of myself and let me know he was still there when the pain hurt so bad I wanted him to get away.

I got a lot bigger because of this. Both he and I gave me enough room to be sick and ask for help. Quite an achievement for a mortal god and a man desperately seeking one.

I put one of the men who helped me understand my life on a pedestal for a while. As soon as I put him there, I started taking him down. He did nothing to warrant getting off the stool, but neither had he warranted being placed on it.

In one of our group meetings, using the very tools he had given me to help myself, I noticed his behaviors towards certain women. A few weeks later, my observations were reinforced. A few weeks later, at the end of a meeting and out in the parking lot, my observations were confirmed.

And he had asked me to walk with him. I was beside him when he kissed a woman from our group, and I realized his affection for one of our members compromised his role to our group. He directed things to lessen group pressures on this woman instead of letting her form her own alliances.

We had been getting bigger all along, so this came as no shock. He is still a role model, but I know now there are only certain pieces-parts of him to which I'll apply glue.

The lesson? Friends are patterns. More correctly, you think not of a friend but of a pattern, a P-C relation. Bits and pieces of various situations match the pattern and evoke the memory of the friend. That's the obvious part. The less obvious part is that a friend's pattern acts as a filter or perceptual organizer. Thus the world is viewed, heard, felt, experienced, and interpreted a bit differently due to having interacted with the friend. When we do this, we are allowing ourselves to be *Noumenon*, an entity in the act of becoming.

I moved to help the freckle-skinned boy and my need made me bigger. Part of Jenreel became part of me.

CHAPTER 54
MAD HORSES

ack to Baltic College, back to one of those hellistic convocations, this one involving a group of middle-aged-to-elderly white men and women who were going to tell us all about sex. They spelled it differently, but both words started with "s." Their word for it, I later discovered, means "to miss the mark". Makes the whole concept a little less, don't you think? Instead of "I sinned" you get "I missed the mark". What's wrong with us that we can't accept the softer of the two as the real?

These people explained to us what GOD WANTED US TO DO ABOUT SEX and we listened. After they completed their white Eurocentric fundamentalist Christian statements - all of which were fine, by the way. Everyone in the convocation knew they were attending a white Eurocentric fundamentalist Christian establishment, whether they accepted it as such or not - we were allowed to ask questions.

The questions were not unusual considering the audience and hardly merit mention here, except for one; "How can I tell if I'm celibate?"

Segue now to a few months earlier. I, a new student to both the faith and the school, am meeting my dorm mates, one of whom is about six-five, lean-thin with a rich tenor voice, a lisp, strong arms, clear skin mottled only with the attempts at a beard, an accent I never could place and never asked about, and black. He was friendly, caring, giving, helping, physically emotive, on extremely equal terms with most of the girls on campus and all of the women, and, when he shook my hand with tenderness instead of a grip designed to elicit orange juice, I knew he was gay.

He wasn't, he said once, not that I asked, but he needed to say it to others who saw me with him, perhaps to let them know I was straight and therefore acceptable in their eyes.

Without anyone telling me so, I came to understand he was celibate. It was his choice and his gift, and I grew to respect him for it.

I don't remember his name, although the sound of his voice and his face and his laughter will stay with me forever. Aside from that one time which was perhaps for my benefit, he never discussed his sexuality, except this one time when someone asked about the possibility of their own celibacy.

The panel demurred from answering. None of them were celibate, said Dean Ted, and they therefore couldn't answer a question outside of their own experience.

Made sense then and it makes sense now.

My dorm mate, sitting two rows behind me and to my left, raised his hand, was called upon, stood, turned to face the man with the question and said, "I think I can answer that."

Maher Circle is clean because it is near the Polo Grounds which is also where some of the NYPD's horses are kept. Whatever litter may sweep around is quickly scoffed by the sanitation crews cleaning up after the horses.

A horse charges at us. I say "charge" but it moves like a warhorse which has charged through too many battles, which wants to get some idiot off its back, which wants humans to finish each other off so it can rest in a field of grass and clover and oats.

Several men and women come running down the street, ropes and whips flying and snapping in their hands. As the horse nears I see it moves awkwardly, favors its right front leg. It's almost as tall as Cetaf although not as wide. It has white near its hooves and looks like it's wearing socks, and each time its front right hoof touches the ground the horse seems to wince like a man who's repeatedly stubbing his toe. The rest of the horse is bay-colored except for a splotch on its brow. Its mane is clipped and what I see is a punker horse. Its eyes are wide and foam flecks its flanks as it thunders towards us.

I try to hurry Cetaf, Beriah, and Jenreel into a door, out of the way, this mad horse bearing down on us like a crippled demon in heat.

Beriah and Jenreel sit on the pavement, their hands in their laps and their eyes on Cetaf. He stands before the horse, his arms open in greeting and tears in his eyes.

The horse slows, gallop to canter to trot to walk to stop, resting its head on Cetaf's shoulder. Cetaf strokes its neck, lifts the horse's head and scratches under its chin, then rests its head back down. He says, "Yes, I am afraid, too," and the horse grunts to him. It shifts its weight to its left front leg, its good leg, and paws the pavement with the favored hoof.

Its handlers approach and the horse fidgets. It limps behind Cetaf.

"We'd like our horse, please."

"It is not your horse. It is its own horse."

A woman with a whip steps forward, "Listen, Citrus or whichever one you are, that's the city's horse, we bought him, and he's glue if we can't make him into a mounted patrol carrier."

The horse snorts at her.

"You make his choice for him. Maybe it's not the choice he would make. Given the options you presented, he created a third."

Another woman, full figured with golden hair, strong like a man and looking nothing like one, fashions a bridle from the rope in her hands. "A single option is not a choice."

The horse moves towards her. It shifts its weight when it stops. She looks down, "Did you see that, Connie?" The strong, golden-haired woman lifts the horse's right front leg, inspects its hoof. "He's got a stone in his frog. God damn it, no wonder he bolted when you tried to tack him up." She starts to walk away, the horse following with no tension in the bridle.

The first woman hollers at her, "That's the city's horse, Cynthia."

"Send me the bill."

They move back to the Polo Grounds. I stare at Cetaf as Beriah and Jenreel rise. "How did you know that horse wouldn't't've mowed you down?" I ask.

"I didn't," Cetaf answers. "All I know is that I am Cetaf, and I was afraid."

"But the horse just came up to you. I don't get it."

"Perhaps my knowing who I am allowed the horse to know who he is and, around me, instead of thinking he had to be a 'mow-you-down,' he knew he could be a horse."

He got no further. That much I know. How clearly I remember, I can't attest, but I remember turning at the sound of chairs hastily pushed back and seeing Dean Ted standing up, his shoulders tight and his Anglican glasses falling from his New Zealand nose as he shouted over my dorm mate's voice, "Excuse me, but if there's a question, our panel of experts will answer it."

But they couldn't answer out of their own experience.

Had any ever had or contemplated abortion? Could any of them see a clothes hanger as something other than a place to hang clothes or a bottle of bleach as merely a way to get your whites white? Had any ever suffered venereal disease? Had any of the men mastur-bated to the point where their penises became open raw stumps festering in their hands? Did any of the women find themselves wanting someone, male or female, with a fire so consuming they penetrated themselves with a hairbrush repeatedly, deeply, until swollen and weeping, they bled and bled and bled? Did any of them ever fellate, cunnilingize, or sodomize?

It doesn't matter. It's none of my business.

The only problem is, they made it theirs. To follow their message, Saturday nights with the lights off, missionary, in the bedroom on the bed with the shades drawn and the doors locked.

My friend looked first at the panel and then, of all the people in the gym he could focus on, at me. He smiled, and nodded, and sat quietly until the convocation came to an end.

I didn't. I couldn't. I couldn't do so much as breathe. "Here is a man who we all acknowledge has the gift, who better to let us know? He can tell us how he found out for himself, he doesn't have to tell us how he can know for us," I wanted to say but didn't.

He is dead now, died of some horrible, flesh destroying, disease. Never Gay, never a lover, never immune to some unspeakable ill contracted while volunteering at a hospice slowly claimed his life.

I would have liked to know his answer.

I tell you this because it illustrates a fear I think I once had but now often forget. It doesn't matter what the fear relates to, it can be anything, because the fear stems from a sense of self-lack.

Your experience is different from mine. There is no room in me for two opinions so different for both to be correct. I know mine works so yours must be wrong.

What I couldn't conceive is "mine works *for me*". Those two extra words allow yours to work *for you*. Suddenly there is difference but there is no threat because there is an entire cosmos between us and we both have room to grow, there is nothing to defend. Your opinion, your difference, is yours and there is no need for me to judge myself against it, which means there is no need for me to attack you because, if I let you stay, I won't judge myself against you and find myself lacking.

I do not know and can only guess the people on the panel feared the peace and serenity my dorm mate had with his choice. There have been those I've feared because of the peace and serenity they found with their choices, choices which worked for them and which I judged myself against.

But when that was the case, I learned to realize either I didn't make the choice or it was, indeed, my own.

I can always change. I can always make my own choice.

CHAPTER 55
ALONE

Walking through High Bridge Park at night isn't the safest thing to do, although I know I'm safer with my brothers than without them. "What happens when we get to the end of the island?"

"The final stage of evolution will occur," Beriah answers, "when the four bodies align."

"Do you ever hear what I ask?"

"Certainly not. Do you?"

I rephrase it. "In about sixty blocks we'll hit water. This land we're walking on stops and we either learn to swim or cross a bridge. That's what I want to know. What happens when the land stops." I'm afraid Beriah will tell me to turn left again, but don't know why this makes me afraid. I have learned that, if I do not force turns where none belong, bullets hit no one, no one is harmed, no one is hurt, and my memory remains clear.

Jenreel looks back towards the way we came. I wonder how he can figure it out with all the turns we've made along the way. "This island never stops."

Cetaf looks in the direction opposite and I realize he's looking to where we're heading. "The journey goes on forever."

Beriah, ever patient, ever watchful Beriah sees a tear streak down my face. "The end of the island isn't here, now, Ben."

I look from one to the other. They are all ever patient, ever watchful. More patient and watchful of me than I've ever been, as patient and watchful of myself as I'm learning to be.

Still, it hurts. "Yeah. Sure. Fuck it."

Cetaf places his hand on my shoulder and starts to lay down. I wouldn't think to spend the night here. "What are you feeling, Ben?"

"I don't know. I feel...I feel angry."

"Tell me about your anger."

"It's just anger." Now I'm angry at him. "Is that okay with you?"

"Fine. I'm curious what you're angry at."

I'm angry at him but denial can give one a sense of power, of control. "Nothing."

"Nothing makes you angry?"

"Yes."

Beriah lays beside us. "Yes. Nothing makes you angry. Right now you need to be angry so you've made yourself angry."

I nod vigorously. "And doing it damn good, too."

Jenreel nods in agreement. I taught him to do that. He, of the three, nods and shakes his head for yes and no. At least I've given them that.

"What is the problem to which anger is the solution?"

"Huh?" I know what he means. I didn't know he remembered or even thought of it. It is something else I told them, how I, as a mathematician, solve problems. I assume I have the solution and work backwards to see what kind of problem the solution answers. This is also how magicians work. Start with the finished illusion, work back to figure out how you did it.

But there is more to it than that. In life, problems are solved. In life, problems don't exist, only solutions do. How so? Much as nature abhors a vacuum, nature seeks balance. Problems, in nature and, by extension, in people, are always solved immediately.

Problems cause tension and neither nature nor people survive long when tension exists. So all that exists in nature are solutions. Which means if I am angry, my anger is the solution to a problem solved so quickly - as is best - I didn't know the problem existed. People, unlike nature, always solve their problems in ways they've already tried. Nature solves problems with whatever nature has at hand. Only people will repeat what didn't work before, thus proving themselves insane for any around to see.

Did you know that some solutions create other problems?

Accept the wrong solution and you've said, "Why, yes, please give me cancer! I think I'd like to try that!"

So, I'm solving a problem and now, with three-quarters of an island behind me, think my solution might not be best for ridding me of the problem.

"I'm angry because...because...because when we get to the end of this island, I'm afraid you'll go and I don't want to be alone."

Who is teacher and who is taught? They have infinite patience. Do they hang on my every word? The same words by which I am hung?

The words ache as they come out of me. My chest and throat constrict like a boa inside my ribs. Cetaf and I cry. He lifts me and places me over his heart. Jenreel takes my left hand, Beriah my right, and each places it over their own hearts. They speak as one. "You are never alone, Ben."

5: There are some other, I think equally interesting aspects to this understanding of relationships, teaching, and life: Changes occur over some measure of time. Taken along any single element, we have the speed of change in that direction.

$$f(e,s,p,m)_k/t = s_k$$

Summing over all elements (as we did in we get item 3), we get

$$f(e,s,p,m)/t = \underline{v}_L \,\|\, \underline{v}_L \mid \text{the velocity of life}$$

and so we now have a quantification of both the speed and direction, or velocity vector, in which changes occur in an individual's life, specifically an individual with whom we are able to learn.

CHAPTER 56
CHANGEFUL REUNIONS

A friend of mine - no, A friend of ours - comes up to us at Sylvan Terrace in late September afternoon daylight. These are the start of the Long Sun Days, when you can see the rays of the sun casting long arms across the face of the planet. Shadows grow long and from noon to dusk takes much longer than in summer or spring, although dusk is usually flushed-cheek red and quickly comes to pass. In a few months, when the Long Sun Days are guiding the planet, you'll know. At noon, the sun seems to use so much energy to make the world bright it doesn't have enough strength left to make it warm, and at the end of the day the sun's so tired it can't hold its arms up anymore. The sunlight still streams across the island, into unshuttered rooms, throbbing instead of blinding people facing it in highrise office towers, but you can hear the sun laboring, straining, waiting to go over the horizon and let its arms drop.

The friend is a man who gave us a bag of groceries long ago when the south of the island felt so secure, a man who took off his shoes when he realized even they didn't know where he'd been. I do not recognize him except when he smiles, the smile lost in the depths behind his eyes, because he has cut his hair.

I stop as he waves and cock my head remembering. "Hi. Don't I know you?"

"It'd be nice if you did."

"I didn't recognize you without your hair."

He laughs. "I recognized you with yours."

"For me, that would have been a brave step, cutting it off."

"I was scared, then I was shocked at how handsome I was."

"I never doubted it." I start to sing "Almost cut my hair..." but the reference is lost on him. He is four years younger than I but it was four years that marked the end of my generation and the start of his and I, for one, will not emphasize my maturity and his lack of it because I don't know which is which and that, I think, is a little of where spontaneity begins.

We laugh. "Better hurry up," he tells me. "Looks like your friends don't want to wait."

A block further is the Wall Street woman now leading children across the street, sneakers and jeans and sweatshirt fitting her more easily than the three-pieces she wore before.

"Aren't you - "

She smiles and the children tell her it's okay to cross. "I was, once, I think."

The children move through the Healers until I'm separated from them, the children grabbing my hands and pulling me with them. "I - I've got to go."

A young man, his face stubbled and lines of pain where there should be tears of joy, stares at me from an alley, behind trash bins like someone scouting us in an old western movie. He is familiar but I cannot place him. I've met so many, seen so many more. He separates himself from the bins. His eyes lock onto mine and he approaches - a confident step, a less confident step, a step sideways, a step back, his movements a constant battle between what he feels he must do and what he'd rather have done - until he stands before me. "It was my fault."

"Beg pardon?"

"We were horsing around. I didn't know the safety wasn't on."

I go back through my life, but not as before. Not reliving, now re-piecing, re-membering. "I'm sorry, I - "

"I put my hand over Buck's holster, kidding around, you know? He thought the safety was on, too. He must have. He pulled his sidearm up and waved it at me over his shoulder. I knocked it down and it went off. I didn't know."

From early in our journey, when the military and others kept a ring around us. "I'm so sorry."

He turns away from me and mutters to no one in particular. "I didn't know. I didn't know."

Beriah, Jenreel, and Cetaf stop and hold their hands out to me, not parents with children but children in a scary place holding the hand of another child to comfort.

Cetaf, who helped me up so often and I'm sure will do so many times more, nods at the mumbling boy-man. "All questions are answered."

Jenreel follows his gaze before returning it forward. "In their own time."

Beriah finishes their thought. "When we're ready for them.

"How much further are we going to go?" I ask.

They point, they shrug. "We don't really know."

I offer a statement disguised as a question. "I'm not like them anymore, am I?"

Beriah comes up beside me, to my left and slightly ahead of me. "You never were. You wanted to be, once. You worked hard at it, we think."

Cetaf stands behind me. "We think you would have died if you had continued."

Jenreel mimics Beriah's position on my right. "Like the warriors of our kind."

With one step I feel myself preparing to fugue. I feel the Healers, their colors, rush through me and wonder if I will awake at the Seaport, Jiminy standing over me as an officer calls for help, another citizen fatigued from the heat. I stare at the Healers as I click my heels three times to flee the witch. "There's no place like home."

This journey, this path change, this self-correcting algorithm suddenly activated in my life, has much of the charm of a fugue - a sudden, unexpected travel away from home or customary work locale. There is no assumption of a new identity although the persona has changed. I recall who I was and am glad for that. There was no blow to the head or stroke or similar trauma. Perplexity and disorientation have occurred. I hope there is no following recovery. I do not wish to forget what has happened during the fugue. They have, for one moment, made me their center, and their gift is so great I cannot speak, only cry, and know those as words are adequate.

Cetaf's yellow hue washes over me. "Do you regret your life, Ben?"

"No. I...I don't."

I am bathed in Jenreel's light. "Good, Ben. Good for you. To say your life didn't turn out as you planned is to hope for different yesterdays."

I am bathed in Beriah's light. Both he and Jenreel turn to face me. Each raised a hand to my face and I feel moisture there. Beriah smiles. "Tell me, Ben, could you understand dolphins and whales now?"

CHAPTER 57
ISOLATING ELEPHANTS

Wayne Martino came to play at my house one Saturday morning without being invited. Actually, his crime was far worse. He was riding by on his bike, saw me outside, and stopped to see if I wanted to play.

My father was working in the yard and, because this was how things were done, so was I. I didn't want to work in the yard. I wanted to play. To admit such would have been death.

You have to understand, no one could have credit cards in my family because that meant someone would know my father's business. By "business" we mean such mundane and abrasive things as age, sex, marital status, approximate income, number of children. You could have learned as much by observing the car we drove, the house we occupied, the clothes we wore, the food we ate. Yes, indeed, the mysteries of life are revealed around us.

So no one could have credit cards, except, of course, when it became convenient for my father to have them.

I caught him on this once. In a braver moment. Spurred on by public surroundings.

Something happened to the car and he had to rent one for a day. The attendant, a black man my father's age, filled out all the paperwork to rent my father a car and asked, "How will you be paying for this, sir?"

"Cash."

"Fine. I'll also need a credit card number. Visa or MasterCard will do."

"I said I'm going to pay in cash."

"I understand that, sir, but our policy is to only rent if you have a credit card. You can pay in cash and nothing will be billed to your credit card. It's merely a way for us to reference."

"I don't have a credit card."

"I'm sorry, Mr.," he looked at the paperwork again, "Matthews. I can't rent you a car. That's just the way it is. I'm really sorry about that."

At which point my father displayed just what kind of a man he was. "Is there something wrong with my money? Or is there something wrong with me that you won't rent me a car?" This, my black as Zeb's ass father said to a man just as black as he.

"Mr. Matthews, I understand how you feel, and if it were up to me I'd let you have the car. But it's not up to me and I can't let you have the car. I'm sorry. There's nothing I can do."

My father looked at the man, cursed under his breath, reached over the counter and took the papers which he folded into a wad, stuffed in his shirt pocket and started to walk out.

"Looks like you shot yourself in the foot, that time," I said. I don't think he could wait to get me outside, around a corner, away from other's eyes.

A man jogged past one day as we worked in the yard, long before jogging was popular or people could recognize Frank Shorter's body-erect, long-distance lean, walrus-mustached form breaking from the marathoning crowd. My father waited until the man was a block away, then stood to look after him and said, "What a waste of energy that is. He puts all his time into that when he should be working in his yard."

Nor could we have a color TV - "I've had color TV for a long time. There are whites and coloreds on all the time, so I got color

TV," he would tell us - until he wanted one to show off to his friends. His friends were mostly his brothers and sisters, his mom and pop. He often talked of friends but never brought any home. We never saw them, never knew them.

It's strange that I think of that now. He never brought people home and was always nervous when people showed up unannounced. A man who lived with a total sense of lack.

I remember well telling Wayne I couldn't play, that I had chores to do. Wayne asked if we needed help and my father, overhearing this and thinking he was acquiring free labor, agreed.

But Wayne didn't want to work. Wayne wanted to play. My father didn't know this. After perhaps a minute of uninspired work Wayne started to play.

"I thought you wanted to help us, Wayne."

About thirty seconds of work then play.

"Wayne, you said you'd help us."

Not even an attempt at work. Not even an attempt to acknowledge what my father said.

"I think you should leave, Wayne."

Wayne kept on playing. He played so demonstratively that I, whether I wanted to or not, was forced into the game.

You have to picture this. My father, big as any adult is big to a small child, standing behind Wayne, his eyes bulging and his face quaking, the muscles in his arms, neck, and chest tightening and straining in an isometric frenzy, his lips pressed white and his teeth grinding so loud I can hear them over his breathing which is coming in as if a mike were stuck in the nose ring of a charging bull, starts walking back and forth between our back door and Wayne Martino.

Wayne paid no attention. My father said, clearly three times, "You better leave, Wayne, now. Now I think you should leave." Wayne ignored him each and every time.

By this time my father's steps are accentuated by his choking breaths. This is how agitated he was, how riotously enraged he was that someone, some dumb-little-pigeon-shit of a kid, wouldn't roll belly-up at the great man's speech.

"I'm," my father choked his rage back down. "I'm going to call your father, Wayne Martino, so you better go."

Now my father had Wayne's attention. Wayne sat down beside me and asked, "Find out when I have to be home for lunch, Mr. Matthews, okay?"

My father went into the house and came back out before the screen door closed. "Your mother says they're getting ready to eat now, Wayne. You better go."

Wayne got on his bike and pedaled away. My father, his body still tight, his breathing still hard, his teeth still clenched, came into his quarter-acre kingdom again, mumbling, "Little bastard thinks he's so smart. Little bastard show him who's boss. Little bastard wait 'till he gets home," and then a little laugh, a little spittle leaping from his lips to the dry ground beneath.

He turned to me, then. I wasn't looking at him but he probably knew I was watching him as best I could and he gave me something to do. He didn't give instructions, he didn't give directions, he just gave me something to do, something I'd never done before, something my six year old arms were too weak to do, then stood back and waited.

The intersection of 179th, 178th, and Fort Washington Ave is busy for more reasons than there being three streets, one major, two parallel, coming together at once. It also lies under the Trans-Manhattan Expressway, is above the Manhattan Island terminus of the George Washington Bridge, is the river delta to the last exit on the Henry Hudson heading north before Dyckman and the second exit heading south, either of which once taken still leave you on the island, and houses the way-uptown bus terminal.

We are surrounded by horns. Some are directed at us, others are directed at drivers unheeding the NO U TURN signs. Two diesel flatbeds are stopped on the ramps over us. Their rumbling and exhaust trickles down to us like Hiroshima rain.

We stop. Beriah gazes in all directions. There are more than four and he peers down them all. "Which way from here?"

I start to cry, not because I'm judged ready to lead, but because I fear where we must go.

Cetaf echoes a statement he made so early when I met him, "It hurts," and joins me in my tears.

I point, not wanting to but knowing I must. "That way" If this were therapy, I would call it "terminal phase". It is when the patient knows the end of therapy is near with neither the therapist nor the patient having admitted it before. It has a paradigm in family systems, as well.

In healthy families, there comes a time when both the child and the parents realize the child can no longer stay at home. Time to push the young ones from the nest. No more regurgitation from papa's belly, no more succor from mama's breast, time for the pups and cubs and fledglings and kits to attempt their own kills. The parents have given all they can and any more repeats what has gone before. The children have taken all they can take and any more, like too many vitamins in the blood, are pissed away. Time to go and learn from others, learn from yourself.

The tears are heavy and thick.

I lead them up Fort Washington, towards the Cloisters. "What if I lead you the wrong way?"

Jenreel lifts his arms and embraces every place we've been. "Isn't it great to be alive!"

6: So what is the greatest velocity at which a teacher can live their life? If any single element changes at a different rate than the others, the equation in item 4 can be normalized so that some terms sum to "0", which negates the conclusion of item 3 by forcing

$$g(e,s,p,m) = 0$$

which is a non-muting life.

Therefore, a teacher can only teach when they are changing equally in all four directions. This causes the velocity equation to be

$$\underline{v}_L = 0$$

because changes in different directions cancel each other out. This can be demonstrated as follows:

It's easier to change direction if you're moving slowly.

7: Which leads to another interesting aspect of what a teacher is and can again be demonstrated:

You can only change direction relative to something else.

and:

You must be in constant contact with some reference point if you wish to change direction rapidly.

Which apparently denies the conclusion of item 6, as the acceleration vector becomes

$$\underline{v}_L/t = \underline{a}_L \parallel \underline{a}_L \mid \text{the rate at which changes in your life occur}$$

and

$$\underline{a}_L = 0$$

which means people must be at the center of all their changes for the changes to be wholly integrated into their life.

It's tough to be young, six and already be the Ancient of Days. Given no directions, no instructions, no guidance, and given something totally new to do, I did what most six-year-olds do.

I failed.

This was excuse enough.

What surprises me most as I think back on this was that my

father performed his leather belt surgery where others could see, in the backyard, where all the world could witness.

Back then, no one did, however. We kept our eyes averted and closed our doors and shutters, turned the radio or TV up loud so we couldn't hear the cries and anguish of our neighbors or the breaking of their bones.

This was another time when the universe moved slightly on its spindle. Before Wayne left, I knew I was going to do something wrong. I didn't know what it was, knew merely that I would, and so the waiting began, the waiting for the pain. When the job was given, I felt the rope upon my neck, heard the guillotine descend, smelled the sweet almonds of cyanide under my seat, tasted the bitter garlic as the needle entered my flesh, jiggled as I rode the lightning, its constricting electric death making my eyes rupture in my skull, and felt my hands, feet, and side pierced, a perfect sacrifice for young Wayne's sin.

Many years later, shortly before I left home, and after a day when I could do nothing right, I said to my father, "Look, if you want to hit me, just hit me and get it over with. I can't stand waiting anymore so just go ahead and do it. I know you want to and the waiting is making it worse. So just hit me, please, alright?" He was shocked that I said such a thing. I noticed something else, something I wish I'd learned earlier in my life: his rage had gone. I said, "Look, here's an elephant," and he had no choice but to clean up the elephant shit which was knee deep all over our house.

But the universe rotated slightly that day. I realized other people's kids were more important to my father than his own. I realized there was something about other people's kids that stopped my father from beating them.

And I realized it was because he'd get in trouble if he did. (really want to cry now?) And I realized he knew it, as well. He knew he'd get in trouble for hitting somebody else's kid the way he hit me.

Is submission as good as resistance when you have no choice? I wonder first, who is the question to? What is the question about?

Only when you have no choice. When you have choice, you lose the option of being a victim. Otherwise you're a participant.

My fear of making a mistake rises in me, gagging me, loosing my bowels and my bladder as it often did when I was six and not six years old. I shake my head, recontinenting myself (yes, it's been one hell of a war) before any disasters - no, this much I've learned - I mean "accidents", occur.

To steady myself, to align myself, to remind myself of the day and time where I am. "*Cognito, ergo sum*. I think, therefore I am."

Beriah stares at me. If this toad-faced being could look confused, perhaps in pain, he does. "If you feel, are you not?"

Jenreel's blue warms through me. "If you do, are you not?"

Cetaf touches my arm. There are tears in his eyes. "If you believe, are you not?"

Beriah takes a step, then stops. He is not facing me and yet he talks to me. I hear his words even though I don't see his lips move and feel my skin tinge red. "It is not any of these separate elements, Ben. You simply *are*. That is all there is. We came here speaking your words and not your language. Were our exchanges, when we shared, spontaneous?"

Cetaf stands beside me, suddenly much larger than I'd known him and suddenly as fragile as a blade of grass. "We think not. It is none of these things. You could not communicate with us until you first *were*, until you allowed yourself the freedom *to be*. Once you allowed yourself to be, you could talk to us, be heard by us." Honey-lemon colors dance on my skin.

I wipe my tears away and don't succeed.

"And hear you when you answered?"

Jenreel's blueness envelops me like a bear rug. "Yes. When you allowed yourself to be - to be - you allowed us to be. Until you could let us be who we were, without prejudice, without fear, without assumption or presupposition, until you were willing to let us be even as you allowed yourself to be, you could never have seen us, never have heard us, never have felt us, never have shared us."

There is a mist around me. It is the tears steaming in my own eyes. There is a whisper coming up the throat of the city and it sings to me with the sounds of the Healers, "Never have been us."

This is the answer. This is where my path lies, what I must follow.

Beriah, still facing away from me, all three continuing their paths, not waiting for me to follow yet allowing me to be with them, continues, "You wish to share with others on your planet; the people, the animals, the fish, and the birds? Perhaps with ones on worlds you don't know exist? Then *be*, Ben, just *be*. And in your being, let them be, as well. You will share lifetimes with them in seconds, and moments together will become lifetimes shared."

They have given me the answer by giving me what I had all along.

I can communicate nothing until I know *who* I am communicating.

8: This apparent contradiction between teaching and what one can teach is resolved when you consider accelerations over all time taken in infinitesimally small increments, in which case you get

$$\int_0^1 (a_L/gt)\, gt = \int_0^1 0\, gt = L \| L \| \text{ a Life constant}$$

What's interesting about the above is the expression "a_L/gt" which is the form for v and can be thought of as the "frequency" at which change occurs, which is constantly by item 7 previously. Now we add another concept via a demonstration:

If your life is out of balance, seek the new balance point instead of trying to maintain the old balance point.

This is the equivalent of "people must be at the center of all their changes", mentioned in item 7.

From the above equation, when your life is changing, you're too busy balancing to notice and when you've noticed the change your life has stopped changing. This is the Heisenberg Uncertainty Principle applied to life and is the indication of our *Noumenon* finally becomes a *Transcendental object*, and is, I think, what Liebniz meant when he said, "The force of the mind is its ability to persist through various states of consciousness." The problem with this is that a negation of change also negates what a teacher is. This is resolved by

$$_{e,s}\prod{}^{p,m} = 0 \parallel {}_{e,s}\prod{}^{p,m} \mid \text{a matrix of a life}$$

which is also the form of gravitational systems, which makes sense, considering the observations of items 6-8.

CHAPTER 58
TINA VERSUS THE MORLOCKS

"It takes
So many thousand years to wake,
But will you wake for pity's sake...?
- Christopher Fry, "A Sleep of Prisoners"

I went to Las Vegas for a convention. There are few cities you can go to for a convention, Las Vegas is one. I knew from someone that Tina Kolas had gone there, had worked as a show girl, had started her own restaurant and lost it, and was doing something else, nobody knew what and nobody knew where.

I went to Las Vegas for a convention, looked in the phonebook and gave her a call.

"Tina, you probably don't remember me. My name is Ben Matthews. We knew each other in junior high and high school - "

"I remember you, Ben." As she talked I heard a refrigerator door open and close, a Tupperware top unseal, and her munching on something which was crunchy and required her to occasionally slurp in some juices. "What can I do for you?"

Back to the A-train, but going towards instead of away-from.

The entrance to the A-train at 190th Street is a building which from the outside looks like a public bathhouse on a beach. Inside are two elevators, only one of which works at any given time, which are operated by a variety of people all wearing transit worker uniforms. One day it is an old black man with one eye cold and white, two days growth of beard, a face so wrinkled and lined the Blind love to read the stories it tells, his hands gnarled and curved into arthritic ghostly brown claws, huddled on an old piano stool, a winter coat pulled tight against the summer chill, withdrawing into the controls of the elevator, humming a tune and rocking as he works. The next day it is a beautiful, red-lipped, blue-eyed Chicano girl, still and always all of nineteen, running shoes comfortable with transit system shorts and shirt, her hair in dreadlocks, gum cracking between strong white teeth, smiling behind a TV-tray with cards kings queens nines aces jokers spread out in some unknown solitaire splay. Their job is both exacting and complex; when people get on the elevator, the operator pushes the single button marked up if the passengers are on their way to gather Eloi, down if the passengers are on their way to feed the Morlocks.

We get on, a ride of nine blocks north and some of the fastest ground yet covered is both over our heads and behind us, the end of the island a funnel and we're caught in its maelstrom scythe, and the operator presses the button "UP".

The elevator stops. Each of us takes a turn saying "Thank you." The old man, humming to himself, fingers twitch, perhaps remembering keys to some Scott Joplin tune. His good eye takes us in one at a time. He smiles and a Satchmo-like "You're Welcome" comes up from deep inside.

The door opens and there are children. Children many rows

deep and moving like the water in the ocean. Children upon children upon children, and Cetaf laughs, walking into them, holding out his hands and arms and they laugh and climb onto this mountain who walks like a man. Jenreel and Beriah join him, taking one child in each of their arms and staying close behind.

I stand behind Jenreel and shudder in a self-induced cold. "Jenreel, I'm afraid."

"Good, Ben. Good for you."

"Good? I'm scared, damn it. What's so good about that?"

"Good because you know what you are right now. Good because you can share who's inside."

"But I need to know what comes after this."

"Don't ask us, Ben. We don't know. Decide for yourself the answer to that."

I'm not satisfied with that. "Give me a clue. Anything. I don't want to walk on unless I know what comes after."

Cetaf takes a step, turns, checks where he walked, turns back, takes another step. "Sorry, Ben. We don't have any dimes. Besides, what is the function of a phone?" He laughs. "We won't know what comes after until it has come after."

I pick up a child. As I open my mouth it pops a piece of candy inside and Jenreel, coming close beside me, says, "Good, huh? Mine's - what's mine, Tom?" he asks of the boy on his shoulders. The boy leans over and it looks like he's eating Jenreel's ear "- licorice. What'd you get?"

"Didn't you know this place existed before you came here?"

"Certainly not. If I don't know that something exists, then it doesn't exist."

"I know about China and I've never been there."

"No. You don't *know* about China. All you know is that somebody told you about China."

"But everybody on Earth knows about China."

"Know about China, Tom?" Jenreel asks the imp on his shoulders. The imp again eats his ear. "Tom doesn't know anything about China."

"There are kids in China who don't know you exist."

"Then to those children I don't."

"But you're right here in front of me."

"And you're not one of those children in China."

Like a flock of pigeons suddenly aware of an indelicate cat, the children move en masse to the elevator door. The four of us are alone again.

I feel there is not much time left. "You haven't asked a lot of questions about my people, my race, this planet, my home."

Beriah turns to me. "Of course we ask questions. We're alive."

"I'm not hearing your questions."

"Perhaps not, but you certainly are giving us answers."

Tina unrelentingly attacked me verbally and emotionally when I was in junior high and the first two years of high school. Because she was tall for her age, well-built in any age, and on the pill in seventh grade, lots of others followed her lead.

Now the truth. Lots of others verbally and emotionally attacked me in junior high and high school. Some did physically, as well. Tina told the truth, and Tina was the only one who ever knew. I didn't even know and I'd like to think I was there. Of course, Robin Williams has said, "Anybody who can remember the Sixties wasn't really there."

"I wanted to thank you for something I've found so seldom in others," I told Tina. "You always told the truth. You always told me the truth. Even when you had me crying and you wouldn't give up, it was only the truth you were saying."

"That's the way it is, Ben. I'm not going to bullshit anybody. Never have and I'm not going to start now. You should know that."

"Yeah, I do. I just wanted to say thanks."

Crunch munch. "You calling local? You in town?"

"For a convention, yes. A few days." I stammer. "You...you want to have dinner...or something...maybe?"

"Can't tonight. I'm working at Caesar's. Private show. But you come in and ask for me. I'll get you in."

I did. I went into a line of people who wore more than I made in a year and asked for Tina by name. She came and grabbed my arm, "Come on in, Ben," then to a man with arms as thick as my waist, "He's with me, Henny. He's okay." She had the same nose, same eyes, same mouth. Different lines connecting the three, but years roll on and what can you expect?

"No, Tina. This isn't my style. We both know that. Besides, I just wanted to see you. I wanted to let you know I turned out okay. Things got good for me after a while."

The lies we tell when we don't know what we're saying.

"You got a card? Write down where you're staying and don't forget the room number. You stay up late? Jesus Christ what am I saying. Ben Matthews. Sleep light 'cause you'll get a call." She let go of my arm and was gone. Henny patted my back and smiled as I left.

She called, of course. Tina doesn't lie. Her idea of a call was a knock on my door about 5:00AM. "Hey, Matthews, open up! I gave up one hell of a party to ball you so don't disappoint me, Boy."

Of all the things she called me in the time I'd known her, it was the first time she called me, "Boy" and I'd never heard it said as a joke in quite the way she said it.

"Wait a second, I've got to put something on."

"Why?" she called from behind the door. "You'll only have to take it off."

I put on my pants and opened the door. "Tina, Jesus. There are people that know me here."

"Oh, Matthews, shut the fuck up."

She scanned my body. Even with pants on I felt naked.

I also felt alive.

Her x-ray eyes came back to mine. "I've been waiting for you to have the balls to come at me for so long I'd just about given up. But if I'd known you were going to turn out like this when you were seventeen I would have invited you in back then."

I actually covered my chest with a sheet. "Are you serious?"

"Ben, you're a good-looking man. You've got a beautiful body. You've got something you should be proud of and nothing to be ashamed of."

She pulled the sheet away and if you want a flavor of the rest start with "It was raining hard in 'Frisco" and end with "Only time will tell".

We talked for a while. She told me how her brothers had died. How her father, when I knew her in school, was the third of four, and how number two had got her on the pill so she wouldn't have his child. I thought she lived at home when I knew her in school but she didn't. She lived with some friends. She decided back then, she told me, to always tell the truth, simply because her mother never believed.

"Ever read *The Time Machine*, Ben?"

After our shared confessionals, after our shared sweating and heavy breathing, it seemed such an odd question to ask.

Yet, Tina always told the truth, and I decided I would, as well. "Yes, many times."

"You don't have to go to the future to find the Morlocks, Ben. They're here. They're all around us. And unless you can figure out who they are, they'll eat you alive." She checked her watch and gathered her things. "Gotta go, Ben. The Morlocks are waiting."

I offered her my hand because I didn't know what else to do. She slapped it aside, knocked me back on the bed, threw her things off the side, and mounted me again. "Let 'em wait. I gotta make up for what I missed out on in high school."

CHAPTER 59
INTERRACIAL INTERFAITH SOCCER LESSONS

Patti Stonesner. Red hair, pale, freckled skin, always in a tight collar so no one would know there was an Adam's Apple bobbing in her throat, lined face and spindly legs. Old hands, too. She must have been a blue blood because her veins clearly showed blue under her thin, knobbly hands. She was twenty-nine and hired me half the country away sight unseen, just from a letter and a little bit of work I'd done which got published widely. I called her Patti Stonesniffels and if I'd known then what I know now as they say...

She never revealed too much to me or anybody, and I doubt she revealed much to her husband who, as I remember, was a pretty nice guy. One thing she did tell me was she practically raised her brothers and sisters even though she wasn't the oldest kid in her family. One thing I noticed was that she never shared much of herself or engaged in conversations with people who worked for her. Because she never let herself be seen by those who worked for her, a wall was created that became impossible to take down.

The wall exploded on a Friday afternoon, around 2:30PM, when I, a mid-level manager, saw everyone dying on their feet after a hellish two weeks, got on the intercom and announced, "Ben

Matthews is going on an Eclair Run, folks. Anybody want some sugar or caffeine, place your orders. You got five minutes."

Corbin Plaza and some Hispanic, Black, and Orthodox Jewish kids are playing soccer with no sides marked, no boundaries set, no goal posts or fences to be seen. All I can think of is the little Jewish boys getting their clothes dirty.

Along the wall, Hispanic, Black, and Orthodox Jewish men open picnic coolers and lay out food. One of the men is a rabbi and is praying over the food of the Hispanic and Black men.

I'm slightly amazed. More amused, really, but what's a vowel here or there among linguists, right? "I didn't think he could do that."

Beriah watches and smiles. "Whatever it is he's doing, he seems to be doing it quite well."

With one minute to go, a woman, Terri, poked her head in my office. "Did you mean that?"

"Mean what?"

Tom was already in my office from the minute I made the announcement, but Tom was always in my office or I was in his because he'd never met anybody like me and I'd met too many like him.

"Are you really going to get eclairs?"

"Sure am."

"How about chocolate donuts? Will you get chocolate donuts?"

"Sure will."

"I'll take two." She handed me a dollar.

I heard her as she walked down the hall, "Hey! He means it!"

The line formed and I walked out with two pages of orders and one-hundred-sixty-three dollars and change. Tom and I made our Eclair Run.

Patti wasn't there that day. No upper management was. Some

kind of management retreat where they learned good management skills they'd never put into practice. They took a paid holiday at a Michigan UP resort while the rest of the company cleaned up after a two week crush and still hadn't had a real day of rest.

But she found out.

I don't know who told her. It wasn't important. There were several people who wanted to tell me. I wouldn't listen.

Patti called me in and drove a meat grinder up and down my spine. Finally I said, "Give it a break, will you? People were dying and feeling like management didn't care, that nobody was saying 'Good job' for the work they'd done, and I thought a little morale boost would be good." And then I put in the killer. "Production didn't suffer and it helped, didn't it?"

Let me give you a clue you can use in your own life regarding this: never, ever, ever, give a control freak reason to believe good things will happen without their control. It's not too bad if they're morons, but if they have a little bit of smarts you'll make an enemy you either can or can't afford to keep.

A month later I quit for several reasons, one of which was Patti Stonesniffels. I gave two weeks' notice. Patti's first question was, "Did you get a better job? Are you leaving because somebody's going to pay you more?"

Like a fool, I told the truth. "No, I'm leaving because I can't stand it here anymore. None of the promises made to me are being fulfilled, I'm not doing what I was hired to do, I'm given projects requiring skills I don't have and am not being given the time to develop them." I said this knowing my feet were firmly planted in unseen sand.

"So what are you going to do when you leave?"

"I don't know. Drive trucks, cook short order on the swing shift; I'll find something. It doesn't matter what I do, all that matters is that I enjoy what I do." Sand wiggled betwixt my toes.

Then it came, "You'll tell me what you're going to do or you'll never work in this industry again."

Because I was sophisticated and mature, I immediately fantasized throwing her on the conference table and fucking her until she jiggled like jello, foaming from the mouth and unable to think beyond a hunger for my cock. Tom, Terri, co-workers and such were, of course, lining the sides of the conference room cheering me on.

Glad to say my focus returned to the red-headed, pale skinned, irrigation-lined face and sack of onions before me, all steam-fitted into a twenty-nine year old body, and the thought of fucking her anywhere anytime dissolved like a Fizzie in superheated water.

An Orthodox lad of perhaps ten, his yarmulke coming loose as he runs, stops and asks a Hispanic man for some fried plantain. As the boy eats, the man secures the lad's yarmulke. He washes down the plantain with some apple juice and rejoins the game.

I scan the multi-cultural crowd. "Excuse me, are you all Jewish?"

A Black man standing beside me points at two Orthodoxers. "Benyamin and Yahood and the children they brought are, I think. There may be others, but I don't know."

"That little boy just ate a plantain. Isn't that illegal?"

"I won't tell the police if you don't."

"No, I mean, plantain isn't kosher, is it?"

The rabbi, overhearing this, comes up to me and takes my arm tenderly and lovingly. "It's kosher now, here. That makes it okay."

"But what if he goes somewhere else and there isn't any? Kosher, I mean."

The Hispanic man who gave the plantain and secured the yarmulke answers, "We'd rather they learn how to eat than to starve."

We gain different things as we move through life. One of them gained from this was an intuitive knowledge that what we learn in childhood we keep with us forever.

In the movie *Splash*, John Candy's character rolls quarters on the ground so he, while ostensibly looking for the quarters, can look up women's dresses. We've already seen a scene where he did this with pennies as a child. His brother, back in adult time, calls him on this and Candy says, "Hey, I don't give up what works for me."

Neither does anybody else, unless they put a lot of work and time into it. Learn "Florida is on the west coast" when you're young and you will continually point west when asked where Florida is as an adult. People will see this and figure something's wrong, decide you're an unreliable witness, and if healthy, move on. Meanwhile you're still pointing west and tell people the Atlantic meets the Pacific somewhere south of Ft. Lauderdale, around Miami, maybe somewhere along the Keys.

If you learn Florida is south and work at it a lot over time, and people come and ask you where Florida is, your hand will perform this insinuous arc starting to go west and eventually pointing south and you'll say something like, "We-outh. Excuse me, I just had a pain in my shoe. South. Florida is south."

You can even get to a point where someone will ask, "Could you tell me the way to Florida?" and you'll say, "Sure, go south."

But if somebody catches you off guard or on a day you feel a little out-of-sorts or something somewhere else is making you a little insecure, your hand will fly, your nose will follow, and like a bird dog proud to have found the last pheasant in the high grass, you'll point and say, "West. Yes, by crackers. Florida is west."

In this, I assure you, there is no shame.

Likewise, there are no Scrooge-like conversions. Miracles of attitudinal adjustment are not performed overnight. Pressure was building up a long time and something just caused the dam to break, as you read. We finally learn which turns need to be made.

Similarly, what we don't get in childhood we spend the rest of our lives looking for.

Somewhere along the way, Patti learned that her survival was intimately, instinctively, insidiously tied up in being in control of what was going on around her, even to the point of controlling the decisions in other people's lives. Part of being in control of what went on around her was being so in control of herself she could never let anybody see, hear, taste, touch, or smell what was going on inside.

This is a lesson she learned early in life. Very early. Probably quite young, when lessons weren't even lessons yet, sometime between the age of three to five. Others will tell you seven to eight.

The key word in the above is "survival". It is important to a lot of what is understanding. To an adult, "survival" means "I do not die". To a child, "survival" means "I am not alone".

It doesn't require hiding behind a shining aluminum trash can while holding a yellow-drawstring kitchen garbage-bag filled with plantain peels to figure out. Anyone who understands they are truly loved can never fight.

CHAPTER 60
AGE MATTERS

found out I wasn't queer when I was fifteen. Sometimes being found out isn't as important as finding out. This was one of those times. What I found out was that I dreamt of spending my nights with Tina but wanted to wake up to Jan.

John Lyles sang tenor in our church choir. No, I said I'd be honest - John Lyles was tenor in our church choir. He was the one of whom it was said, "I don't mind him having opinions, I just wish he wasn't always right."

John taught me a lot about a lot. I don't know why he befriended me. He was ten years my senior. This isn't important now, it was then, for reasons both foolish and curious. Perhaps our friendship grew out of a mutual love of Bach. I grew fond of Bach early on. Here was a mathematical precision put into sound. Bach was never unexpected, yet always intricate, highly structured and never formalized. I know why I became inured and have no idea what John's excuse was.

A mutual love of Bach led to mathematics, then to physics, then to Lincoln Labs where John worked. Eventually it led to my being thrown out of my parents' house.

Prior to that blessed event, it led to one-hundred wooded acres on a dirt road in Lyndeboro, NH, very late one very dark night, which is what this is about.

John, you understand, was queer. Not gay. We didn't have gays back then. We had queers. We had homos. We had fags. We had sallys. But we didn't have gays.

How did I know this?

Easy.

My mother told me so.

How did she know?

Easy.

He was twenty-five and I was fifteen. He was white and I was black. He was a thin, frailish guy (*guy*, not *gay*) who spent most of his time in his lab, doing his research. I was a strong, nicely-built kid who spent most of his time reading, studying, and generally avoiding social contact. What interest could John have in me except that he was queer and wanted me for his love-slave?

The real kicker is, because of my mother's in-depth understanding of John's hormonal selectivity, my parents were faced with the question or not little Benny was indeed doomed to be the Queen of Spades.

My mother told me matter-of-factly that John was queer and that I should spend more time with kids my own age. I didn't want to associate with kids my own age and not a lot of them wanted to spend time with me.

So I took to spending lots more time with him. He was good company. He started teaching me deductive, inductive, and abductive reasoning, advanced mathematics, physics, and programming. Basically, the foundations of logical thought and argument.

My mother, upon hearing this, straightened herself at the stove and, using the spoon she was stirring a stew with as the Sword of Heracles, stated, "I told you he was queer."

And one night, one night when I wasn't home and wasn't at church and I really don't remember where we were right before, John took me out into the woods.

Deep woods.

Woods with so many twists and turns in the road, woods so deep I hadn't seen a light, either city or porch, for about half an hour, woods so deep that the road had been untraveled dirt for longer, woods in which I couldn't see the stars when I looked straight up, and he stopped.

He pulled off the road, as it was, drove perhaps another fifteen feet into what looked like fallen timber, and stopped.

Then he said nothing. He just sighed.

And everything my mother said in her kitchen, everything my father refused to say in his den, everything every gym teacher visited upon me yea those many years ago, came rushing back with a vengeance.

North on Broadway, approaching 204th. What I knew once as distinct ethnic boundaries have become a city-long slur of people, words, and places. Pablo McDonnell and Kam Fong Rabinowitz co-own a Native American Crafts & Supplies store.

A tall Aryan looking woman comes out of the store. She's wearing expensive red shoes and black patterned nylons which go up towards an expensive looking red skirt. I see by the muscle tone of her legs she takes care of herself. Where there should be a blouse then jacket matching her skirt and shoes, where there should be a tasteful purse on a gold chain over her shoulder, where there should be an accountant's briefcase weighing down her side, there is a Lakotah Ghost shirt, its colors and symbols telling all she works for the natives reclamation of the land, there is a healer's pouch, open, its herbs and feathers available for healing, there is a turtle-shell rattle, letting those who know she studies and performs native midwifery.

"There was a time when I would have seen her and asked, 'When is she going to decide what she wants to do?'"

Beriah stands aside so she can pass. "And now, Ben?"

A pause. A moment so I, too, can Understand.

"Now I realize I spoke out of my fear. I was afraid of her ability to explore, her freedom to investigate, her desire to challenge herself in so many ways rather than take the safe road of only challenging herself with things she knew she could master. Now I envy her."

"From fear to envy. What are these, then?"

"Judgment. Both are judgment."

"Which is worse, do you know?"

"The former, I think. It is true, both are judgements, but the latter only judges me. When I know I envy, I'm feeling what I think about what I do. When I express it, when I share it, it is my spirit which asks and answers. And when all parts of me are engaged, I can find forgiveness, for myself and others, if I want it. Then judgment ceases."

"Yes, Ben. Yes."

I waited for John to make his move, for his hand to slide across the seat, for his frail, white frame to fall against me. I sat there, thinking, "Oh, Christ, ma is right. Fuck it fuck it fuck it."

But rather than say, "I don't go that way, John," which is what was bursting from my lips, I thought, "Hey, you've never had any reason to wonder or worry about the guy. Until he does something, do nothing."

Which is what I did. And John, bless us, said, "This is my property. I plan on building a house out here. It's going to be a geodesic, like Fuller's. I'm going to build it myself. If you want, I'd like your help clearing the land. I'm going to pay for the excavation and foundation, but then I'll need help with the building."

We talked about his dreams for the next hour or so, the two of us sitting in the car, looking out at nothing but darkness. He saw a cleared acre or so, a well dug deep, stacked wood on the side, and a geodesic dome some two stories high in the middle of nowhere. I, without realizing it, was gazing out into a desert of sand with three not-quite-men walking across it.

My parents were determined to teach me that John was queer.

He was interested in getting me to think clearly, cleanly, to observe and use logic - this, even though he'd never heard of Mr. Spock - as a way of understanding all I could see.

Several years later, having left the hospital and finding my way back, I told him that I appreciated his gift, then gave him one of my own: that all the while I had been struggling towards consciousness, that he, like my family, had been unconscious all along. He, in applying a filter which never changed his world, was as dead to the world as were mom and pop. Consciousness, I told him, only occurs when it is necessary to incorporate new information into our personal worlds. Therefore consciousness is the ultimate perceptual filter.

I then gave him my gift, the same I had given myself in that moment when, at the age of fifteen and alone with him in the very dark woods, I decided he wasn't queer because I knew I wasn't and there had only been opinions, no hard facts, otherwise: I gave him self-awareness, the act of consciously separating ourselves from our environment.

This, I know, isn't an implicit memory. This is how awareness and understanding and language mix, this is where they come together.

In that moment of not knowing, I decided to become aware of myself. In becoming aware of myself I understood. Because I understood I could Understand. And in Understanding, I decided to go for a new language and I let what came come spontaneously, no longer student or teacher but equal.

Equal. Whatever is on the left is the same as is on the right.

If you gave an oyster a little hole or wad of cloth balled up at the toe of your sock, do you think it could make a pearl?

CHAPTER 61
APPLYING FORCE

The language we use defines who we are."
- Linda Anfuso, Mohawk Indian

Did I ever tell you about my time in the hospital? It was a good place, as far as such things go. It is interesting to me, now, how the universe puts the things in our path we need regardless of whether or not we take them up, how often we'll walk around the Circle until we accept being its center.

Did I tell you about Debbie and her first counselor who at that time was an orderly, who would take Debbie with him to get supplies so she could give him blow jobs? I think she met God. Probably when He came to collect.

Did I tell you about Fred wanting to marry Lill even though he was married to one woman and seeing another?

Did I tell you about Mary, mother of God?

Did I tell you about Sandy, who called me after I left the hospital and she had returned home, asking if I would go to bed with her?

Did I tell you about my case worker who was afraid of me?

Did I tell you that while I was there, I discovered my past, and having discovered it, decided I would not allow it to become my future?

Did I tell you that until I started thinking of myself differently, speaking of myself differently, seeking out those who would listen to and see me as me, I could never have made the choice this journey started with?

"When I was a child - "

"Ben?"

"Yes, Beriah?"

Don't force things to happen. They will if they must, won't if they must not, no matter what your will is in them. Hell, that thing you call 'Hell', is nothing more than striving against the way things want to go. Haven't you ever felt it, a sense of lost place, a sense of no time, that occurs when you fight the stream of life? Make your choices. Know your decisions. But do not fight What Is when your path takes you away from what you want. Perhaps what you want isn't what wants you."

"When I was a child - "

"Ben?"

"Yes, Jenreel?"

"When you work at making things happen, often they don't, or not as well as you would like them to. Also there are stops and starts, evaluations and re-evaluations at every step or at certain steps, instead of letting it happen, letting it go. Become part-of instead of an appendix-to. Don't you ever wish you could just let life happen around you and not worry about where you're going in it or how it will happen around you? Life is just like this story. When you don't let it happen, there're missing paragraphs or too many words. Things happen that shouldn't and you don't know where you stand. When you let things happen, you always know where you stand. You are always the Center.

"When I was a child - "

"Ben?"

"Yes, Cetaf?"

"If you don't like the theme of your life, change the story. Remember: Learn from your past. It is your lessons, not your prison."

"When I was a child - " and I stop. "No more of that. Move on without it."

And so I learn one can grow out of pain into joy.

If one is willing to do the work.

To change their own story.

CHAPTER 62
THE FAR DISTANT SHORE

I do not know how long this journey has been, only that now my path is my goal, my journey is my prize. How much time has passed since South Street Seaport became a sand-baked desert and three men differently the same said, "We are Healers from the Land of Barass" is impossible to decide because there is only now and absent. My past is a belief, my future a hope. All I have for anyone, myself included, is this, here, now.

The Hopi language does not separate time and space. They are the same, like energy and matter, which means energy is time and time is running out.

The end of the island is clearly in sight. To our left is Kraft Field. Soon Tenth Ave will tread water to Marble Hill. We slept in the Dyckman Farm house, just south of here at 204th and Broadway. I thought the floodlight might keep me awake, but few things interfere with my rest when I need it anymore.

So saying, as night wraps its late September warmth around us, I wonder if I will sleep tonight. I am here, now, yet know tomorrow will be different.

I do not know what will happen, but know Bronx County will change.

We pause, Beriah, Cetaf, and Jenreel gathering around me as if I'm the eye of some storm. I feel their arms around me and they kiss my face then bow their heads so I may kiss their horny crowns. I am finally and totally loved, by creatures I lie myself into believing will always be an arm's length away and know I will not see again, not as I see others around me. I take in as much of and all if possible of their attention I can, washing myself in their love for me, their celebration of me, and watching them wash in my celebration of them, my love for them. My mind wanders and my eyes close. "I ask a lot of questions, don't I."

"That's true, Ben. You are an excellent teacher."

"We've covered most of the Island. It's not the way a tour guide would have done it. I'm sure the mayor's office and civil defense would have preferred we took different paths."

Jenreel looks ahead. "The Great Way is not difficult for those who have no preference."

"What do we do now?"

"It is night. Tomorrow we travel far. Let's rest," says Cetaf. He pulls me to him, holding me against his chest as he lies down. I hear "Kitty, mommy, kitty" although no words are spoken.

In the middle of the night I dream myself awake. The four of us sit around a campfire on a high plain. There are stars overhead but no constellation I know. To our west are two mountains like columns which reach up into the sky. A meteor flares high overhead, slows, and seeks a place to land. "This is a dream, isn't it?"

Beriah closes his eyes. They move under his lids. Is he dreaming? Or seeing something I don't yet see? "Your life is dreaming a dream, Ben. It isn't real."

"Then I'm dreaming you."

"Yes."

"And if I wake up?"

"You will be us."

"How will I know what is real and what isn't?"

Jenreel's hand passes in front of Beriah's eyes. A chickadee pecks at his palm. Where did it come from? How come I didn't see it? "Nothing real can be threatened. Nothing unreal exists."

The chickadee turns into a winged homunculus. It waves at me and is gone.

Was it ever there?

Or will it always be there, ready for my being willing to see it, and I become Lettvin's frog?

Cetaf watches the sun glistening on the Harlem. "What does it take to realize your dreams, Ben?"

The three of them look to Marble Hill and a slight, warming breeze starts. I feel it. I feel the dirt of the city smiting my cheeks, neck, and arms. I smell the Harlem growing warm - smells are now clearly demarcated, not arousal but anger; anger, which I now know, when it was confused, became rage - and grab Beriah's arm. "Who am I?"

"You don't know?"

"Who do you think I am?"

"I will tell you. You must know that who I believe you are is exactly that. It is who I believe you are. Who I believe you are may not be who you believe you are. Taking on a role because it's who you think I want or need you to be forces you to lie to both of us; to me because you are no longer you, you are a shadow of my needs and wants. To you because to be who I believe you are denies you the right to be fully who you need to be."

I am in agony, no longer aware of who I am. All my self-beliefs have slowly, agonizingly been stripped away in four month's time. "Who do you think I am?"

Beriah speaks, his voice the voice of the three, "I think you are 'China exists'. I think you are 'I lost my little boy'. I think you are 'How can Jenreel feed that beggar?'. I think you are holding Cetaf's hand when his mate chose a path he could not as yet follow. I think you are fear and confusion when we chose each other. I think you are the four things without which nothing else can exist.

. . .

9: What if we assume these changes don't start at some time

$$t = 0$$

but at

$$t = -\infty?$$

We can integrate and get

$$\int_{-i}^{i} {}_{e,s}\prod^{p,m} dt = F_L \parallel F_L \mid \text{the Force a life exerts on another life}$$

10: How does F_L get maximized or minimized? By determining the distance at which we let others into our lives, by becoming aware of and a participant in our own P-C relationships, which means moving from *Transcendental object* to being a *Thing-in-itself*, recognizing and rejoicing in the mystery we are and therefore recognizing and rejoicing in others being Things-in-Themselves, all of which is based on boundaries and limits - and follows a $1/r^2$ formula, which completes the gravitational metaphor - and is developed via trust and mutual respect, which is developed via rapport, which is language, which is communication in its purest form.

"I think you are, Ben Matthews."

The three of them look across the water and suddenly the bridge, The Bronx, and everything beyond is gone, lost in a strong wind. In their place is a landscape, bright white sand and harshly brilliant night sky. Far off, what I take to be a city. Above the city and spreading out over the plain, the horizon is the color of wine. As if to ground me, to provide a center to the realities behind me, a window opens on the second floor of the building across the street. A blonde, thin man in a tie-dyed muscle shirt waves at us and smiles, then places a radio in the window. I hear

Now everybody has got the choice
between hotdogs and hamburgers
every one of us has got to choose
between right and wrong
and givin' up or holding on

I feel the song is a lie. I look upon the three men I $\int_{\{have\}}^{\{ed\}}$ journey with and know, yes, life is a series of choices. Over time, through the eternities of our lives, our choices become shadowed gray lands of wide expanses given weight, substance, color, brightness, fever, timbre, and depth by who we are. But this is only over time. Moment by moment, as each particle of infinity reaches into the next, our choices are simple, binary: Yes, No, Up, Down, On, Off, One, Zero. Either you Do It or you Don't.

Sometimes one choice shadows or brightens the landscape for the rest of our days. That is where the graylands originate, too, when we journey to one side and our path lies to another. We divide ourselves, and nothing divided against itself can long stand.

So my choice, now, I realize, is to journey my path, which limits my choices for the rest of my days. All *is* vanity, and I'm glad of it. I choose to be as selfish as I can. I choose to cry for my own pain, to tend to my own needs, to tell you how I feel. I choose to be all the colors of the rainbow and not a white man in a black body or a black man in a white world. I choose to hold those I care for and kiss those I love and celebrate their life and not be ashamed or fear what others might think. I choose to be, because in so doing I give you the room to be, as well.

And in doing so I condemn myself to no longer having choices. I choose to let all things exist because, inside me, they do, and why should the universe I walk in be smaller than the one which walks inside me?

It seems they hear my thoughts, read my mind. Could they always do this and I wasn't aware?

Beriah: "If you are to become anything, to do anything, recognize the hodologist in you."

Jenreel: "To the best of your ability, obey the hodologist."

Cetaf: "You will never lose your child."

They unify, their three voices harmonize in a song only I can hear. "You will find yourself."

Cetaf begins to move and I slide off his chest back to the ground. Beriah says, "It's time for us to go, Ben."

I cry. "I don't want you to go."

"Don't cry because we go on. You can journey with us whenever you like."

This puzzles me. I know enough of their metamathemagical ways to know they do not share them. Whatever magic this might be, it already exists inside me. "How?"

"Obey the rhythms of your life. They can be a drum, a hammer, even the beating of your own heart."

The three of them join me in my tears and I wipe their eyes. "I thought only Cetaf cried."

Beriah: "I am telling you how I feel."

Jenreel: "I am tending to my own needs."

Cetaf: "I am crying for my own pain."

My words are unspoken yet they nod. "And so am I, to all of you." I no longer have to speak to be heard.

They walk and I, unable to move, shout a final denial. "Will you write?"

Jenreel pauses. "When you need, yes."

Cetaf faces me and slowly, considering his response, nods. "I think you would understand the gibberish." They walk on.

Beriah, his feet shifting into the bright white sand, turns to me. "Did you ever find your little boy?"

I laugh and cry and laugh again. "I never lost him. I just forgot who he was."

He joins them and they walk together, the same slow pace, the same light step. For one instant the four of us are aligned and a new baptism fills me, erupts me, washes over me. The four bodies - Physical (tending to his own needs), Emotional (crying for his own pain), Mental (telling how he feels), and Spiritual (finding my own child, my own self) - align and I see hear feel taste touch smell know understand use become my own healing.

My companions call themselves "Healers from the Land of Barass" and tell me they heal their own wounds.

What kinds of wounds can three such creatures carry that they go on this journey of... Enlightenment?... Salvation? ... Finding?

As they move, I notice a slight variance in their color, a momentary change, as a brief shading the color of my skin shines through them. The wind kicks up fiercer and both they and the land they travel in are...are.

God told the Jews, "I am." It became something to fear. Maybe God was only agreeing with them. Perhaps it was God's greatest lesson to them: a recognition of independence no matter what their desires, beliefs, hopes, and dreams might be. Maybe he wanted to teach them "to be" regardless of others' desires, beliefs, hopes, and dreams for them might be.

Maybe God was only saying "Yes."

Part of who we are is our desire to lingualize our experience. In the final analysis, because we can only communicate with those we have something in common with, some similar basis for understanding, the only way we can communicate with dolphins, whales, other earth lifeforms which might be sentient in a way we don't yet understand, with aliens, is if those we wish to communicate with also wish to communicate, also have as a part of themselves the desire to lingualize their experience. They can be so alien as to not recognize us as life and us not recognize them as life. But if they wish to communicate, that will be the base for our spontaneity, for our development of a mutual language.

The only way you can understand this is if you, like I, am a self-correcting algorithm, and if I, to the best of my ability, share the equations which I am. Reality is not a consensus of opinions. It is a consensus of Understandings.

Of compassion.

It took 4,989,600 heartbeats - a little more than one summer's worth - to change my world.

You?

WALKABOUTS

Would you like to schedule an online One-on-One Wounded Healers WalkAbout with Joseph? http://nlb.pub/WalkAbout

Online and Live Group WalkAbouts are available. See http://nlb.pub/GroupWalks for details.

COMING FROM NORTHERN LIGHTS PUBLISHING IN 2025

Tales Told 'Round Celestial Campfires Volume II

"...a plethora of delightful and thought-provoking stories that run the science fiction gamut from on-world to off-world to dream-world to surreal-world. Each tale is meticulously crafted and well researched, with most of the stories featuring relatable—or at least sympathetic— characters, each with something to gain and something to lose, each navigating their world as best they can and hopefully helping us learn something about ourselves along the way. I am not exaggerating when I say that several of these tales are worthy of inclusion in any best-of science fiction anthology.

...Worthy of Philip K Dick himself. ... the stories are pretty much all gems. Intelligent. Thought provoking. Each with its own unique voice, setting, tone and message. And a few delightful surprises along the way."

"I enjoyed all the stories, their mix of the commonplace with fantastical twists, and their incredible descriptions – just one example of the latter: "...the fog was hanging on you like a sweater soaked in snow...". "Mani He" was my favorite of the collection, with its nice surreal feel and a number of great life-lessons. "Those Wings Which Tire, They Have Upheld Me" brought tears to my eyes. And "The Settlement" caught me completely by surprise; I had not expected that twist at all!"

"I couldn't put it down. I kept reading and reading. Reminds me of Stephen King's "Night Shift," and John Christopher's "The White Mountains," "The City of Gold and Lead," and "The Pool of Fire," or, maybe The Twilight Zone."

That Th!nk You Do Volume II

Without question, the right book at the right time for so many who will look upon this as a mirror, reflecting many situations and circumstances resembling those we've encountered. Stories told with candor and an extraordinary level of honesty, along with advice which becomes the magic elixir we can all draw from as we continue to navigate that unpredictable journey called life.

Dennis J. Pitocco, Publisher & Editor-in-Chief, BizCatalyst 360°

A true polymath, Carrabis blends the astute wisdom of Covey, the practical guidance of Ferriss, and the sagacity of Dear Abby into an eclectic potpourri of advice and opinion. This assortment of insights is a veritable box of chocolates, each one sure to please. Drawing from multiple disciplines— principally psychology, sociology, anthropology, and busi- ness—the author shares his unique perspectives. Throughout the chapters covering a wide variety of topics, readers are encouraged to think and behave in new and improved ways.

Victor Acquista, M.D., award-winning international author

I sipped at Joseph Carrabis' That Think You Do. Change,

choice, connection, and conversation (inner and outer) make for a hearty brew. Hooked by the exacting sensory images; neuroscience and wit added spice. I stopped often to digest the richness of resonant principles he weaves throughout.

This is a book I'll put on my library shelf and return to again and again.

Susan Sneath, co-host of the internet tv talk show "The Change Zone"

and more!

ABOUT NORTHERN LIGHTS PUBLISHING

Northern Lights Publishing/Press is an association of five professionals (one graphic artist, one marketer, one editor/book designer, one copyeditor, one editor/educator/author) and a rotating group of ten published authors and poets all of whom are passionate readers. Financial backing is provided by a small group of investors led by Susan and Joseph Carrabis through the NextStage Evolution Corporation. Everyone receives remuneration and owns an equal share of the company with the exception of Susan and Joseph Carrabis.

We're developing our publishing/marketing model so we're not accepting submissions at present.

We'll open our doors to submissions (and announce it through various social networks) once we're sure we can break even and preferably turn a profit. Until then, wish us well.

It's an exciting journey and one we'd love to share, but only after we're sure we can successfully navigate the publishing seas.

Join Northern Lights Publishing's Journey
http://nlb.pub/JoinNorthernLights

ABOUT THE AUTHOR

Joseph Carrabis is a master storyteller with a sharp sense of humor and linguistic expertise. Hailing from New Hampshire, USA, his passion for writing began at the tender age of seven while washing dishes with his older sister, Sandra. She'd read 'Mission to the Heart Stars' for a book report and shared her fascination and excitement over the story. Joseph, a plate in one hand and a dish towel in the other decided, "I want to give that to people." With a career deeply embedded in evolving technologies, Joseph served as Chief Research Officer, Chief Neuroscience Officer, and Senior Research Fellow at several institutions and agencies while earning numerous awards for his journalism and trade technical writing.

Joseph refers to himself as boring - something loudly debunked by his readers and peers - and weaves wildly imaginative stories that dance on the boundary of the known and unknown sciences where natural, preternatural and supernatural intersect. Fans' comments regularly mention Carrabis' ability to bring together advanced mathematics, quantum physics, cybernetics, and neuroscience with believable multi-dimensional characters and spellbinding future technology. Joseph has been nominated for the Pushcart Prize, recommended for a Nebula Award, and received an honorable mention in 'Writers of the Future'.

Outside of writing, Joseph spends his time with his wife, Susan, reading, walking his dog, talking around campfires, flying kites, and befriending wildlife. He thinks of music as a language of sound and movement and enjoys listening and playing the piano, clarinet, saxophone, and guitar. A facilitator for open-minded conversations, Joseph runs a monthly forum, Roundtable 360°, where creatives from a range of fields discuss what drives their souls to create.

Reach out to Joseph online at: https://josephcarrabis.com